BY

Erna Fergusson

MEXICO REVISITED (*1955*)

NEW MEXICO
A PAGEANT OF THREE PEOPLES (*1951*)

CUBA (*1946*)

CHILE (*1943*)

OUR SOUTHWEST (*1940*)

VENEZUELA (*1939*)

GUATEMALA (*1937*)

These are Borzoi Books
Published in New York by ALFRED A. KNOPF

Mexico Revisited

≑ BY ≑

ERNA FERGUSSON

MEXICO

REVISITED

ALFRED A KNOPF   NEW YORK

1 9  6 0

L. C. CATALOG CARD NUMBER: 54–7203

© Erna Fergusson, 1955

THIS IS A BORZOI BOOK,
PUBLISHED BY ALFRED A. KNOPF, INC.

Published September 19, 1955
Second printing, April 1956
Third printing, December 1960

Foreword

THIS BOOK *does not propose to be a history of Mexico or a sociological or economic study of that country. There is a considerable library of scholarly books in English. But in a country as vigorous and lively as Mexico statistics go out of date faster than books can be published. In these rapid changes, filled with ferment, confusion, and hope, lies Mexico's present fascination. The country has lost none of its former beauties. Its mountains and coasts are as magnificent as ever; its archæological fields grow in wonder and significance as new finds are made and as better communications make them more accessible. Improved communications, tending to destroy the picturesque, are also opening up new areas and hitherto unknown tribes. Primitive life and quaint customs may still be found on every hand, but the most interesting Mexicans are those who are going ahead. Fast as they change, they must inevitably develop along lines laid down by their own character and experience. They change most rapidly in Mexico City, which in a way sums up the country, and which I have therefore left for last in this book.*

This book, then, tries to present fairly some actual Mexicans with enough sidelights and backward glances to explain why they live and think and act as they do. Two years' travel among them suggests that their over-all characteristic is a tough invincibility. People with such a gift for life and laughter, not to mention intelligence and ambition, will inevitably carry their country on to a unique and important place in the modern world.

Contents

Contents

Illustrations

Illustrations and Maps

Maps

PART ONE

South Toward the Center

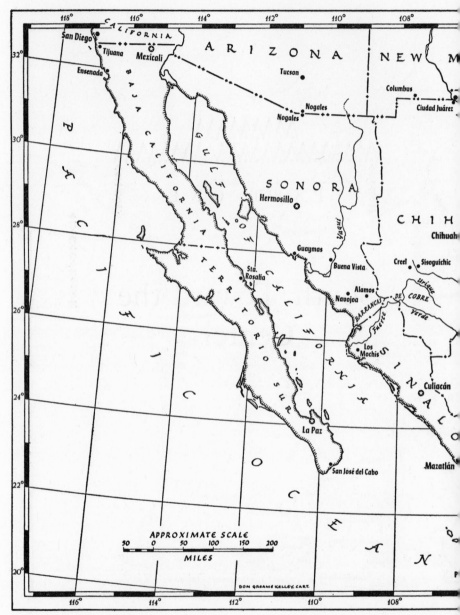

APPROXIMATE SCALE

50   0   50   100   150   200

MILES

DON GREAME KELLEY. CART.

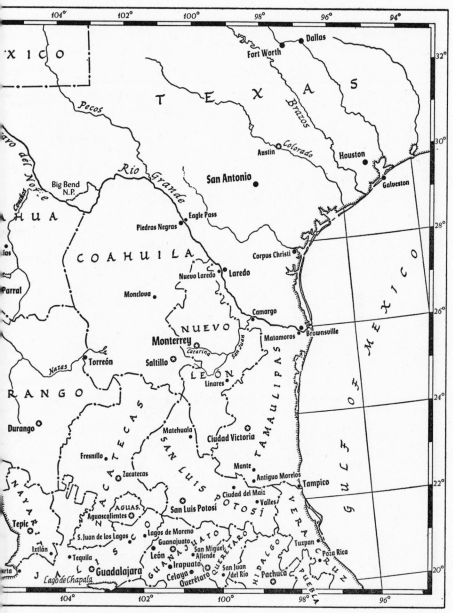

❧ ⊂ ❧

I

CIUDAD JUÁREZ AND HOW THE LAND LIES

⊂ I ENTERED Mexico by the international bridge across the Rio Grande from El Paso, Texas to Ciudad Juárez, Chihuahua. I was returning to a beloved land after twenty years with only brief visits in the interval. What should I find? Would the people be as engagingly friendly as I remembered them? Could the country be as magnificent as my nostalgic recollections made it?

On the bridge, the last lanky Yankee drawled his "So long" and the first Mexican smiled his welcome. Immediately I heard the word that was to greet me every day. "*Sola?*" Was I alone? It might be disapproving, but it always resulted in friendly offers of service. A kind man directed me to a parking-place, and another walked a block out of his way to show me the post office. There a plump matron, waiting in line, addressed me. "In Chihuahua, don't fail to see Luz Corral, the legitimate widow of Pancho Villa. She was married in church and has her papers." This was indeed a distinction. Villa's own defense of his many irregularities was that he married them all, didn't he? I promised to visit Luz Corral, and we parted with the gentle *abrazo* (embrace).

Ciudad Juárez was proving as friendly as the Mexico I remembered, and its streets that day could only have been in Mexico. Women walked crowned with huge baskets of marigolds, and burros were all but hidden under panniers

5

of yellow flowers. It was November 2, *día de los muertos*, when Mexicans celebrate All Souls Day by decking their graves with marigolds, the Aztec death flower, and picnicking in the cemeteries on the ancient Indian foods of turkey with chile sauce, tortillas, and chocolate.

Mexicans habitually celebrate Catholic festivals with ancient Indian observances. The roots of modern Mexico are long and tenuous, reaching back beyond any white man's history. The United States of Mexico is a republic with twenty-nine states and two territories and a rapidly growing population of over twenty-six million. It is not a homogeneous population. One of Mexico's greatest problems is how to make citizens out of its large Indian population of people who are tribal rather than national.

Even in the border town of Ciudad Juárez I saw evidence of this tribal division. I met long files of men not militarized, but ordered and led. A few carried suitcases and wore clothes bought in the stores. More wore straw sombreros, *huaraches* (sandals) or serapes or carried baskets or string bags whose color and design marked them clearly as regional or tribal work. These men were *braceros* (arm-workers, hands) going under work contract to the United States. Their migration amounts to an international problem. Mexicans have always been desirable workers in the United States. Mining and railroad companies used to ship them in, underpay them without scruple, and abandon them when times got hard. But during the war years Mexico and the United States entered into an agreement that guaranteed Mexican nationals a living wage, decent housing, and an adequate diet. There were even provisions for helping them to send money home. For Mexican *braceros* this was Utopia. Thousands came, hundreds of thousands continue to come. Mexico's Secretary of Foreign Affairs reported that 193,285 registered workers had crossed the border in 1952. In addition, untold numbers cross the frontier illegally. These are the "wetbacks," who are presumed to swim the Rio Grande, though that capricious stream is often too dry to wet the sole of a foot. Wetbacks as well as *braceros* are in demand from the cotton fields of Texas to the orange groves of California and the beet fields of Utah and Colorado; many go farther north.

Altogether this labor drift promises to be permanent, though unions in the United States complain that *braceros* upset our labor market, and Mexican employers inveigh against luring their workers away with high pay. A representative of the United States Department of Labor estimated that *braceros* took some ten million dollars back to Mexico in one year, as much as tourists spent there. Most *braceros* return to their own states with new ideas. Unfortunately many return embittered by harsh treatment or discrimination. The two governments try constantly to stem the flow of wetbacks and protect the registered workers. But the movement flows on like a tide.

Much of this was unknown to me as my car purred smoothly along the highway to Ciudad Chihuahua. I was following the Central Highway, which was opened in 1940 and has brought the whole western United States and much of Canada closer to Mexico. At intervals a uniformed guard popped out of a police shelter to ask for my papers. He always commented on the New Mexico license on my car and made the usual remark about women driving alone. Was I not afraid? I soon developed a standard reply. How could I be afraid in a country whose police were so courteous and efficient? The road was fast, the land was enormous with gold and silver swells rippling with dry grass under the breeze and shaded only with angular cactus or cloud shadows. Now and again a whirlwind picked up its skirts and danced madly past. Just before Villa Ahumada, where one is warned to take gas, the road crosses fifty miles of sand dunes. Beautiful on a still day in bronze and gold, but what a scouring they must put up under a stiff wind.

This Central Highway crosses seven states between Ciudad Juárez and Mexico, the capital, which lies in its Distrito Federal like Washington in the District of Columbia. One should know that Mexico refers to the capital; the country is customarily called *La República*. In its 1,340 miles this highway climbs from an altitude of 3,700 feet at Ciudad Juárez to Mexico's 7,334, but it is a gentle rise with few dramatic moments. This is the Mesa Central held between the two long arms of the Sierra Madre, the Oriental and the Occidental. Eastward there are a few passes through the sierra; but to the west the mountain ranges are so forbidding that Mexico's daring highway department has only now breached them with a road from Durango to Mazatlán. From Chihuahua to Sonora one still goes by horse or burro—or by air. Mexico often gets ahead by skipping a few eras of development.

The country's greatest physical handicap is that it is mountainous. Geographers, always cautious, classify about a third of its area as "more or less level." This long north central plateau, which ends in a jagged line along the southern boundaries of Zacatecas and San Luis Potosí, is its largest extent of flat land. And this, unlike our fertile Mississippi Valley, is not well watered and fertile; it is arid or semi-arid like our southwest, which is its extension. Its annual rainfall averages about fourteen inches, a scanty supply that is often curtailed by droughts that last for years. The government has undertaken irrigation projects along some of its few streams, but, as in our southwest, it is questionable that such expensive projects will justify the outlay.

Any gringo tempted to preen himself on our rapid development as compared with Mexico's slower advance may regain his balance by recalling how fortune has favored our country. To begin with geography, our two great mountain ranges were comparatively easy to cross, first by Conestoga wagons, then by railroads. Once over the low crest of the Appalachians, the frontiersman found all the rivers leading him into the vast Mississippi Valley, one of the most productive areas on earth. After that the stiffer Rockies were crossed with "a whoop and a holler" in the knowledge that gold lay beyond.

In Mexico, on the contrary, only twentieth-century skill and equipment could conquer the sierras, which rise from the central plateau and pitch steeply down over hundreds of miles of escarpments to the Gulf of Mexico on the east, and on the west to the Sea of Cortés, now known as the Gulf of California. Rivers tumble down these western steeps, making beautiful and often fertile canyons; the coastal plains vary between dusty dry and lushly tropical; along the shores are some fine beaches and few good harbors. The eastern coastal plains, which produce coffee, cacao, hard woods, and pineapples, curve around the Gulf of Mexico to form the Yucatán peninsula. Mexico's shape suggests a horn of plenty, but students agree that the old notion of its inexhaustible wealth is ill-founded. Less than half its area is even potential farm land; no more than ten per cent can be added to its agricultural lands by irrigation. Soil experts classify much of Mexico as grazing-land; yet it has been farmed for four hundred years, with tragic depletion of the soil. This becomes more clearly evident as one reaches the central valley, where the splendid capital city lords it over one of the loftiest cultivated areas in the world. The capital city itself is constantly bedeviled by the perennial woe of arid lands: too little water or too much, drought or flood.

South of the capital the sierras come together in formless confusion. Inaccessible canyons have served revolutionists better than farmers, though there are occasional peaceful valleys. A line of volcanoes crosses the country like a row of snowy signal towers from Colima, which mariners on the Pacific watch for, to Orizaba, whose 18,000-foot peak is visible one hundred miles out in the Gulf of Mexico. Mexico is a country of incredible beauty, but of near invincibility.

It is in this setting that Mexico's people have tried and are still gallantly trying to make a modern democratic nation. No honest student of its situation and of its people can fail to respect the courage and high intelligence with which this Republic—just over one hundred and thirty years old —is facing its manifold difficulties. Nor can one fail to recognize that as this nation moves forward it offers a fine example of what may be done in so-called backward areas. That Mexico is living on many levels of development is everywhere apparent. Burros and airplanes. Charcoal for chimneyless cooking and factories run by natural gas. The most primitive living and the most advanced social planning in the civilized world. To the bafflement of the visitor as well as to his goggle-eyed delight, all these contradictions exist in the same place, seem often to produce conflicts in the same person. There is no understanding the Mexican people without some knowledge of their vigorous and varied heritage and the extraordinary handicaps they have had to overcome in their advance.

Mexico's population is founded on a broad Indian base. Census figures do not list Indians as such, but scholars estimate that some ten million Mexicans still live at the "Indian cultural level." Over half of this number speaks Indian dialects rather than Spanish. They live and farm and, in many ways, think as their ancestors did. They provide picturesqueness for the visitor's delight and pose appalling problems for the educator. Somehow these Indians must be brought into the current of Mexican life, sharing its language and culture, playing a part as citizens. If this can be done without destroying the Indian's own culture, so much the better. Certainly his fate will determine that of his country as a whole.

The history of the Indian mass is simple—and tragic. Before the Conquest, they labored for Indian masters. The Spaniards substituted a Spanish conqueror for an Indian chief, a Catholic priest for an Indian shaman. The toiler, still weary, hungry, and despised, worked as before, ate the same food, built the same wattled shelters to live in. The conquerors, forcing European culture and Catholicism on the Indian, inevitably denied him any advance along his own lines. They also gave him an enduring sense of inferiority. Twenty years ago one often heard the phrase " I am only a poor Indian." This is infrequent now, but the acceptance of white superiority persists as social snobbery. Dark-skinned people of obvious Indian extraction boast of blond relatives; mothers blondine the hair of tiny girls and call them Güera (Blondie). Spain's feudal system transplanted produced an exploited class of Indians held in debt peonage, in ignorance and superstition. This is not the stuff of which a democracy is made. Mexico has had to produce its middle class. And this is its story.

One may again contrast Mexico's hard luck with our good fortune. For more than a century Europe sent to the United States useful and knowing people; not lily-handed aristocrats seeking easy wealth, but men who brought skills, who were willing to work, and who found vast unoccupied lands free for the taking. Mexico had no such immigration. Its two classes consisted of the descendants of the conquerors and others who came to enrich themselves, and the Indian whom they deliberately held in ignorance as easier to control. Our south under slavery is comparable, and in our south advance was long deferred, as it has been in Mexico.

As the third deterrent to Mexico's progress one must reluctantly name the Church. Not the Catholic religion.

The Church as represented by its higher clergy, which,
throughout the colonial era, was generally Spanish and
drawn from the privileged classes. It is true that during
Mexico's long history not a few churchmen have been
aware of social evils and active in combating them. Soon
after the Conquest, Bartolomé de las Casas, a Dominican,
wrote and preached so vigorously against abuse of the Indians that he reached even the monarch in Spain. As a result Spain, in 1542, enacted the most humane laws ever
promulgated for the protection of a conquered people.
Missionaries taught their converts and interceded for them
when they could. A priest, Padre Miguel Hidalgo, set the
spark that started the War of Independence from Spain in
1810, and a few years later Padre José María Morelos called
Mexico's first constitutional convention.

But the Church in Mexico, as an organized force, opposed the War of Independence; and in every nineteenth-
century conflict it backed the party of property and privilege. Quite naturally Church leaders believed in the class
that had produced them and was their main support. For
this reason devoutly Catholic Mexicans, who also believe in
democracy, have had to distinguish between the religion
they revere and the clergy who have often opposed social
advance.

Mexico has made three strong strides to get out of the
morass composed of unassimilated Indians and the obdurate,
rich, and clever anti-democratic forces. Its hope and its
glory have been the many Mexicans of all heritages with
the vision to foresee their country's potentialities and with
the courage to fight for them. The Wars of Independence
freed Mexico from Spain, but left the basic pattern of life
unchanged. The years between 1820, when independence
was achieved, and 1876, when a dictator seemed to promise
peace, were turbulent. A people unaccustomed to self-
government and used to domination was easily led by petty

and often vicious demagogues, best known by the Spanish word *caudillos*.

Throughout this period, learned men of great integrity were trying to free the people from the domination of landowners and to help them to become landowning, self-governing citizens. Liberal leaders got tithes declared voluntary; monks and nuns were left free to renounce their vows; church courts were abolished; and secular education was declared compulsory. These laws aroused the clergy to a fury that was to last into the modern period. In the constitutional convention of 1856, the Church party's banners bore the device "Long Live Religion! Death to Tolerance!" The liberal party, largely Catholic, won, and the constitution it framed is still Mexico's basic law. Streets and plazas named La Reforma and La Constitución refer to these enactments. The most important declared for freedom from forced labor, freedom of speech and press, and the right to assemble and petition. There was no attack on religion; religion was not mentioned. But there were articles designed to break the land monopoly that kept a majority of the people in peonage.

It is estimated that when Mexico became independent, five per cent of its people owned ninety-five per cent of the land, and that half of that was owned by the Church, which, in the absence of banks, was the moneylender and held mortgages on much property it did not own. The Constitution now decreed that all lands held by corporations must be sold. It was hoped that Church lands would be bought by small investors who would develop a new middle class. But two things went wrong. Clever lawyers construed the law as applying to lands owned communally by Indians—the *ejidos* that became so politically important a century later. The Indians were forced to sell, and devout Catholics, who would not buy confiscated Church property, gladly bought Indian lands. And foreigners, having no scruples against either, became owners of some of Mexico's finest lands.

The guiding spirit of Mexico's era of reform was a quiet, imperturbable, liberal Zapotec lawyer from Oaxaca, Benito Juárez. He believed in honesty, in legal methods, and in his people. As president, he appointed a cabinet so honorable that its members enjoy the unique distinction of having retired no richer than they were when they took office. But they were ahead of their time. Disgruntled landowners kept revolt flaming, and finally the growing national debt led to French intervention. Mexicans at the court of Napoleon III in Paris invited the Austrian prince Maximilian to become emperor of Mexico. So the country, in the midst of civil war, saw four fantastic years of a European court in their capital while the elected president, Juárez—more often in a plain dark carriage than in an official residence—tried to carry on legal government. By 1867 the French were driven out and Maximilian was shot. But Juárez died in 1872, leaving his country again in tragic confusion.

The strong man who took over then was Porfirio Díaz, part Mixtec Indian, from Juárez's own state of Oaxaca. Díaz, who had fought bravely against the French as a liberal, soon became the typical *caudillo* and ruled Mexico for thirty-five years. His cabinet of *científicos* (men of science) enriched themselves, but they also put their country on such a sound basis that it enjoyed its first period of international respectability. They accomplished this by inviting in foreign capital on easy terms, especially as regards Indian lands. Mexicans and foreigners built up a new landed aristocracy upheld by the army, now rich and powerful, and the Church, again wielding political influence. Only the Indians, at that time eighty per cent of the population, were left in peonage, ignorance, and hopelessness.

Mexico's third strong step forward was taken in 1910,

when a rich young planter of Coahuila came out as candidate for president. He was Francisco Madero, who had acquired his ideas abroad and whose slogan was "Effective suffrage and no re-election!" He proposed peaceful political changes, and he proved quite unable to control the popular forces he released. Peons who had worked without hope and lost their lands without recourse rose in many places under such leaders as Pancho Villa in Chihuahua and Emiliano Zapata in Morelos. Zapata's battle cry, *"Tierra y libertad!"* (Land and liberty), expressed the real meaning of the revolution. Madero was sympathetic, but he was too idealistic, too inexperienced, perhaps too weak, to cope with the power-hungry men who surrounded him. And the United States Ambassador, Henry Lane Wilson, made an intimate of the officer who betrayed President Madero. Madero was assassinated. The Ambassador was recalled—too late. And Mexico was in for fifteen years of bitter battle. This was revolution. It is not what Mexicans mean by their Revolution.

Le Revolución means to Mexicans the ceaseless effort to build a modern democratic state with equal opportunity for all, special privileges for none, universal education, and complete freedom of expression. Many of these ideas were expressed in the Constitution of 1857. The Constitution of 1917 also included laws to protect labor, to restore lands to Indians by breaking up oversize estates, to extend education, and to provide medical and social aid for all. It was the most socially advanced constitution in the world. But it was only on paper. The brilliant and dedicated Mexicans who have formulated its programs have faced all the evils known even to people accustomed to self-government. Inevitably they have met malfeasance in office and have suffered many failures due to inexperience. But forty years is not a long time in which to produce an intelligent electorate out of such material as four centuries of suppression had left. Mexican leaders say that their Revolution will go on until every Mexican has a chance at good health, decent living-conditions, and all the education he can use. It is a noble and inspiring program.

The traveler from the north will do well to change his slant on Mexico. He may still revel in primitive Indian costumes and customs and admire the magnificent stone churches, forts, roads, and bridges the Spaniards built. But he will do well also to notice the village schools and social-service centers, the agricultural banks and co-operative farms. Even the noisy, smelly trucks that threaten him on the highways mark real progress toward industrialization and better living.

The United States of Mexico is a progressive country that has cleanly made its first hurdles. It has a constitution under which a modern democracy can develop. It seems to have outgrown the period in which every defeated candidate took up arms. It is hard at work at education, industrialization, reclamation. How fast it can advance depends upon its people—that heterogeneous mass of unassimilated, ill-educated Indians and backward-looking conservatives, as well as keen businessmen, social-minded clerics, ambitious and eager young people, and farsighted and honorable leaders.

I proposed to know as many of them as I could, to try to understand our neighbor country as its people understand it.

II

CHIHUAHUA

Chihuahua seems an empty land, uninhabited to its horizon of distant blue mountains. But it is a great cattle country, with some of the biggest ranches in the world. Its Barrancas de Cobre (Copper Canyons) dwarf the Grand Canyon, and America's last cave-dwellers are hidden away in its forests. Spanish explorers crossed these wastes after they had learned to make their way north without swinging out to the coast. For a couple of centuries their caravans of wooden carts and burros carried supplies to the New Mexico missions and brought back Indian blankets, tanned hides, and ore from the mines. But Spain did not settle these wastes. Nor did Mexico until the sweeping land-grabs of Porfirio Díaz resulted in kingdom-size ranches. Díaz granted over thirty-five million acres to seven families in Chihuahua, among them the Terrazas, who, in 1910, owned fifteen million acres, the largest estate in Mexico. Díaz also favored foreigners. The Cananea copper mines in the mountains of Chihuahua enriched a United States company while miners worked in hideous conditions, and William Randolph Hearst acquired enormous ranches.

The Díaz peace and order, so vaunted by Don Porfirio's admirers, were maintained by his *rurales*, federal police magnificently mounted, snappily uniformed, and well armed. They arrested freely and as freely shot prisoners in the back under the *ley fuga*, law of flight. These conditions, including powerful dominant families and stern repressive measures, produced such revolutionists as Doroteo

17

Arango, who, as Pancho Villa, became the archetype of the guerrilla fighter. The legend is that, as a boy, Doroteo saw his sister raped by a ranch foreman and killed the man. He took to banditry and changed his name to Pancho Villa, becoming the adored protector of the poor and the terror of their oppressors. His band rode the best horses from the best stables, wore the finest leather coats and breeches, the heaviest silver braid on the biggest sombreros. They were armed with guns and ammunition bought in the United States.

Mindful of the lady in the Ciudad Juárez post office, I called on Luz Corral, Villa's "only true and legitimate widow." She was in a house bursting with plants, caged birds, and a roaming parrot. She said she was of pure Spanish descent, but she looked Germanic, with graying fair hair and a heavy dignified mien. Proof of her marriage's legitimacy hangs over the piano; it shows the bride veiled in white and the groom in a broad "Texas hat," a cartridge belt around his middle, and an expansive grin. But the savage was there. Villa was a ruthless killer and a ravisher of women. Luz Corral has for sale her own book *Pancho Villa en la Intimidad* (*Pancho Villa in Intimacy*) and volumes of clippings in Spanish and English.

The Villa legend was really made in the United States. It was the thing to do for adventurous young reporters to slip across the border and ride with Villa. Some of them wrote exciting boyish books about raids, troop trains loaded with women and children, highhanded shootings, and bodies lying bloated in the streets. These books are awash with pulque, glaring with sun, and funny with sketches of dumb peons strutting in stolen finery, trying to manage tableware in raided houses, trying to like fine liquors.

Villa first appeared in the international press when, in defiance of Madero's orders, he rode north with Pascual

Orozco, a revolutionist from southern Chihuahua. Díaz's troops in Ciudad Juárez expected a trainload of munitions, but when the train stopped there, a bandit army debouched from it. They took the city while delighted gringos watched the fight from housetops in El Paso across the Rio Grande. Villa and Orozco then rode south and captured Chihuahua City with an army disguised as burro-drivers.

Villa soon developed skill as a strategist and won battles against Díaz's trained officers. Perhaps the federal soldiers had no heart for the fight. The revolutionists were a people on the march, and Villa had a magic to make a man take his rifle out of the thatch, steal a horse, and join up. Their supply problem was simple. Each man had his *soldadera*, his woman, who stole chickens and ears of corn, cooked, and carried reserve supplies on her back along with the baby. In battle, the *soldadera* handed ammunition, even handled a gun; she served as a nurse. The Ballads *La Adelita* and *La Valentina* honor the *soldaderas*. Their like may still be seen trudging along the roads with marching soldiers or bringing a soldier his lunch in barracks.

Villa and Orozco ranged across the northern states and even as far south as Mexico City. After Madero was killed in 1913, the revolution became a free-for-all among marauding bands. Villa captured great houses, destroying what he could not appreciate, won the people by distributing largess. When money ran out, he ordered bills printed. Everywhere he married, but—perhaps with a tender thought for Luz Corral—he always ordered the record destroyed. His most preposterous raid occurred in 1916, when he raided the small New Mexico town of Columbus. That brought General Pershing on a punitive expedition, so described to avoid a general war. Villa's fighters, like their Indian ancestors, ate cactus, drank its sap, tightened their belts, rode their horses to death, and ate their flesh.

They could disappear over cliffs or into sandstorms; they never stood, never gave the heavily accoutered gringos a chance.

Villa soon became a problem to the revolution's responsible leaders; in 1920 President Álvaro Obregón gave him a ranch near Parral, in the state of Durango. Luz did not preside there, but she willingly shows the battered Dodge car in which Villa was shot, as she says, " by enemies who dared not meet him face to face." This was in 1923. By that time the Revolution in its larger sense was emerging.

Thinking about Chihuahua's bandit tends to people the empty land as a car speeds easily along. Few cattle were in sight, though roadside signs warn *Cuidado con el ganado* (care with the cattle). Most other signs indicate only MEXICO, as though nobody would care to visit any town short of the capital. Distances are given in kilometers; one kilometer is five eighths of a mile. Gasoline is sold by the liter, and that calculation takes less arithmetic, especially if one is satisfied to know that one gallon is about four liters.

The sign for gasoline and oil is *Pemex, Petróleos Mexicanos*. Mexico's oil is government-owned since 1938, when President Lázaro Cárdenas, with extraordinary nerve and daring, expropriated the holdings of the British, Dutch, and United States oil companies. His critics foretold dire failure of public ownership; even now they warn one that Mexican gas soon fouls filters and spark plugs, that mileage is low. My experience is that none of this is true. Mileage was as good, and my car remained as clean, as on good old Standard at home. As at home, it is well to buy the highly refined Super (pronounced su'pair) for mountain driving.

Mexico's north and our southwest live so close together that business and the easy crossing of the border have modified life and speech on both sides. The border speech is *pochismo*, a hybrid of Spanish and English, named from *pocho*, a slang word for the Mexican-American. José

Vasconcelos first used these words in print in his auto-biography, *Ulises Criollo*. Scholars hate *pochismo;* they say it has added no beauty to the language. This may be true, but it has produced many useful words and made life much easier for the tourist. Learn to give your tongue a Spanish twist and many English words will serve you well, especially in northern Mexico. You may *parquear* your car alongside the *traque,* a word the track workers brought in along with *chante* for the shanty they lived in, *overoles* for their levis, and even switch, which has spread throughout the Republic to wherever an electric wire ends in a push-button. Boys at filling-stations greet one with a cheerful *"haló!"* and offer to *checar* or *chequear* the *brecas,* to look at the *batería* and the *tayers.* Coil and clutch have crossed the linguistic border unchanged. The car itself is generally *carro*—only purists use *coche;* and *troca* is of general use.

Any wayside stop has its *lonchería,* offering *sandwiches* as well as *tacos; hamburguesa* and *perro caliente,* a literal translation of the hot dog. Pretentious places will offer *bistec,* though the cut itself is practically unknown south of the border. Mexico is a land of mysteries; none more baffling than what happens to the edible portions of an animal when a Mexican butcher operates on it. What is served as *biftec, bistec, filete,* or even *tibón* is any sliver of beef, well pounded and fried quite juiceless. It is then usually served mildly warm. Only in a few top restaurants and hotels can one get a decent steak. It is best to settle for Mexican meats —chopped and highly seasoned; or for fish and shellfish, which are superb and well cooked in most places. But in the north, sandwiches or *tacos* are the best bets, especially if chicken is available. Ices are everywhere and so are *donas,* which are certainly easier to spell than doughnuts. *Soda,* in endless variety, is ubiquitous; sometimes even the smaller places will offer it iced. Mexican beer is better; Mexican beer is very good indeed.

Pochismo is the language of sports, and whoever remembers that *j* is pronounced like *h*, *a* like *ah*, *e* like the *a* in labor, and *i* like the *e* in we, can readily learn what *tim* is playing *beisbol* and who is *umpayer*. Somebody makes a *jit* or a *jom ron;* another knocks a *flay* to *en autfiel*. Each sports writer follows his own ear in writing, but in spoken *pochismo* the pronunciation is close to the English original.

Chihuahua is a busy state capital with fine clear air, hotels designed for tourists, and enough night clubs to attract week-enders from El Paso. The hotels, tiled and patioed, lack Mexico's old unconscious grace of flowers both indoors and out. Nor do hotel people realize how much tourists like Mexican pottery and glass; meals are served on heavy china dishes. But clerks speak English, and an English-speaking *pocho* presides at the newsstand that offers only magazines from the States. Why no Mexican periodicals? "The gringos can't read Spanish, and Mexicans prefer to read English." The first hint that Mexicans are learning English fast. It is strictly a vocational speech, but it serves them well.

At the Hotel Victoria, the snappiest bellhop was Alberto. A baffled clerk referred all problems to Alberto; he carried more luggage, answered more questions, and was more smilingly pleasant than any other of the staff. He seemed to be always on duty, a phenomenon he explained readily. Both he and his brother have jobs at the hotel. One month Alberto works as himself from seven to three. From three to eleven he works as his brother. Meanwhile, brother is running a tractor on a ranch. Next month Alberto will operate the tractor while brother does double duty at the hotel. They expect some day to own the ranch where they operate the tractor now. Alberto was the first of many Mexicans who disproved for me the fallacy that Mexicans are lazy.

The men I saw in Chihuahua's hotels look like movie

westerners: tall, heavy, slow-moving, and sun-browned, but with no trace of Indian. Many have long Spanish faces with prominent noses; many are ruddy, with sandy hair and gray or hazel eyes. It is fun to guess which is the gringo, which the Mexican. They use *pochismo* words and slide from English to Spanish and back again without accent in either. These are the men who produce the ore, the lumber, and cattle, and who have lately gone into cotton. Now that Mexican law requires that fifty-one per cent of all corporate stock must be owned by its nationals, Mexican capital—formerly shy about investments—has ventured into international partnerships that have proved successful.

Chihuahua cattlemen were complaining about measures taken to prevent the spread of hoof-and-mouth disease to the United States. Mike King, who had run cattle in Chihuahua since his discharge from the army in 1918, spoke freely. "That was just a deal put over by U. S. stockmen to protect their market. They know there is no foot-and-mouth disease in these northern states. It is a tropical disease, virulent only in the Vera Cruz swamps. It never came north of Zacatecas, and the few cattle who died there probably starved because their mouths were so sore they couldn't graze. Their feet probably got cured walking over dry land. It was a Texas dodge, I tell you, and I'm a Texan myself."

Chihuahua's enterprising cattlemen met the emergency by going into the canning business. The Regional Breeding Association, by assessing its members, has built a slaughterhouse and a factory where they pack chunks of beef in oak barrels for shipment to the United States. Mr. King, outlining this project, went on to discuss some Mexican traits, which he knows well, as his partners are Mexicans.

"Mexicans," he said, "just won't spend money. I've just spent ten thousand dollars for feed to get us through this drought. No Mexican would do that; they let the cattle die.

So at the end of a drought they have to start from scratch, while the gringo has a herd. There are no feeders in Mexico; Mexican cattle go to feeders in the States to be readied for market. But this may change with the growth of the cotton business." Mr. King laughed at my effort to follow his thought. "You see, in the States cotton men needed an outlet for waste, so somebody invented cotton seed cake, which is a fine feed for cattle. Something like that may happen here. Mexicans are not inventive, but they are quick to adapt a new idea that they think is good."

The people met on Chihuahua's streets are brisk moderns, pedaling bicycles or driving automobiles. They could be anywhere; few of them show the warm brown coloring characteristic of the south, where Indian and Spanish have fused into the true Mexican. Two groups of immigrants from the United States move among them. Mennonites, hatted and hooded in their style, and making friends with nobody, come to town only to sell their fruits, honey, and cheese. Dour, silent folk. The Mormons provide a perfect contrast; they are friendly, expansive, and progressive.

A tall man swung into a small restaurant and took a table. A Texas type for size, complexion, and hat width, this man was speaking Spanish with the amusing colloquialisms possible only to long habitude. We began to talk and soon reached the inevitable question: "Where are you from?"

"I," said he, "am a Mexican. I was born in Chihuahua." Soon he was telling me how it came about. "My father was sent here by Brigham Young. Do you know who he was? . . . Well, my father was one of a group of colonists. I've never wanted to go back. I'm a Mexican citizen by birth and inclination. . . . There is nothing these people can't do." He paused. "When it occurs to the men in power that they must double wages without raising prices and be content for a while with lower profits, they'll begin to make such profits as they never dreamed of." Another pause. "Do you realize that they did not find that out in the States until Henry Ford tried it? And remember what they said of him when he led off with a five-dollar day? Well, that can happen here. It must."

III

TARAHUMARA AND THE BARRANCAS
DE COBRE

⊄ THE STATE of Chihuahua does not lack Indians, but
they are Tarahumara, one of the country's most primitive
tribes. They appear in the city only to trade. They live in
caves, scratch the ground a bit to raise corn, run a few cattle and sheep, tan hides and weave blankets, and, incongru-
ously, carve out and string very good fiddles. Tarahumara
men are quite tall; the man in a dirty white shirt and turban
around bushy black hair looks like a dusty bundle on top
of stringy dark legs; he wears a small G-string and a cloth
triangle, seemingly quite useless, fluttering out behind.

Asked if his legs were not cold, a Tarahumara said: "Our
legs are our faces. Is your face cold?" The women wear
full skirts and the same headdress as the men. They all carry
blankets and are shod only in sandals, often made from
old tires. They are shy people who trot silently along in
family groups. They speak their own tongue, and at night
they disappear into the hinterland or into noisome slum
courts where they sleep. Only the Jesuits know much about
the Tarahumara, and I was directed to the Jesuit school.

Father Elizalde welcomed me pleasantly, quite undis-
turbed by the clatter of closing hour with boys charging
out to the ball courts. He wore civilian dress in conformity
with the law against clerical garb, but was a Jesuit who had
learned his scholarly English at a Jesuit university in the
United States. He had served in the Jesuit mission to the
Tarahumara. The first Jesuits reached Chihuahua early in

26

the seventeenth century. They departed in 1767, when Charles III expelled the order from all the Spanish dominions. But in 1799 they returned to their remote mission in the Sierra Occidental. In 1934 President Cárdenas, enforcing the Constitution of 1857, closed their school. The more lax administration of President Ávila Camacho, who announced himself as "a believer," permitted the Jesuits to establish their present mission at Socoguichic, which claims four thousand converts.

Professor Elizalde said that the mission teaches farming and the crafts of carpentry and metalwork. Several girls have become nurses; a few boys have been graduated from the school in Chihuahua; two became priests, and one served in the state legislature. But in school they are unhappy and maladjusted. The tribe remains apart and all but unknown. Census-takers could only guess their numbers as some 40,000 or 50,000 people. They have acquired from the white man only domestic animals and Catholic forms that are weirdly confused with ancient pagan practices.

The Tarahumara habitat is the mighty Sierra Occidental, which rears up against the limitless sky like a blue rampart. But tourist-conscious Mexico is planning to invade these fastnesses with roads, landing-fields, and hotels to lure the world to their Barrancas de Cobre (Copper Canyons), which are said to dwarf the Grand Canyon of the Colorado. Missionaries and miners had long known these stupendous gorges, and a few explorers had penetrated canyons so deep that unclothed Indians lived in tropical heat at their bottom while snow fell on the brink. The only known approach to these wonders was by a long and arduous mule-ride in from the sierra's western slope. But in 1949 Chihuahua's tourist bureau and the *El Paso Times* organized an expedition to prove that Las Barrancas de Cobre were in their territory. Bill Latham, managing editor of the *Times*, wrote up the adventure, which took sturdy young men, heavy-duty trucks, full camp equipment, and a guide who knew every passable trail.

The Barrancas de Cobre, unlike the Grand Canyon's one stupendous gash, are gorges cut by several rivers that unite to enter the Gulf of California as the Río Fuerte. The main stem of the Río Urique is only 150 miles long as against the Grand Canyon's 280. The *barrancas* vary in width from one hundred feet to several miles, while the Grand Canyon is from five miles to fifteen across. The *barrancas'* greatest depth is 8,000 feet, the Grand Canyon's about 6,000. Comparisons are silly; the splendor and the wonder of both is inexpressible. I know because I saw one *barranca*; without organization, newspaper financing, guide, or even the blessing of the tourist bureau, which did not answer my letter of inquiry.

It seems standard in Mexico that organizations may fail, but friends never; and I found a friend in Ingeniero Manuel Muñoz (*Ingeniero* means engineer; this and other titles are used in Mexico as we use Dr.) Ing. Muñoz assured me that the world held no grander view than that from his mine on the Río Batopilas. He cordially offered me hospitality at the mine and the companionship of a nurse who would be traveling on the same train to Creel, at the end of the railroad.

It was a tiring day, from seven in the morning until eleven at night, on a chilly train that jerked to a stop at every water tower. I do not recommend it. But Ing. Muñoz was right about his view. And I found the trip richly rewarding because of three young Mexicans I met: a nurse, a doctor, and an engineer, all of the type that is making possible Mexico's amazing advance.

The nurse boarded the train just before its first jerk. She was a sweet-faced girl, wearing unmatched skirt and jacket and a lace blouse. Her slipper's heels were ladder-high, and her hair made a mist of black ringlets. My Spanish proving adequate for chatting, she settled happily. Within the hour I recognized Srta. Berta Méndez as a soundly trained professional, fully aware of the difficulties of a career dedicated to improving Mexico's low health standards. She had worked as a public-health nurse in Chihuahua's slums, and she had taken this post to enlarge her experience.

A representative of the mining company, Los Minerales de Chihuahua, met us when the train had jerked its last at Creel. He established us in the hotel, where lack of comfort was fully compensated for by friendliness. Early in the morning we were ready for the truck, after taking hot coffee at the *chino*'s cafe.

The dust stayed behind as we left Creel, and our noses delightedly sniffed the fresh scent of morning. The air was crisp at first, but the sun soon warmed it, bringing out the aroma of pine and spruce. We could see how the forest had been tragically hurt by bad lumbering, but the government's conservation program was permitting new growth to establish itself. The driver had little to say; he made this run four times a week. Now and then he stopped to leave supplies with a road crew. The mining company had built the road and kept thirty-five men always at work repairing bridges, clearing off landslides, filling holes. We met a few trucks: one from a lumber camp, several loaded with ore from the mine at Batopilas.

A road-runner sped ahead of us in a hopeless effort to win. As he darted off the road, we caught a flash among the pines like that of a deer. But it was a half-grown Tarahumara, as still against the tree's bole as the tree itself, except for startled black eyes under bushy hair. The driver said he was probably following a trail no white man could see.

Finally the road burst out onto the edge of the Barranca de Batopilas, and we could peer down past dozens of its loops to the mine town looking like a toy village on the river. The canyon there is 4,950 feet deep, with deeply fissured walls rising sharply against the sky or sliding into deeper fissures where sun and shadows carved out the cliffs. Their colors ranged from silvery white and sulphur yellow in full light to rose, copper, and purple in shadow. The driver gave us plenty of time there while he leaped down over a baby cliff to greet his family, living in a hut perched on the brink of nowhere.

The road, snaking around those sharp descending curves, gave us ever more detail of sheer cliffs weathered into turrets and towers and streaked with purplish water stains. Every swing showed us another silvery gleam from the river, which, as we dropped, grew from a tiny trickle to a wide stream. Beyond the bridge, we rose again, topping the concentration plant, leaving Srta. Méndez at the hospital, and finally delivering me to a well-appointed guesthouse. This stepped-up series of buildings was the town of La Bufa.

I met the staff at supper. And the cook, the most important man on the place. He had cooked for years in mining camps on both sides of the border, and he promised me my favorite breakfast food, whatever it might be. Ing. Sánchez, in charge of operations at the plant, could tell the entire history of mining in this sierra. Ing. Antonio Obregón, graduate of Texas Western College of Mines at El Paso, was plant manager. Dr. Ignacio Aguilera was putting in the tour of social service which every doctor owes his country before his title is confirmed.

The *medico's* social service is one of Mexico's ideas that the United States might advantageously adopt. It means six months of dull or uncomfortable living for the doctor in some forlorn village or isolated mine or ranch. But it brings medical service to people who have no other. Most physicians agree that they get invaluable experience. Working alone, the young doctor has to meet many problems that he would refer to an older physician if he could.

In the morning I saw La Bufa. I saw Srta. Méndez at the hospital. She was the trimmest, neatest, starchiest professional nurse imaginable, from her white cap to her flat-heeled shoes. The doctor was washing up, but he took time to assure me that he could not have asked for a more competent nurse. If only she—an attractive city girl—would like it well enough to stay!

Machinery is not my primary interest, but I can appreciate enthusiasm. Ing. Obregón loved the plant and gloried in its complete modernity. The mine's daily output of five hundred tons of copper ore is reduced in this concentrating-plant to four tons of concentrate to be shipped out by truck. The mine also produces gold, all of which must be sold to the government. Ing. Obregón also showed pride in the pleasant modern cottages for about thirty office workers and two-room frame houses for four hundred miners, who pay no rent and have water piped in. Men coming off shift were entering bathhouses and drifting off to the union hall that the company had built. The Sindicato de Mineros (Miners' Union) is one of the most powerful in the Republic.

Speaking of labor, Ing. Obregón suggested that the mining company was doing more to civilize Indians than either government or schools. "When we first hired Tarahumaras," he said, "they were completely undependable. A man would just disappear when he got bored. But after eight years they are learning to stick to the job. They even like what money will buy. And they will wear trousers. . . . No, they won't live in the company houses; their women still like their caves better."

I had not seen the full glory of the Barrancas de Cobre. But Chihuahua, state and city, had given me a fairly comprehensive view of Mexico's most pressing problems and most telling achievements. I had caught a glimpse of its cave-dwellers. I had seen a thriving city. I had touched the country's growing industrialism and science in the mine; and the doctor and the nurse embodied its most advanced social effort. Chihuahua was a good gateway to the Republic.

IV

DURANGO AND ZACATECAS

◖ Durango and Zacatecas—both are states as well as cities—mark fairly well the difference between northern, cattle-raising Mexico and central Mexico, which the Spaniards found richer in mines and where they built more and more stately edifices. Durango, without too great violence to the facts, may be considered the last northern town, and Zacatecas the first town typical of central Mexico.

Mexico, as I drove southward through Chihuahua, with the Sierra Occidental to the west, seemed to be becoming always more Mexican. Small adobe villages were shaded with cottonwood or pepper trees and brightened with geraniums in pots. Many dooryards were fenced with ocotillo, a desert candlewood with wand-like thorny branches that in the spring are tipped, with fiery red blossoms. I saw some mechanized farming before crossing the state line between Chihuahua and Durango. Government irrigation projects near the towns of Delicias and Camargo have turned semi-desert lands into cotton fields and filled the towns with cotton-brokers in Texas hats. Many peasants were tilling their fields with oxen; and women, always the last to profit by modernization, were beating out clothes along the streams and making the bushes bloom with their colors. Laden burros or skinny horses trotted along, all but hidden under rustling loads of dry cornhusks. Now and again the load moved on human feet. But, in contrast with the Mexico of twenty years ago, most produce is now shipped by truck, and most people travel by bus.

33

Buses passed me at high speed. First-class buses are as commodious as any in the States. Second class is, as Mexicans say, *regular*, meaning so-so. Third-class buses carry as many passengers as can be pushed aboard and stacks of bundles, baskets, and crates on top. People and baggage are handled by the *ayudante* (aide), who takes tickets, assigns seats, and directs the driver with whacks on the bus. Two knocks mean all clear for backing. One means stop! When the bus is rolling, the *ayudante* swings aboard wherever he can. No seat is reserved for him; he perches on top of the baggage, on the spare tire, on the step. Sandstorms, pouring rain, or blistering sun never seem to quench his cheer; he seems to glory in his hardships as sailors are said to do.

Durango, which tourists find little more than a handy overnight stop, has a long history as an important center. Mountain and valley trails met here before the white man came. The city was the seat of a bishop whose diocese extended, in the eighteenth century, to distant Colorado. It became a shipping-center as mines were discovered, lumbering developed, and cattle came north. In time federal irrigation projects watered wide fields of wheat, barley, and cotton along the Nazas River. The railroad from Ciudad Juárez to Mexico City meets near here the eastbound line which hauls Durango's most important product, iron ore from El Cerro de Mercado. Mercado was a sixteenth-century gold-seeker who was disappointed that his hill contained no gold; its solid iron was appreciated only much later. But it faces a two-hundred-mile haul to the coal fields in the state of Coahuila. Again Mexico's misfortunes contrast sharply with the luck of a country whose iron and coal lie close together in Pennsylvania and Minnesota.

Durango is now a thriving city of some 50,000 inhabitants. Its downtown streets are animated with well-dressed men and shopping women, cars and buses, delivery boys on bicycles, and much destruction of old buildings to make way for new. And, as a recommended overnight stop, Durango is thoroughly tourist-conscious. The sight of a foreign license brings out the *chamaco* (urchin) found everywhere. His insistent *guachucá* (watch your car) has given him a new title. He knows the way to everywhere; he says he can drive (but don't trust him!); he warns you that thieves will strip your car of hubcaps, gasoline-tank tops, even tires and luggage, unless he is left on guard. I found thievery less general than all *chamacos* and most tourist agencies warned me. But the *chamaco* does know his way around and is often a diverting companion. Businessmen doubtless are amused by the tourist's peculiarities, but they respond kindly to a request. I asked a well-tailored gentleman to recommend a restaurant; businessmen do know where to find good food. He named one, adding: "It is completely hygienic, just like in your country." The hygiene was not apparent. The waiters' jackets and the tablecloths were spotty, and flies abounded, but the gentleman knew the words that would appeal.

Durango's plaza is dominated by the Palacio de Gobierno (State House) and Cathedral. The palace, a full block long, retains its lacy upstairs balconies of wrought iron, but the original heavy door has been replaced with an iron shutter and its patio has been roofed. The eighteenth-century palace of the first Count of the Valley of Suchil is, by happy contrast, one of Mexico's best examples of churrigueresque architecture.

Churrigueresque, named for its inventor, José Churriguerra, is Spanish baroque that went quite wild in Mexico. Its masses of cherubs, flowers, fruits, shells, and interwoven vines suggest Indian toys with their gay detail. Durango is rich in such fancy among its gold-plated altars and saints in gaudiest garb. The effect is handsome, and the Cathedral seems to dominate the city. Its bells sound the hours. And at every hour businessmen, office girls, old ladies, and children slip quietly in for a prayer.

Durango's domestic architecture recalls its colonial days, when most houses were built of adobe with the odd rippling cornices that are the city's distinct feature. I found many such homes on quiet streets; they were well kept, freshly plastered in beige, blue, pink, or terra cotta, and adorned with the owner's crest or monogram. The Mexican colonial house is quite different from anything that name recalls to us. Spaniards built their dwellings flush to the street and with no space between them. The only entrance is the big front door, large enough to admit a coach to the patio. Such a house would serve as a fortress; many did so. Entering one is still a formidable undertaking. The visitor, on the sidewalk, lets fall the brass knocker; sometimes there is a tiny electric button, well concealed. In time, a servant comes to ask one's business. Only then is the caller asked in. He has doubtless been under observation from long barred windows that give fascinating glimpses of family life through lace curtains. Rooms opening on the patio have no windows, but only glassed doors into the patio, the center of all activity.

Some large houses have a second patio; if not, the kitchen opens on the main patio. There is no back door. Everything passes through the *zaguán* (wide passage from street to patio). Servants, deliveries, garbage, vendors with live turkeys, freshly killed pigs, baskets of fruits or vegetables. Bargaining goes on in the *zaguán;* there the family pensioners come. Few families lack the old servant or unacknowledged relative who comes for the daily coin, leftover food, or worn clothes. Laundry is done on the roof, where its bright flutterings in the sunshine enliven the distant view of any city. Turkeys and chickens, tied by one leg, await their doom on the roof; and there the servants live in the pleasantest rooms, sunny and with a view.

Life in such a house follows many old conventions. Ladies observe the streets through the iron-barred windows to which the suitor comes to chat with his girl. Only the accepted fiancé may call, and then he is received by the whole family. Sunday and often one other evening the band plays on the plaza, and young people walk there, girls going one way, boys the other. And, as old customs break down, young married couples may include unmarried friends in their evening plans. These conventions are changing in the capital, but in the provinces young people often asked wistfully: "Is it true that nice young people are allowed to go out together?"

Durango's *alameda*, the tree-shaded parkway that was the nineteenth-century social center, is now a dusty walk where poor people sun themselves. I crossed it to the Franciscan boys' school of Santa María. A tonsured friar received me pleasantly, but when I offered a handshake he quickly covered his hand with his robe in order, I presume, not to touch a woman's hand. It was the hour of vespers, but he had time to tell the story of the Blessed Virgin's miraculous appearance in Zacatecas. I must, he insisted, visit the Franciscan convent there. And he made sure that I knew the tale of the appearance of the Virgin of Guadalupe, Mexico's Holy Patroness.

I repeated the well-known tale of Juan Diego, a humble Indian, who saw the Blessed Virgin on a rocky hill near Mexico City. She directed him to build a church in Her honor, but when the amazed Indian told his priest of his vision, the padre did not believe him. She appeared again; and on the third day She offered proof, filling his *tilma* (rough cotton mantle) with fresh roses. Juan Diego carried this to the priest, who with his own eyes saw the roses fall, revealing a picture of the Blessed Virgin Mary standing on a crescent moon, draped in a blue mantle, and crowned. She was not the pink-and-white maiden of most religious paintings, but a Virgin as dark as an Indian girl. (So the popular belief maintains.) She became known as La Morena (Dark One), the patroness of Mexico and of Mexicans wherever they are. Her basilica at the foot of the hill of the miracle is one of the grandest in the Americas.

The Franciscan, satisfied that I knew the story, said: "Now I shall tell you what happened in Zacatecas." About two centuries ago a devout friar in the Franciscan convent there had a vision of the Virgin of Guadalupe. She asked him for a ring for Her hand. The friar, dazzled by the loveliness of his vision, told no one. The second night the Virgin came again. Her hand, he saw, was bare. When She came the third time, he told his superior, who assembled the brothers to consider what to do. Their conclusion was that the Blessed Guadalupana should by all means have Her ring. So they, brothers vowed to poverty, bought a ring. I might see it, the smiling young friar told me, on Her hand in the Convent of Guadalupe near Zacatecas. Perhaps this is why I drove on south to Zacatecas before taking the new road from Durango to Mazatlán. A good itinerary must be subject to revision.

The highway crosses the Tropic of Cancer between Durango and Zacatecas, but at altitudes of from 6,000 to 8,000 feet there is nothing tropical about it except the full noon sun on one's head. But the country, at every southbound turn of the wheels, took on a different aspect. Adobe construction gave way to stone, a faded pink church seemed to top every hill, and the people looked darker and more Indian than people farther north. I had seen Zacatecas several times from the train, and had vowed to come again to see if its rosy-pink towers and stately aqueduct against dun-colored hills were as dreamlike as I remembered them. They were indeed. I paused on a hill as bells were ringing for vespers and the lilac haze of late afternoon was washing over the Cathedral towers and

houses built along the canyon walls. Zacatecas is comparable to Taxco and Guanajuato for picturesquesness; and,
like them, it has been named a national monument. This
means that old buildings will be preserved and new ones
built in the colonial style.

The road, dropping into the canyon and under the aqueduct, reached the town's center, where a policeman on a
box pointed out the Hotel Ruiz. It was only a block away,
but it was a drive of several blocks to reach it. Cars barely
squeeze through narrow streets crowded with files of burros expanded to three times their width by rustling corn
stalks or balanced crates. Pedestrians dart among them with
a heedlessness that Mexicans take for independence. "We
have much more independence than you have," they say.
"Just look at our traffic!" Only the main streets are paved;
most of Zacatecas still bumps over the cobblestones that
were Spain's first efforts to get out of the mud. Streets
mount the canyon walls like stairs, and houses stand above
their neighbors. A jar of water splashed out to dampen the
dust cascades down a block or so. I could watch this from
my window in the hotel.

Heavy stone mansions have done their best to adapt to
modern life. Old families have their stores or offices on the
ground floor while they live above. Many *zaguanes* have
been turned into workshops where tailors sit stitching,
women mend runs in stockings, tinsmiths and leather-
workers ply their trades. These people represent the latest
recruits to the growing middle class; they are just emerging
from peonage by changing pick and shovel for lighter tools
or a shop. The marvel is that they do not put their eyes
out; daylight is scanty, and they work until full dark,
squinting more and more intently.

Zacatecas has two plazas, either of which repays hours of
quiet sitting. The larger, busier one is full of modern business, which is still impeded by loaded burros and slow-

moving country folk. Motor salesrooms and garages shine with glass, and display windows impertinently take over old barred balconies. Men with briefcases dash about, and motorists honk their impatience. Somehow Mexico has taken on much modern rush while retaining its ancient leisureliness. Individuals are often quick; the process remains slow.

The tourist learns this if he tries to cash a traveler's check at a bank. The cashier watches the signing, scans the two signatures, and consults his superior. On that one's nod, the cashier passes the check to a man or a girl at a typewriter, who, clearing his desk and arranging papers and carbons, copies at high speed and in quadruplicate everything on the check. The patient signer is then handed a coupon and directed to another window. There a fourth functionary receives from a messenger written permission to hand out the cash. Five employees to cash one self-identifying check! Is Mexico trying to give as many jobs as possible to the emerging middle class? No Mexican can explain it. *"Es la costumbre,"* they say; custom is Mexico's unacknowledged god.

The other plaza, tucked away behind the Cathedral, has changed little since Don Juan de Oñate opened the mines and laid out the city in 1546. Its two-storied houses are stout enough to resist attack, its windows are iron-barred, its doors reinforced by heavy iron. Motors in general leave this plaza to old gentlemen and sleeping dogs, who share the mimosa-scented sunshine. Most people who come enter the Cathedral. Poor women, fingering rosaries, bring a few coppers. Old ladies in delicate black lace mantillas and gloved hands walk attended by maids or young relatives. Younger women stoop to kiss a padre's hand. Few priests appear in the forbidden clerical garb, but a few do. Nuns habitually wear long black dresses and Mexico's typical stole, the *rebozo*. But they walk in pairs with lowered eyes, folded hands, and introverted air that mark them as surely as the habit could. In Zacatecas I first noticed young women in the brown Franciscan habit with floating panels and long sleeves. So clad, they served in stores or beauty shops and went about their affairs. They are not an order; just pious maidens fulfilling a *manda,* a promise to wear the garb as a penance or in gratitude for a favor granted.

The Cathedral of Zacatecas is one of Mexico's finest churrigueresque churches. Its twin towers and its over-carved façade are so perfectly balanced that they give a sense of dignified repose in spite of a plethora of intricate design. The color is the soft rosy terra cotta of all Zacatecas. The Cathedral's interior is a treasure house of gold altars, silver altar rails, excellent paintings, and carved and inlaid statues. Such extravagance is found only where mines yielded vast wealth and mine-owners expended it with lavish piety. This is one of the cities that claim the mine-owner who paved with silver coins his daughter's path from his house to her wedding in the Cathedral.

The original Zacatecas Indians had scratched enough metal from these hills to tempt the Aztecs to demand tribute from them. And when the Spaniards came to see where the Aztecs got their gold, they found mines already dug in along the veins. The Spaniards then brought in *indios mansos* (tame Indians) to help control the *indios bravos* (fierce). Mines near Zacatecas are still producing gold, silver, and copper. But the miner's situation has changed with revolutionary governments, labor unions, and laws to assure safety measures, decent pay, and health insurance. The miner walking the streets with his tin hat and lunch pail is no longer an underground peon; he is a Mexican citizen.

Mindful of the young Franciscan friar's tale of the Virgin's ring, I drove to Guadalupe, ten miles out of Zacatecas. The convent, which once housed two hundred friars, is occupied now by one priest, a tremulous old verger, whom we found playing a wheezy organ, and the caretaker. Collecting thirty centavos, the caretaker led me through vast cloisters, up worn stone stairs, and into huge chambers, furnished with ancient carved pieces, dim pictures, and statues. Its library of ten thousand volumes—many of parchment and hand-illumined—smells of antiquity and medieval lore. Students have scarcely touched this wealth, said to be only a small part of the treasure hidden by the friars during various revolutions.

In time we stood before the Virgin of Guadalupe. It is a copy of the original, but with an extra star in her robe. On her hand is the ring the friars bought for her. What a touching reminder of the eternal feminine love of adornment—even in a goddess—and of the masculine desire to grant a loved one's wish—even in holy and celibate men!

These Zacatecas churches typify the ecclesiastical architecture of the colonial period, during which religious orders built sixteen thousand churches in Mexico. The Wars of Independence and anti-clerical legislation in the nineteenth century curbed the Church's passion for building, but it has revived since 1940, when Manuel Ávila Camacho, taking office as president, announced himself a loyal son of the Church. Tourists used to be told that Mexico's typical sound was the soft patting of *tortillas*. *Tortillas* can be shaped by machinery now, but Mexico's unchanging note is the chipping of stones. The ancestors of today's masons hacked out boulders to build the pyramids. They used stone hammers instead of steel, but ever since the Spaniards came they have been pecking just as patiently away with steel.

I think of a village near Zacatecas as typical of hundreds of villages I was to see in many parts of Mexico. I sat in a refreshment booth and watched workmen hacking away at stones to pave the church's atrium. Women passed, lugging water in oil cans. Children played in filthy streets. The padre, paunchy under his spotty cassock and unshaved that day, stood chatting with the druggist and watching the work. He extended a hand for a parishioner's kiss. He did not wish to talk to a stranger.

The scene, so picturesque as a seventeenth-century survival, so shocking as a twentieth-century actuality, impressed me in itself. It became unforgettable as I talked with two young government men in the hotel.

The engineer said: "I am a Catholic, I wish to be a Catholic, but it is hard because the priests will not help us in what we need to do."

The agronomist, answering the unspoken question in my face, carried on. "Many of our generation feel the same, Señorita. What we are doing is not irreligious! And so important. We work for better living-conditions, cleaner, healthier. That makes for morality. Think how the priests could help if they would put their influence behind our work." He paused. "Can you imagine, Señorita, what it would mean to Mexico if all the village priests began to think that a clean water supply might be for the glory of God?" He laughed at the preposterous idea. But it was a hopeless laugh.

PART TWO

Mexico's North

V

CROSSING THE SIERRA OCCIDENTAL

MEXICO's ambition to pierce the Sierra Occidental has been achieved in a daring but safe road between Durango and the port of Mazatlán on the Sea of Cortés. Joining the Durango-Monterrey road, this would make the first west-east crossing of the Republic north of Vera Cruz. It would expedite the shipping of oil from Tampico on the Gulf of Mexico and open up much territory to trade. It would also make accessible such mountain splendor as is seldom equaled.

This would be something to see, but I decided to leave my car in Durango. Driving ten or twelve hours over a twisting mountain road could not be classed as diversion. I decided to patronize the Transportes del Norte, paying thirty pesos, then about $3.50, for a front seat on the bus. At seven in the morning I found the bus station occupied by a sleepy clerk and two nondescript men, probably traveling salesmen. We all showed our tickets, surrendered our suitcases, and sat shivering in the morning chill. Nobody feels chatty at such an hour.

It was Sunday. Bells had been calling to Mass, and shrouded women and children were crossing the plaza toward the church. Suddenly our polite reserves were broken by the entrance of a small, untidy man carrying a battered carton carelessly roped. He began at once to talk, as though we had been a party of friends awaiting his arrival. "You should visit the Templo de San Agustín," he urged. "It is

47

beautiful. Mass is just over now. There will be another Mass."

The others, appealed to separately, assured him they had already been to Mass. But nothing stemmed the flow of his amiable chatter as he extracted a bottle of mescal from his carton. Catching one young man's eye, he explained. "It is my heart. I need mescal to keep my heart functioning at high altitudes. Did you know that this road crosses the Sierra at an altitude dangerous to the heart?" He addressed me as the certain ignoramus. But his greatest need was to account for the mescal. It was, he assured me, the very liquor of the gods. Any other liquor could do one damage, but never mescal, which is of purely vegetable origin, made with scientific cleanliness from the uncontaminated juice of the lordly maguey. He wound up with the old rhyme:

> *Por todo mal,*
> *Mescal*
> (For every evil, mescal)

and was pleased that I could cap it:

> *Por todo bien*
> *También*
> (For every good, likewise)

The two young men, warming up a bit, now included me in a smiling pact of amusement against our fellow traveler, who, quite unabashed, opened a fat wallet and dealt out his cards.

> *Profesor Duarte*
> *Mentalista y Ocultista,*
> *Consulta a toda hora.*
> Hotel _____.

Doubtless he would fill in the name.

"In life only he triumphs who is well prepared. We all have problems to solve, the poor to better himself, the rich to keep his wealth. Every problem has its solution, however difficult it may be. Consult me today, as later it may be too late."

Professor Duarte now dusted his unshined shoes, retied his carton, and was ready to greet new arrivals. A stout middle-aged man with a leather suitcase arrived in a taxi. Another taxi disgorged a tall, brisk young man with full lips, red against the pushing black stubble, oiled black hair above a high brow, and brilliant almond eyes. Altogether he suggested Moorish ancestors back in Spain or recent Levantine arrivals. He carried a good suitcase and wore both overcoat and gloves.

The driver strode briskly in. Well built, thoroughly barbered, and crisp in fresh khaki suit and polished brown boots, he was a man to inspire confidence. He checked with the ticket agent and rolled out the bus, a shining station wagon. He supervised station attendants as they stowed the luggage on top and roped on its canvas cover. We were then invited to take our seats. As he took our tickets the driver warned us that we were starting fifteen minutes late and that the drive was closer to eleven than to ten hours long. A man of honesty and no nonsense.

The shining young Levantine shared with me the wide front seat beside the driver. The Professor, with his bottle, was installed in the rear seat, and the traveling-men and the stout elder were on the middle seat. Clearly the *señorita* was to be protected from possible annoyance. I was surprised to note that the bus had empty seats. But we were only starting.

Out of Durango we should drive a couple of hours across arid land before beginning to climb the mighty sierra. Everybody was quiet, and I had time to ponder what a triumph this road was, and what thirty years of road-building have meant for Mexico. No government project ever meets such widespread approval. Roads get the poor man to market, speed the rich man on his business or pleasure, and bring in the tourist with his welcome dollars. Moreover, Mexico's fine system of highways is sure proof of the skill of Mexican engineers. One of the criticisms hardest for Mexicans to bear is the assumption—often only too explicit—that Mexicans are inefficient and incapable of organization. But Mexico's road-builders have proved this assumption false, as they have crossed their country's lofty mountains and all but impenetrable jungles with all-weather roads. Between 1925 and 1950 they had built some 15,000 miles of new highways. By 1952 the nation had expended over 620,000,000 pesos on 82,000 miles of national, state, and local roads. This is considered only a beginning. Each presidential candidate pledges more roads, though the emphasis may shift from Miguel Alemán's superhighways to super resorts to Adolfo Ruíz Cortines's modest program of farm-to-market roads.

As we left the city the driver turned on the radio. If he ever turned it off for a second, the Professor's voice came plaintively: "I liked that music we had." Music we had uninterruptedly from the Central Plateau to the Sea of Cortés. Mexicans like noise, and one may as well be resigned to that.

Just before the stiffest climb we stopped at the hamlet of El Salto for breakfast. Once known only to the *arrieros* (muleteers) and the bandits who lay in wait for them, El Salto now serves trucks and buses all day long. The Professor knew a better place than the one the driver indicated, and there we ate very well. When we returned to the bus, we found the driver making room for an extra passenger on the back seat and accommodating two country men on boxes upended between the seats. Mexico's old habit of overloading buses had not changed even when a good driver and a fine motor faced some of the stiffest grades in the country. Laboriously we pulled out.

The plateau now lay spread out below, shimmering in pastel tones patched with darkness where trees of an arroyo gave shade. Rising on hairpin turns, we could see above us the route ahead and below us the road we had just traversed. Ears popped as we gained a thousand feet of altitude; the air was lighter to breathe. Desert cactus had disappeared; as we climbed, piñon and scrub oak gave way to tall pine and gray cedar, whose aroma came strongly in the sunshine. The road reached one ridge only to sink again into a canyon's shaded depths and climb to another summit. On the almost level ridges the car ran smoothly, but the driver's alert caution never relaxed. Strong hands on the wheel, keen eyes on the road or lifted only to scan the curves ahead. Once he pointed out the rusty remains of a truck that had pitched over, a hundred feet or more, killing four people.

At a turn-out we met another driver with news. A truck coming from Mazatlán had gone over, killing the driver and two passengers. The bodies had just been removed by the Red Cross; we could see the truck as we passed.

The crossing of this stupendous range is beyond compare, but its incomparability dawns slowly. Mountain roads anywhere reveal widening vistas of distant plains and other ranges muted in shadows or highlighted in sunshine as clouds shift, lower, or drift away. This road alone does not offer a series of magnificent views; it is an unbroken wonder as the road, between deep gorges, rises higher and higher to reveal new glories without giving the traveler time to let out his breath and relax before the next revelation.

At last we reached El Espinazo del Diablo (Devil's Spine), where the width of the road was that of the ridge and the altitude was over ten thousand feet. From there we

could gaze straight down into the tropics, where an isolated people live in palm-thatched huts as they have
throughout the ages. Trails led down, the driver said, but
he did not think the villagers often came up. He knew of
nobody who had even gone down. He had heard church
bells in the early morning. It gave an eerie feeling to look
down from our complicated world into a life so remote.

The lunch station was a tiny hamlet awkwardly overlaid
by gasoline pumps, Coca-Cola signs, and the smells of eat-
ing-booths. In the open-air restaurant the Professor, whose
bottle was all but empty now, offered drinks all around.
The younger men took beer at the bar; the stout gentleman and the Levantine were deep in talk; and the driver
explained that he never drank on the road. What a man to
trust!

After lunch, quiet settled on us all. Even the cries for
music were stilled and the motor's purring let small sounds
come through the afternoon's warmth. The road still swept
around alarming curves; any view would be worth a day's
journey anywhere else, but hours of trying to encompass
such splendor produce satiation. I began to observe lesser
beauties—wild flowers beside the road and the way clouds
dragged their shadows over the pine tips—and to sniff for
the scent of the sea. It was late afternoon when we came
slowly down to the gulf and the water was striped with the
sunset's lavender and green under glowing clouds.

I remembered Mazatlán as a lovely little city where pink,
jade green, lemon yellow, and French blue houses climbed
the hill above the beach, and magenta bougainvillea, flaming hibiscus, and pink oleander burst out like music. I
planned to stay in the old Hotel Belmar, where I recalled
snakes and parrots in the patio, a Spanish *mayordomo* suggesting delicious sea foods, and an upstairs veranda above
the seaside esplanade. It was an alluring prospect, only a
bit dampened by the Professor's promise to call that eve-

ning to plan for showing me the city next day. I was sorry, I said, and the gentlemen and the driver quickly agreed that the lady must need rest after such a drive.

The problem was solved because the Belmar had no space for me. So I proceeded to the Imperial, far less impressive than its name, but as charming as so many Mexican inns are. My room was furnished with an iron cot and an Empire wardrobe, and its long French windows were iron-barred. The patio blossomed with the variety of flowers possible in a climate that has tropical growth along with northern daisies, snapdragons, and bachelor buttons.

The city of Mazatlán I found disappointing. The pretty pastel-toned houses that used to climb the hill were destroyed in a hurricane in 1943, and their owners have replaced them with dull gray apartment houses that enjoy the same sea view but add nothing to the town's beauty. Too often Mexican progress seems to lie in the direction of more cement and fewer flowers.

In one of the battered victorias that are considered a tourist lure I set out to see the city. The coachman, flapping the reins over his bony horse, drove the length of Olas Altas (High Waves), which would soon be extended along a silvery beach where a few homes have already been built. A modern hotel, a club, and boats and guides for fishermen are promised. Mazatlán hopes to rival Guaymas, up the coast and connected with the United States by paved roads, as a fishing-center. Here too is prime sport with tarpon, giant ray, and shark. And in the high sierra, where Huichol and Seri Indians still hunt with bow and arrows, the white hunter may find rabbits and quail, turkey and deer, mountain sheep, and the exotic jaguar, often called Mexico's tiger.

The coachman proudly pointed to the oil tankers from Tampico and the new docks a-building against the day when Mazatlán becomes again one of the country's busiest ports. But it was pleasanter to watch the mottled blue sea as the lazy horse climbed the hill. The sixteenth-century fort had seen galleons bringing shawls and sandalwood from the Orient, and New England clippers coming ashore for water, or had now and again fired on pirates. Happily the old dungeons have now been breached and conquered by a rush of marigolds and wild cosmos.

Better than driving was strolling along Olas Altas to watch swimmers beyond the breakers and children on the sand or the paved walk. In Mexico the family is a unit. Here are no rich old women dragging out an arid old age; the gray-haired woman performs her natural function of leading or being led by children. Mother and father bring the whole family; and not a puny two or three but six or eight children, attended by nurses. Parents chat or bathe, but are always ready to share the children's games. It seems easy and happy. Children seldom cry, rarely squabble; the larger look after the smaller fry. Dressed for the afternoon, the little girls in frilly white dresses and the boys in sailor suits suggest Cassatt's paintings of half a century ago.

Mazatlán anticipates a busy future as a shipping-port and a profitable tourist trade as the highway that now reaches it from Guadalajara is completed to the border towns of Nogales, Sonora, and Nogales, Arizona. Meanwhile, it remains a lazy, sunny resort for Mexicans who still outnumber the motor tourists, the sportsmen, and the yachtsmen who come from South as well as North America to anchor in the bay.

VI

WEST OF THE SIERRA MADRE

◧ MEXICO'S northwest, isolated beyond the Sierra Madre, has been the least-known part of Mexico, even to Mexicans. I had motored over worn wagon tracks in the states of Sonora and Sinaloa long before there was a motor road, and had traveled by train when the Southern Pacific of Mexico ran three times a week. I now decided to see that region again, approaching it from Guadalajara as sixteenth-century Spaniards had done. The new paved highway will bring Mexico and the United States closer together in the the west, as the highway north from Guadalajara enters the United States at Nogales, Arizona. It will connect many sources of wealth with the rest of the Republic, lure unassimilated tribes out of the mountains, and bring on a new tourist invasion. This is the pattern of all Mexico's northern states, which have been more closely linked with their nearest neighbors in the United States than with Mexico to the south. Tamaulipas, on the Gulf of Mexico, is bounded by the Río Bravo, which we know as the Rio Grande. Nuevo León, whose Nuevo Laredo faces its twin town of Laredo, Texas, across that river; Coahuila; and Chihuahua all meet Texas on the Río Bravo. West of Ciudad Juárez, the line between Chihuahua and New Mexico and Arizona, between Sonora and Arizona, is only a surveyor's trace as far as the Colorado River, which crosses Mexican territory to enter the Gulf of California. The long peninsula of Baja California lies beyond. Its northern half was admitted as a state in 1953 and hailed in the press as a coming agricultural area because of irrigation projects.

All these states, on both sides of the border, face the problem of drought. The two countries have tried to meet it by damming the Rio Grande with Falcon Dam in the east and with Hoover Dam on the Colorado, and by sharing their waters. But the north was riven, as we have seen, by the impenetrable Sierra Madre, also known as the Sierra Occidental. Sonora and Sinaloa were connected with Chihuahua and Durango only by mountain trails. The only motor road across the sierra to date is the one that connects Durango and Mazatlán. But a railroad is proposed, and planes fly high over an area still marked *incognito* on the maps.

This west-coast route, called new in the twentieth century, was one of the first known to white men. Sixteenth-century Spaniards, tempted by tales of golden cities, followed the route of Cabeza de Vaca, who had crossed the continent afoot, healing Indians as he went, and paralleled the Sea of Cortés to the south. After that, the regular route was north from Guadalajara through Culiacán and Alamos. The Southern Pacific built that way, and the motor road is never far from its rails, which the Mexican government bought in 1953. The highway crosses *barranca* country, climbing to dizzy heights with dazzling views and spiraling down into leafy canyons only to rise again. So it cuts the length of the sierra, always in sight of the hazy blue ridges of the mighty mountains.

Guadalajara is in the state of Jalisco, north of which lies Nayarit, whose capital, Tepic, is interesting only to antique-collectors or to people who see beauty in bulldozers crashing into the future. It is good to leave the highway at Tepic and drive down to San Blas on the shore. The road runs through big-leaved plants and lianas dense enough to give the dank feel of jungle. I was lucky enough to scare up an emerald parakeet; some people are chattered at by monkeys. San Blas is an ancient, somnolent fishing-village that seems quite unaffected by the tourist hotel up the beach. The hotel, with only a scattering of guests, is one of those comfortable, unstudied places which are often more attractive than the glamour spots.

The state of Sinaloa, which the highway enters between Tepic and Mazatlán, is as lovely as its name. It sweeps grandly down from the sierra's tall peaks through myriads of tiny gullies, sizable canyons, and vast *barrancas* to the narrow Pacific plain. Canyons that look ferny from above turn out to be heavily wooded when entered. In February they were bursting into regal purple and yellow bloom. Sinaloa's most important city is Culiacán, once a brilliant colonial capital, which is now bidding for tourists with hotels, restaurants, even a night club.

Road engineers, when I passed that way, were working hard to close the last gap in the highway that would make smooth and easy going from Canada to Jalisco. Long stretches were still not surfaced, and occasional detours led off into the old wagon track that was passable but washboardy in the dry season; it would be boggy when it rained. I crossed two rivers on ferryboats, manned by efficient men who knew the key words in English. And I crossed one ford with so many *chamacos* perched on the car's hood and shouting instructions that I could hardly see the way.

Los Mochis, north of Culiacán, advertises its beach resort of Topolobampo, which may be more fun to pronounce than to visit. Los Mochis is a bustling town and the center of some twenty thousand hectares of land irrigated from a dam on the Río Fuerte. This is one of several great dams either built or projected in these northwestern states. Together they are one of Mexico's most vigorous efforts to make agriculture as productive as mines ever were, as inexhaustible as mines were not, and profitable for Mexicans rather than for foreign exploiters. President Miguel Alemán, taking office in 1940, recommended a department of hydraulic resources, which was founded as a ministry. Its statement of purpose promises a study of national resources and "the entire biophysical chain, including man," and their best use in the national interest. Official Mexico never forgets man in its planning. President Alemán's administration saw forty-three major irrigation projects begun, most of which the president inaugurated in person.

Navajoa, north of Los Mochis, showed no trace of the dusty adobe town I had seen in 1927, but I found a good mechanic to make a minor repair, and I enjoyed a savory *taco* in an outdoor restaurant. I had begun to notice many California license plates instead of the Texas plaques so numerous in the central valley. Mexico's northwest is becoming known as a California vacation land. Even Alamos, a town known to American mining engineers for a century, was taking on a California tone—so I was told. I decided to pass up Topolobampo to drive east to Alamos.

The road to Alamos is unpaved, and most of the town's inhabitants hope to keep it so. They like being a bit inaccessible. Alamos lies in a dimple of cedar-tufted hills. Its most impressive monument is the old prison on a hill with the finest view; the charming entrance leads the newcomer along the Alameda to get lost near the outdoor market. The plaza is complete: church with legends, pigeons, pealing bells, and processions on all local saints' days. Bandstand for the weekly concert, where the young meet circumspectly and their elders sit on benches to watch. Almost every house in Alamos was a mansion, and many belonged to the Almada, one of Sinaloa's richest families, who claimed descent from Cortés's Captain Hernán Alvarado.

Almos's church records date from 1686, when it was an important station on El Camino Real, the royal road from Mexico to California. In the eighteenth century Alamos suffered from Mayo and Yaqui Indian uprisings, but its mines were too rich to abandon. Its eight silver mines, operating at once, shipped annually from 1,800 to 2,000 bars of silver to the capital. The Wars of Independence set Alamos back, but it recovered in the nineteenth century when United States investors extracted large fortunes from its mines. But when the revolution hit the town in 1915, the foreigners flooded the mines and escaped, leaving the inhabitants to watch their city crumble into ruins. From a population of about 25,000, it withered into about 2,500. Then came the gringo discovery, headed by Levant Alcorn, who bought one of the Almada mansions on the plaza and turned it into a hotel.

The hotel prospered because so many people who drove in for lunch stayed a week. If they stayed longer they probably bought a house through Mr. Alcorn, who also helped them remodel it. Perhaps thirty-five families from across the border have made homes in Alamos; many others make regular visits. The roll of visitors has grown so long that an enterprising young Californian has opened a hotel at ten dollars a day. Not pesos, dollars. This seems reasonable to people accustomed to California and Arizona resorts and caught by remarkable food. One evening's menu included Guaymas oysters, quail from the hills, a steak cut under the proprietor's eye, strawberries from the Río Yaqui farms, and wine from an old Almada cellar.

The restorers of Alamos have consistently used good taste; only the unoccupied house of a revolutionary general is out of tone. Younger members of the old families had moved away, but older people, left with the grand piano, the pier glasses, and the portraits in leaking rooms, were glad to sell their treasures to purchasers who appreciated them. The new residents joined the priest, the mayor, and others in asking the government to declare Alamos a colonial monument. Regulations now require the colonial style in all buildings and forbid neon lights, though electricity will be extended to permit movies oftener than weekly, and a sewer is contemplated. All these developments have stimulated modest industries to serve and supply residents and visitors. Some progressive thinkers are considering handicrafts; but the most realistic has made Alamos the center, actually the world capital, of the Mexican jumping bean, which contains a bug to make it jump.

The towns of Navajoa and Ciudad Obregón seem, in contrast with Alamos, noisily, even obstreperously, mechanized. Ciudad Obregón, named for President Álvaro Obregón, has engulfed the adobe village of Cajeme I remembered as quietly snoozing under its cottonwoods. It is now a city of stores, banks, and exchanges that handle the produce from the million acres irrigated by the Río Yaqui project. This was the dream of Álvaro Obregón, the Sonoran rancher who made good fighting-men of the fierce Yaquis during the revolution and did much for education as president. He tried out his ideas by organizing illiterates into co-operatives to raise chick-peas and made a fortune himself by raising tomatoes to beat the California market. Naturally he is the most revered patriot in the northwest, and the great dam on the Río Yaqui bears his name.

The Álvaro Obregón Dam is the greatest of three, including also those on the Río Mayo and the Río Fuerte, which—so enthusiasts claim—will irrigate enough lands to feed all Mexico. The Álvaro Obregón hydroelectric station cost $17,000,000 and the main canal, financed by a loan from the United States Export Import Bank, an equal amount. The Mexican government, with its concern for the human end of the "biophysical chain," has helped small farmers to build pretty homes and to provide such education for their children as previous generations never knew. One Sonora businessman said that the people of the northwest have changed even more than the landscape, which has turned from desert to farm. "All workers," he said, "now do business with checks. It was not so long ago that Indians and country men generally were not only fearful of checks but of paper money; they wanted to hear it clink!"

Guaymas has been known for a quarter of a century to fishermen who would endure a hard train or motor trip and small-town hotels for prime sport with sea bass, Spanish mackerel, marlin, and other game fish. Now winter visitors can live with splendor at La Playa de Cortés and other hotels, at motor courts almost as glamorous, and find the same good sport. Guaymas does a big business exporting its lobsters, which are small crayfish with delicate meat. Guaymas oysters are small too, but with a delicacy that makes them a feature wherever they are known. These tiny oysters also produce pearls—at least enough to provide high hopes and romantic tales.

Guaymas is the last bay the northbound traveler sees; it is one he will never forget. Mornings are so still that its smooth green water sharply reflects the deeply indented shore line and straight cliffs. Even the midday light does not wash out its mother-of-pearl tints, and its sunset brilliance is beyond belief. Leaving the Sea of Cortés and the line of Baja California, which may be seen on clear days, the road swings inland into the desert.

This is the same desert that visitors to Arizona know well. It rolls gently toward distant mountains, and it carries the same infinitely varied angular cactus forms, softened by occasional mesquite and the palo verde's soft green stems and yellow blossoms. The road is fast, and few drivers stop or turn off to visit the small towns with saints' names that might, given the right discoverer, be advertised into a second Alamos. The only town of city size is Hermosillo, capital of the state of Sonora. It too has profited by irrigation. Dams on the Río Sonora have surrounded Hermosillo with groves of citrus fruits, especially limes and tangerines, and with figs and pomegranates. The original desert climate, warm in winter, hot in summer, has taken on a pleasant dampness. Altogether, Hermosillo offers a delightful approach to western Mexico.

VII

LA LAGUNA AND THE EJIDO SYSTEM

THE FIRST considerable city northeast of Durango is Torreón, which is the most un-Mexican town imaginable. No medieval churches, no colonial houses, no unshod Indians bringing wares to market. Its wide and often tree-shaded streets are swept and watered, its sidewalks uncluttered; rows of drooping palms center the avenues. The architecture in general is modern and utilitarian, if not stylishly contemporary. An up-to-date business town.

Torreón dates only from 1887, when La Hacienda de Torreón was presented by Porfirio Díaz to General Eduardo Guerra. Its growth began when the railroad built through on its way from Durango to Monterrey, making the town a shipping-center for cattle and ores. With the damming of the Río Nazas for irrigation, the wide Laguna area began to produce cotton and wheat for the British, Spanish, United States and some Mexican *hacendados* who worked the land or ran cattle with peon labor. La Laguna's later importance is social. With the expropriation of the great ranches for the benefit of former peons, it became the outstanding example of the Revolution's effort to develop former serfs into dignified, landowning citizens. Torreón is one of the best centers from which to hazard a guess as to how the program of land-expropriation and *ejido* agriculture is working out.

Torreón looks like a businessman's town, in spite of one of the finest women's shops in the country and bookstores better stocked than the average. Most of its glass fronts display mechanical electrical gadgets, motors of all sorts, office supplies and stationary, and men's high-laced boots, broad felt hats, excellent leather wallets, briefcases, and jackets. Few women are seen in the streets. One or two sit in the lobby of the Hotel Galicia waiting while their husbands do business with the smelters, cotton gins, or flour mills. But at all hours men gather in the Apolo Palacio café across the plaza. Torreón is Mexican enough to have a plaza. The pleasant young man who became my guide explained that women are busy at home; girls who work in offices are not allowed to leave during business hours; "But men find it very convenient to transact business in the café." A man's town.

Among these men doing business in the café are khaki-clad government men—engineers, agronomists, directors of the Banco Agricola and the Banco Ejidal, and the office workers whose jobs permit café conferences.

The *ejido* is not a new thing. In Spain the word was applied to commons at the village exit (*ejido*). In Mexico, prehistoric Indians had a similar system. It permitted a man to work a patch of land and use its produce; land that was not worked reverted to the village. This system held up fairly well during most of the colonial era. Indians were allowed to work their own fields after their dawn-to-dark hours on the haciendas. Then the Díaz administration, taking advantage of the badly worded Ley Lerdo of 1856 against corporate ownership, declared the Indian villages corporations, and their lands reverted to the state. This was the opportunity of foreign investors, who swarmed in to buy up Indian lands for little or nothing; naturally Mexicans were infected by the free-land fever and many haciendas expanded enormously. Peonage grew ever more oppressive as landlords lived abroad and overseers worked the lands with no regard for workers.

Madero was aware of these evils, but he did little to relieve the peasant's agonizing desire for land of his own to till. This need came to be personified in Emiliano Zapata, a peasant who led the sugar workers of Morelos in raids on that state's sugar plantations. Zapata's rallying cry, *"Tierra y libertad,"* inspired certain intellectuals, who joined him, wrote his plans and letters, and in time got some workable laws on the books.

The Constitution of 1917 includes the epoch-making Article 27, which declared all lands, waters, and sub-surface wealth the property of government, which leases it to individuals. Government therefore had the right to divide private holdings in the public interest. Its formula included the restoration of village lands fraudulently acquired and also grants of additional lands to villages that needed them. Altogether, a law strong enough to break the hold of the landowners and to give the peasant a chance to develop into that needed independent, sturdy, and prosperous farmer.

Nothing came of it. Politicians continued to talk about land for the landless, but only one president, Álvaro Obregón, undertook some land-distribution in the 1920's. But only about 64,000 acres were restored to the villagers. In 1930 Plutarco Elías Calles, a strong president dedicated to large industry and with followers avid for large incomes, declared land-distribution a failure and suggested an end to it.

Then came Lázaro Cárdenas, a man who believed in the laws, believed in Mexico, who above all believed in Mexicans. During his administration more lands were distributed than in all the years before: in 1937 alone, over 12,500,000 acres were put into the hands of peasant farmers. But Cárdenas was a realist. He knew that illiterates just out of peonage would not be transformed into intelligent farmers by a gift of land. He encouraged education, founded agricultural schools, and set up agencies to give practical advice in farming and stock-raising. He inaugurated irrigation projects and organized co-operatives to work the reclaimed lands. Best of all, he established banks to lend the fledgling farmers money for tools, equipment, and seeds. The peasant farmer's utter destitution is hard to visualize, as is the downright meanness of some of the dispossessed landowners.

A young man of such a family told me how his uncle met the situation. "When his lands were taken, he just rode out to the farm with all his trucks and he took every tool and every implement on the place. The peons just stood there looking. They didn't have a hoe or a shovel, not a strand of wire or a rope. 'Now you see,' said my uncle. 'You disapprove of capital. Well, this is capital. Just see how you get along without it!' "

Such men naturally claim that land-expropriation has failed. They make sweeping gestures across weed-grown fields, claiming that they used to farm them most productively. They cite figures to prove that most *ejido* lands produce less than privately owned farms. But Cárdenas's was a farsighted program. Doubtless efficient farmers could, in fifteen years, have made these lands bear richly. But fifteen years is not long in human development. These ex-peons will probably not produce more and better crops for generations. But leaders of the land-expropriation program were thinking of people as well as land; they hoped that men who owned land and were given a chance would learn to work it well. This Laguna area is considered one of the most successful of the *ejido* projects, both as to men and crops. So I had to come to see how the program worked when it worked well.

Sr. Carlos Chairez offered to leave his desk in the Banco Ejidal to show me some *ejidos*. "I need to look at them anyhow," he explained. "The Banco has oversight of twelve divisions. We oversee experimental plots, try out fertilizers, guard against crop diseases; we make economic

studies and report to technicians." Young Chairez spoke
easy English acquired during four years in the United
States Army. It promised to be a good day as we drove
between greening brown fields under a sky glowing with
sun. "I'll show you what I consider one of the best," he
said, "one of the worst, and one that we Mexicans call
regular."

We were driving across the wide alluvial valley of the
Río Nazas, one of Mexico's few extensive flat areas. By
1946, 90,000,000 acres had been distributed, about one
sixth of the area. Under the law each *ejidatario* received
about ten acres, two and a half of which are classed as ara-
ble; the rest is grazing-land. The dispossessed owners were
allowed to keep their homes, barns, and farm equipment;
the law was later amended to require the sale of some farm
machinery to the *ejidos*. Each *hacendado* kept at least 250
acres of land, chosen by himself. Naturally he chose the
best land with the best water supply. Alienated lands were
paid for, but on terms enraging to the point of apoplexy.
In the first place, the owner's own valuation was accepted
—as he had given it for tax purposes! And payment was in
government bonds, which owners complained were never
redeemable at full value, or "in kind," meaning lands elsewhere.

Sr. Chairez took me first to visit Sr. Porfirio Campos, the
elected leader of the Ejido de Nueva California. Sr. Campos
was a heavy-set, slow man with an earnest manner and a
look of strength. He told us that his *ejido* of twenty-six
members owns 390 acres. Two hundred acres are planted
to cotton, which they work co-operatively and gin at a gin
owned by a neighboring co-operative. Each *ejidatario* raises
corn for his own use or to sell and has a few fruit trees.
Sr. Campos is proud of his record. He watches each man's
working-hours, pokes up the laggards, and, if necessary, re-

ports them to the monthly meeting of the *ejido*. "I'm stern," he says. "I allow no lazing on the job, and maybe they like that."

Ejidos, considered from the standpoint of people, are an effort to produce democracy by letting people work at it. Sr. Campos explained that the *ejido* is governed by a body made up of one man from each family. Most widows are represented by a son or by a man who works the land on shares, but one widow who had no man to appear for her attended meetings and had a vote. The widow or her eldest son is heir to the father's *derecho agrario* (agrarian right), allotted under the original *ejido* grant. Other sons may get their own right if there is land to spare; otherwise they drift to town and into jobs in industry, or go as *braceros*.

This peasant leader, probably fairly typical of those throughout the country, spoke with an engaging combination of humility and pride. "Of course I had no education. There was a school, but I had to work. I was born on this hacienda when it belonged to Juan Castillón; he was a good man, but not a very good farmer. Production was with God; there was no irrigation, no fertilization. Then with the *ejido* they elected me. I tried, always with God and what head God gave me, I thought." His brow wrinkled in bewilderment. "It was hard; I knew nothing. But I learned, bit by bit. There were always those in opposition. They used to say: 'I was born under a mesquite. Why should I try to live like the *ricos*?' But once they got their houses and two and a half pesos a day for their work on the *ejido*, they began to like it."

Sr. Campos invited us into his home, which was just like the other twenty-five homes owned by the other *ejidatarios*. Crossing a pergola shaded by bougainvillea, we passed through a sitting-room with electric lamps and a radio, and entered a kitchen with a white sink and oil stove. Beyond was a laundry with tubs and an ironing-board, and a patio where a pig grunted in a tiny pen and hens scratched the dust under a couple of fruit trees. This was a far cry from the typical hacienda-peon's hut. Perhaps it was above the average of *ejidos*, but it was an indication certainly of what could be accomplished where conditions were good.

As we drove on, Sr. Chairez talked about Porfirio Campos. "He is a good businessman, though he can't make out the monthly report required by the bank. He shows up with a few grimy papers clutched in his hand and accurate figures in his head, and we make out his report. All *ejidos* borrow money every year to get the crop in. His *ejido* has borrowed about 140,000 pesos at four per cent. They have always paid up promptly. In one month Porfirio Campos had spent 5,000 pesos on interest, repairs, new machines, and tools. And he is preparing his children to do what he cannot. He has two sons in preparatory school in Torreón; one is planning to enter an agricultural school."

Mexico, which inherited from the Díaz regime a population eighty-per cent illiterate, is providing night schools for adults, specialized training in high schools, and primary schools. But the results seem scattered and inconclusive so far. Most villages have primary schools; some freshly stuccoed modern buildings, others only abandoned adobe rooms with poor light and bad seats. Few children finish even the six-year primary course; only a handful goes on to the secondary schools, which are found only in the larger towns. "And almost none," mourned Sr. Chairez, "reach the technical schools, though we need technicians so much. We need more technical schools too."

We visited one technically advanced *ejido*, La Paz, which owns its cotton gin, has 150 members, who plant 1,750 acres in cotton, and in one year cleared 1,800,000 pesos. With this sum it repaid the loan advanced by the

Banco Ejidal at planting-time and had a surplus to divide among its members. Some of these *ejidatarios* got as much as 15,000 pesos.

"How do they spend such an income?"

"They seem to want a better house first. Then a car. They send their children to secondary school in Torreón and sometimes on to an agricultural or normal school. Or—" sadly "—they get into politics and try to gyp their neighbors."

The *ejido* Sr. Chairez showed me as their problem village was forlorn. Unkempt houses, dirty children in dusty streets. The school showed no care. "This is what our enemies point to as proof that the *ejido* system has failed. But we keep struggling. One good, strong leader might change it all, and we think we have that man coming up now."

Ejidatarios, like all Mexican citizens, are entitled to the benefits of Social Security, which was organized, under President Ávila Camacho, from several welfare agencies. The medical service in the Laguna area reaches some 120,000 individuals. Each family pays one hundred pesos annually toward the support of the Hospital Ejidal in Torreón, two regional hospitals, and a clinic of specialists. Fourteen medical units tour the region with one doctor and his aide, one midwife, one nurse, and one druggist. They teach sanitation, with emphasis on boiling water. When this work began, only fourteen per cent of the farms had potable water. The medical services hope in time to control endemic diseases by means of clean water, vaccination, inoculation, and prompt care. Malta fever is more prevalent than anywhere else in the Republic, with venereal disease and tuberculosis of high incidence. Health measures have, however, cut down infant mortality and brought up the world-wide dilemma of a growing population and a food supply that cannot keep up with it.

The Laguna project, admittedly one of the most favored

in the Republic, is showing a creditable record of production. Some *ejidos* have produced as much as $212 gross per acre of cotton or wheat and, within three years of their establishment, were paying off 8 per cent on the original loans. Farm Security loans in the United States are repaid at the rate of 3.5 per cent. Other regions with ample rainfall or large rivers for irrigation and enough flat land for mechanized farming promise similar success. But much of Mexico's mountainous and semi-arid lands are unsuitable for marketable crops, suffer from thin or depleted soil, or lack water. Consequently the *ejido* system, as originally conceived, had not proved the over-all success hoped for. The titles of two serious studies of Mexico reflect a changing attitude toward this problem. Eyler Simpson's *The Ejido, Mexico's Way Out*, published in 1937, was followed in 1950 by Frank Tannenbaum's *Mexico: the Struggle for Peace and Bread*. What seemed a sure way out is now recognized as a struggle, and in a struggle any outcome is possible.

Sound economists agree that the *ejido* system, designed to help people, may contribute to depriving people of their actual living because of its failure to consider proper land-use. Land has been awarded without regard to natural contours, drainage, or soil. A farm that could feed a family well in one state might produce only near-starvation in another. Agronomists believe that any one of the systems discussed —the *ejido*, the privately owned farm, small or large, or the co-operative—would work well in favorable conditions. But all will surely fail, and probably soon, if Mexico's over-all land problem is not solved.

Mexico, like all semi-arid lands, faces the problem of soil-erosion. And erosion-control begins far from the *ejidatario* on his small plot or from the wealthy *hacendado*. In last analysis it begins with the forest, which should catch and hold rainfall, permitting it to emerge later as clear and useful streams. Mexico's forest cover has been diminishing for ages. Historians estimate that over half its surface was forested at the time of the Conquest. Now only ten per cent of its lands produce merchantable forest, including the heavy tropical jungle. Even this is being destroyed at a rate of some 300,000 acres annually. Mexico's National Department of Forests is well-intentioned but miserably underpaid and subject to political influence. Legal cutting exceeds forest growth; illegal cutting is incalculable. And so is charcoal-burning.

That picturesque Indian driving his charcoal-loaded burro to market has burned off trees that are his land's best guardians. Charcoal is still Mexico's prime cooking-fuel; gas and oil are used only in the best homes. That same Indian is even more destructive working his *milpa* (corn patch), which he plants to exhaustion as his ancestors did. Then he burns off another farther up the hill. So the tiny *milpas* make patterns on the hillsides, leaving barrenness behind them. They may be *ejido* lands, lands worked by their owners, or—more likely—lands worked by men hired by large proprietors. The 1940 census showed that three fourths of all Mexicans were *ejido* families and that one fourth of all *ejidatarios* were working full or part time as farm laborers or had gone to the industrial centers. This is largely because their eroded lands will no longer support them.

Mexico's land-distribution policy, conceived as a way to make a landowning citizenry, has rather pointed the way to a larger problem: how to manage the country's resources so they will support its people. This is a problem of national scope; it may be one of national survival. The gloomiest prophets foretell that if erosion continues at its present rate Mexico will become one of the world's most desolate deserts. Intelligent Mexicans are fully awake to this dire possibility and are trying to prevent it. The government has invited the United Nations Food and Agriculture

Organization to study and report on its situation. Experts recommend such farming-methods as European peasants have practiced since the Middle Ages, but which are now brought to Mexico's Indians for the first time. They include protection of the water supply at its sources and also by the extension of meadows which hold water as well as pasturing animals who give fertilizer. The aim being a better and more balanced diet, including meat and vegetables, there must be studies to establish the right size of land units for the greatest and most economical production; they will vary greatly throughout the Republic. This program will require a trained extension service to teach largely through demonstration, as many Mexicans do not read instructions easily. It will be necessary also to induce political-minded legislators to pass laws to control such interests as the lumbering industry. Clearly Mexico's *ejido* has not proved the way out, but its very failures may have pointed the way.

VIII

A GRINGO MEXICAN

Don Raimundo Bell had invited me to visit his Hacienda de Atotonilco, which is in the state of Durango just off the highway from Durango to Torreón. Don Raimundo is a cattleman whose ranch is a model of modernity, but it is perhaps most famous as "the only large property in Mexico that lost no land during the expropriations."

I drove out from Torreón, watching for a railroad siding with a sign marking the hacienda's entrance. There a smiling man swung wide a barbed-wire gate and asked me to take along a young couple going to the ranch headquarters fourteen miles away. They introduced themselves. "Juan Contreras, your servant," and "Isabel López de Contreras, to serve your mercy." We drove through typical cattle country thick with grama grass, reinforced—as I learned later—with twenty other varieties. Huisache and mesquite trees indicated where the ground water was, and in their shade we saw a few bunches of cinnamon-colored, white-faced cattle.

The country was dry. "This drought," said Juan, "has made much suffering, but Don Raimundo has saved his cattle with water pumped. *El patrón* has much knowledge." Windmills were spinning against a sky fading now from sunset crimson and yellow to pale opal. At another wide gate a man rolled out from under a mesquite and opened it. "He has much shame," Juan explained. "Don Raimundo threw him out for being drunk and now he has no work.

He hopes, but who knows? *El patrón* does not hire drunks."

At a gate with stone pillars we stopped near neat rows of workers' houses. Inside, a curved driveway bordered by sage and maguey swung around a central planting of native cactus, and there a group of people went shuffling through the dust. Men bearing a saint's image were chanting without much unison; women wailed a muffled plaint.

"Thus they pray every day," Juan said, "asking San Ysidro to end the drought that does much damage." Then he and his wife bade me farewell with the polite phrases: "May you go well" and "May God go with you."

Don Raimundo met me at the heavy carved wooden door that he had rescued from a Jesuit church in Durango just in time to save it from an attack of modernization. In the patio a fountain's spray tinkled into a wide ferny basin, palms shaded the grass, and flowering vines curtained the heavy arches. Birds chirped sleepily. "Here," my host said, smiling, "you have your house," and ushered me into a large room where stately mahogany was eased by a few cushioned chairs. The whole house was furnished with that perfect combination of well-chosen period pieces and modern comfort.

Don Raimundo is a narrow-hipped man with slim legs ending in English riding-boots, and his narrow head is set on shoulders that appear bent, perhaps by a lifelong habit of examining the ground before him for tracks of Indians, animals, or rattlesnakes. His black eyes flashed, as we talked, with the quizzical humor of a man who has lived much without souring, and his manner was warm with a delightful blend of the western cattleman's politeness and the Mexican's more elaborate courtesy with a woman. Don Raimundo led me along a hallway hung with brocade strips and fine old *santos*, stopping to point out a splendidly carved Spanish desk with hidden drawers incrusted with old family crests in pure silver. Later, as we sat in the *sala* with Oriental rugs on the floor and crystal candelabra on carved chests, he told me his story.

Raymond Bell, as a kid in Kansas, never doubted his destiny; he wanted to be a cowboy. He started right by working on ranches and doing fancy shooting at cattle shows. After a turn in the Chicago stockyards and a term at the Iowa State Agricultural college, he began trailing cattle westward.

In El Paso he got his first breath of Mexico. It smelled good. His uncle, J. S. McCaughan, who owned a ranch in Durango, offered young Ray a job. The boy had enough money for a railroad ticket to Durango, but not enough to pay the forty-five-peso duty on his saddle, which he had to leave.

Working for uncle was good. There was no pay, but he had a horse to ride and his days were filled with sun and dust and the scent of sweaty animals. He learned *vaquero* Spanish and designed for himself a saddle that he still rides. A similar one, designed later for his cowboys, is still made by an El Paso firm as the Raymond Bell Special.

Young Bell was soon offered a better job, on which he showed his spirit by capturing five cattle-rustlers single-handed. This earned double pay, but not long afterward he was injured and spent weary months in a hospital. When he finally got back to his uncle's ranch, he was broke and too lame to mount a horse. But he improved the opportunity to perfect his Spanish and to learn the language of the Tepehuan Indians, who became his fast friends, as they still are. Hearing their tale of buried treasure on the ancient trails, young Bell spent some time searching, but fruitlessly.

But more certain treasure was at hand in the cattle business. When he was able, Ray became his uncle's foreman, with the privilege of accumulating his own herd. He branded them with the down-pointed horseshoe he still uses.

Bell, who was often in Durango, making nothing of the ninety-mile ride from the ranch, began selling beef to the mines. One company offered him a job guarding their payroll of between 30,000 and 40,000 pesos, which had to be carried fifty-five miles over broken-lava country. Bell was known as a crack shot; he shot from the hip, never missed by more than a hair. The company provided him with plenty of ammunition, and he let everybody see him at practice. He usually faked several starts; he never set out twice at the same hour. The money, mostly in coin, was packed in a steel chest bolted to a coach drawn by six mules and attended by two men. Bell rode behind. He always got the money through; he was never attacked. But this was not the cattle business, and, after one ill-advised real-estate venture in Durango, Bell returned to his uncle's ranch and began to build a herd again.

"By the time the revolution broke, I was ready to do business. I made a deal with the Cudahy people. They wanted Mexican cattle; big owners like the Terrazas wanted to sell; a big bully like Villa wanted whatever he could get. So it was easy to make a three-cornered deal, buying stock from the Terrazas interests, paying off Villa, and selling to the Cudahys in El Paso. Sure, I knew Villa; he was a likable roughneck. I knew them all, but the most interesting was old Don Luis Terrazas, who had acquired his lands under Díaz. He was a small man and polished; a graduate of the military college at Chapultepec. In his top-floor suite in the Hotel Paso del Norte the old don used to give audience like a Roman emperor to suppliant Mexicans, gringos with business propositions, and to his own sons, who called daily to kiss his hand and get the day's allowance." In spite of Villa, the Terrazas interests could often deliver 10,000 to 20,000 head; the duty was small; and when the United States established a quarantine against live cattle because of the tick, Bell and the Cudahys opened a sausage factory in El Paso.

As Mexican affairs grew more stable and cattle were in demand, Bell reversed his procedure and began shipping cattle from the States into Mexico. This was profitable, but Bell, living in the capital, yearned for a ranch in Durango, which he considered the best range land in the entire Republic. He knew the Hacienda de Atotonilco, an Indian word meaning hot springs; one of the fifteen springs on the ranch runs hot. This ranch he coveted for the beauty of its situation, its dependable water supply, and its splendid stand of grass, which waves as much as two feet high to the distant horizon. During the revolution he had become a close friend of Don Atanasio Sarabia, whose family had owned Atotonilco for ninety-two years. Don Atanasio had yellowed parchments to prove it.

Awarded as a *sitio de ganado* (cattle location) to José de la Campa y Cos in 1560, Atotonilco had changed hands only two or three times before young Don Atanasio assumed its management. Working with Raymond Bell, he had salvaged enough land for a good comeback after the revolution, but he had later moved to Mexico as subdirector of the Banco Nacional de Méjico. He loved the ranch, but was willing to sell it to his good friend Don Raimundo.

"What I bought," said Don Raimundo, "was a typical Mexican ranch, running mostly sheep and horses, and with little developed water. Its one small stream, the Cuencamé, gave its name to a hamlet famous then for its cattle thieves and revolutionary generals." I remembered Cuencamé; the young men in the gas station there boasted that it was the only one between Durango and Torreón and that it gave twenty-four-hour service.

With Don Atanasio's proposition in mind, young Raymond Bell turned to his friend Edward A. Cudahy, who asked: "Will you be short of money?" "Only one hundred per cent," Bell replied. Mr. Cudahy advanced the amount, sine die, and taking no note. This was in 1922. Later Bell bought out Cudahy and another partner, H. F. Wilkins of Omaha, and became sole owner of Atotonilco's 155,000 acres. He also owns 100,000 acres near San Juan de Michis, a mountain ranch still accessible only by trail.

"When I bought it, the house was a shell." Don Raimundo gazed, as he spoke, over the lovely gardens with the blue swimming-pool, the guesthouses, and the shooting-range where he keeps in practice. "A general from Torreón, one General Cheche Campos, had heard of Sherman's march to the sea and believed he could prove himself a good general by demolishing every fine house he came to. These walls were practically indestructible, being of adobe and stone, but he piled up the furniture and burned it, burned door and window frames. I had a big job to do, but the thirty rooms are the same."

The range also required building up. Average rainfall at Atotonilco is twenty-three inches per year, better than in many places, but not enough to keep the waterholes full from October to May. Thirty windmills now whirl mistily to pump the basins full. Salt licks are so placed that the cattle walk not too far, but far enough to graze widely in getting from salt to water. One hundred and fifty-five men operate the ranch, riding like old-style *vaqueros* or driving cars, oiling pumps, dumping salt, or replacing worn parts.

We visited the large, swept, airy workshop where a blacksmith, a carpenter, a tinner, and a harness-maker worked at bench or forge. The huge storeroom contains a duplicate of everything on the ranch that might wear out—parts of gates, bolts or screws, rolls of wire, auto parts and tires— and, under each *vaquero*'s name, his gear neatly placed. A man removing any item from its place signs for it and returns it in perfect condition.

All ranch employees are Mexicans, from the English-speaking office manager to the rawest hand, with the single exception of Chong, the Chinese cook who turns out delectable meals in three idioms. "Chong," said Don Raimundo, "has been with me for twenty-three years up at San Juan de Michis and here, and I must have fired him fifty times. Sometimes he beats me to it and quits. But in every case he's back on the job for the next meal and we never refer to the unpleasantness."

Most ranch employees and their families—between four and five hundred people—live in the rows of plastered houses I had seen near the gate. Each house has two rooms, a patio, an outdoor kitchen with charcoal brazier, and garden space. "Baths?" I inquired and received the old *hacendado*'s typical reply. "No, these people are too indolent to know what to do with a bathroom, but they have wash-houses and a swimming-pool and two fountains for household water." There is a school, the usual three years of primary teaching. Don Raimundo has helped a few bright youngsters to go to secondary school, and even to business or technical schools. There is no hospital, but a doctor makes weekly visits. For his convenience there is an operating-room as fully equipped as many in the cities.

Don Raimundo's pride is his cattle. He buys registered bulls from the States, constantly improving his original herd of 3,000 heifers. Producing heavy beef requires plenty of range per head, adequate water, and gentle handling. No rodeo tricks are tolerated. Calves are not roped and thrown, but held in "a squeeze" for branding or vaccination. Cows with calves are kept on rich grass, and breeding bulls are given supplementary feeding during breeding season. All this, and much else, results in a calf crop as high as 96.04 per cent. Cattle are shipped from a railroad siding on the ranch, going to the United States when the border is open, otherwise to Mexico City. Atotonilco has taken prizes in both countries. Mr. Bell makes a point of showing in Mexico as one method of encouraging better stock-raising. Atotonilco is a show place with visitors from many countries. But its greatest fame is as "the only large property that has not lost one hectare in expropriation." And how was that?

"I've known every president," says Don Raimundo, "since Madero. Some good men, some bad, some so-so. In the early part of 1937 President Cárdenas spent several weeks in Torreón dividing up large cotton plantations for expropriation. The government had received three applications for the division of Atotonilco lands as *ejidos*. But prominent Mexicans had appealed to Cárdenas, assuring him that the undivided ranch was a benefit to Mexico and an education to stockmen in range-management. On their suggestion, I invited the president to look over my layout. He came, and we rode all day. He saw the headquarters, the employees' living-quarters, the range operations. Chong gave him a bang-up Mexican dinner. Result was that he gave orders Atotonilco was not to be touched. After he left the presidency, General Cárdenas visited Atotonilco twice; he has often praised it, and he has sent men to study our methods. It is plain to me that General Cárdenas has always had the interest of Mexico and Mexicans at heart. And I believe he thought the people were doing all right here.

"The people seem to think so. Few of them leave; those that do usually come back and, if they're any good, I give them jobs. Boys grow up to take their fathers' jobs, and if they show promise I help them through agricultural or technical schools. All my top hands, my bookkeeper, ranch manager, and secretary were born on the ranch. . . . No, there is no union, and no labor troubles. The people are really loyal to the ranch." The humorous dark eyes, I thought, misted a bit. "Do you know that last year when the drought was bad and San Ysidro didn't seem to help much, I found them making special prayers on the Fourth of July? They understood it was a gringo saint's day and they hoped he would intercede."

In 1948 Raymond Bell became a Mexican citizen and cast his first vote. Loyal to his new country, he brings it what he can from the land of his birth. So he is Don Raimundo, proud both of his origin and of his present affiliation.

IX

FRANCISCO MADERO

C FRANCISCO MADERO, idealist who precipitated the revolution of 1910, was a northerner, son of a wealthy rancher and industrialist of Coahuila. He was a small man, whose fine, domed head barely reached above the saddle of his horse. But his eyes burned with the conviction that political democracy could come true in Mexico and could solve all its other problems. Francisco left no children, but his extensive family reveres and loves him as Panchito, the diminutive for Francisco. The Madero family, still active and important in many parts of the country, is typical of old-style Mexico in its unity and its loyalties. Panchito's niece, Chita Madero de Heyn, giggled as she said: "You should see the Madero family when we get together; more than six hundred may gather for a family saint's day or a reunion at Parras. Once I asked an old uncle how many grandchildren he had, and he said: 'I heard there were two hundred and five, but I haven't got today's report yet.'"

Francisco was born at Parras, Coahuila, just off the highway between Torreón and Saltillo. Turning off the highway at Paila, I was at once in another, gentler world enfolded in friendly hills that at sunset were shading from golden-beige through amethyst to purple—the colors of the fine wines the valley is famous for. The valley was named Parras (vineyard) by a Jesuit who there made sacrificial wine from wild grapes. In Mexico even the winepresses claim missionary origin. Driving driftingly into that gracious dusk, I met boys lingering along with milch cows and a bunch of sheep being settled for the night. Doves cooed in the willows along the slow stream, and there was little movement around San Lorenzo, where a huge stone building bore the legend *Bodegas de la Casa Madero, S.A.*

San Lorenzo was the seat of the gentleman who received the first land-grant from the king of Spain in 1597. By the end of the next century its lands were so vast that one cornerstone stood where the St. Anthony Hotel of San Antonio, Texas, is now. These dates make the first Madero, Joaquín, seem a mere newcomer. His early history is obscure, but he too accumulated lands. He and his son Francisco owned properties that covered most of Coahuila and touched the Brazos and Nacogdoches rivers in Texas. This Don Francisco threw in his lot with Mexico when Texas revolted in 1836, and died so poor that his son Evaristo, then eight years old, had to support his mother.

With a pack on his back, little Evaristo began to trade, always profitably. When he was twelve he owned a *carreta* with solid wheels and a span of mules. A few years later he was able to gratify his mother's wish for a cart with spoked wheels. His own ambition was to regain his grandfather's haciendas of El Rosario and San Lorenzo. Always he read what books he could get; he was probably fairly well educated, and he amassed a fortune in the north's expanding business, acquiring not only the coveted haciendas, but additional land to the amount of half a million acres. He owned coal mines in Coahuila, foundries in Monterrey, and flour mills that ground wheat from Argentina. In 1894 he founded Casa Madero, S.A. (Sociedad Anónima—incorporated).

Don Evaristo married twice, and as each of his children married he built another house in Parras of gray stucco with white trim, heavy doors and window gratings. Twenty Madero families live there now, occupied with the family businesses of textiles and wine-making. Parras is clearly a gentleman's town, with plenty of trees, park

Ejidatarios discuss their problems over lunch

MEXICO APPLIES MODERN TECHNIQUES

Monterrey: The Technological Institute and the Sierra Madre Oriental (*above*)
Workers on the Tepalcatepec reclamation project, Michoacán (*below*)

space, churches dedicated to the family's titular saints, and pleasant homes for workers. Francisco, the revolutionist, was born in one of the quiet family homes in 1873, son of Evaristo's eldest son, Francisco, and Doña Mercedes González of Monterrey.

Panchito's childhood and youth were typical of his time and class. He liked to dance, he was an expert horseman, he knew the hills and ranch life. He spoke both French and English well, as he had been educated in Switzerland and the United States. When he returned home, life in Parras seemed to offer everything a young man could wish. The family mansions were open to receive ranchers and businessmen of the north, important political figures from the capital; the older men were friends of Porfirio Díaz and his cabinet. But Panchito had other ideas.

I have been permitted to read in manuscript *Francisco Madero, Mexican Apostle*, a biography by Stanley Ross, which is soundly based and sympathetic. The young Panchito was a vegetarian, a non-drinker, and a spiritualist. Even as a rancher at San Rosario he displayed outlandish ideas by building houses for his peons, providing schools and a hospital, even inaugurating co-operatives. Before 1910 this was advanced indeed. His devoted aide was his wife, Sara Pérez, a Mexico City girl of good family, who shared her husband's ideals and hopes. Madero was convinced that universal suffrage and honest elections could solve all Mexico's problems, overlooking the fact that Mexicans had no experience of self-government on which to build. It was going to be a longer road than he foresaw.

Politically advanced as he was, Francisco Madero was a devoted son who moved slowly while trying to convince his parents and old Don Evaristo that he was right. His letters are filled with requests for permission to express his convictions. He made no overt move until after his grandfather's death.

In 1908 Francisco Madero, with his family's consent, published *The Presidential Succession of 1910*, which advocated the free election of a vice-president; it was a foregone conclusion that Díaz would be re-elected as president. This book made Madero the rallying-point for the many groups, led by Mexico's intellectuals, who were seeking leadership. They knew Madero as editor, as organizer of clubs, and as an indefatigable worker with money to spend. His five sisters had already begun to impoverish themselves in his support; the men of the family stood loyally by. In April 1910 Francisco Madero was nominated for president at a convention in Mexico City dominated by his Partido Anti-Reeleccionista, but attended by representatives of other parties from all parts of Mexico. He set out on a campaign tour, covering all the railroads in Mexico, speaking often. He was always accompanied by his wife. Contemporary photographs show her in the wide plumed hats, feather boas, and dragging skirts of the time quietly beside her husband. Madero smiled through a soft brown beard, and his voice was light and high, but he drew enormous crowds wherever he went.

Porfirio Díaz, who had begun by belittling Panchito as too puny to notice, ended by fleeing Mexico. In 1911 Madero was elected in what was probably Mexico's first honest election. But the revolution his pronouncements had unleashed had become a terrific storm that Madero could not control. Dr. Ross believes that Francisco's brother Gustavo might have saved the administration. Francisco was too confiding to recognize that among his closest advisers were evil men plotting against him. He believed that, having been honestly elected, he could not be overthrown. He thought he had time to work out his program. But there was no time.

Díaz had fled, but interests that had profited from his preferential policies had not. Henry Lane Wilson, U.S.

Ambassador, so reported the situation that Washington refused to recognize Madero as president. Madero protested directly to President Taft, but got no reply. Against the agonized advice of Gustavo and loyal followers, Madero appointed Victoriano Huerta as chief of his guard. Huerta, with Porfirio's nephew, Félix Díaz, and others, conspired to take over. After ten days of shooting in the capital city's streets, Gustavo was brutally killed in the prison. Sra. de Madero, swathed in black, called on the United States Ambassador, begging sanctuary for her husband in the United States. Ambassador Wilson refused on the grounds that he could not interfere with Mexico's domestic affairs. But he announced the change in government even before it was effected. The Cuban Ambassador protested. The Chilean Ambassador spent the night in prison with President Madero and Vice-President Pino Suárez. But at dawn the prisoners, under pretext of the old *ley fuga* (law of flight), were shot in the back. This was the night of February 22, 1913. Ambassador Wilson was recalled, but too late. Too late for Madero. Too late to save our country from a black mark in Mexico's books. Our diplomatic representative had conspired with traitors in revolt against a properly elected government. This is an evidence of *"yanqui imperialismo"* that Mexicans do not forget.

X

MONTERREY

☙ MONTERREY, with a population nearing 400,000, is third city for size in the Republic and the northeast's trade and industrial center. Its pre-eminence is hard to explain. Monterrey is neither port nor river town; the Río Catarina is a dry rocky bed except when it is in dangerous flood. Coal and iron for the city's steel mills come over a long haul; its food is largely shipped in. Yet Monterrey is a thriving city, businesslike and alert; its citizens believe in it, invest in it, plan for a long future. Less thrifty Mexicans find Monterrey folk tight-fisted; they also say that the city's canniness and enterprise are due to proximity to the United States. Its citizens heatedly deny this charge. "Yankified," they snort. "Just because we dress decorously, eat well, travel widely, and speak English!" Such patriots insist that Monterrey's development would have been the same if there had been no United States.

Monterrey's 1,500-foot altitude gives it a climate like the southern parts of our southwest, hot and arid, but humid in the rainy season. Monterrey admits to a hot summer—"though not as hot as many a city in the U.S."—and names 90° as its summer average. Humidity is not mentioned, but when one is sweltering at 100°, with humidity too high to name, the thought of a winter average of 75° is not very cooling. Monterrey in summer is hot with steaming, suffocating, day-and-night heat. Happily, most restaurants and some hotels are air-conditioned, and Monterrey makes only a few perfunctory efforts to make one linger. It is an inevitable overnight stop for tourists by automobile, being only 148 miles from the port of entry at Laredo. But the city's real life is little affected by the thousands of cars that stream through daily. So a busy hostess might say: "I throw the place open to you. The servants will look after you, but you will forgive me if I am occupied elsewhere."

The elsewhere in Monterrey is as apart as though it had been planned. The business streets are wide between modern office buildings, often arcaded against the sun's heat and glare, and fresh with color. Shopwindows reflect the demands of a modern city, and there is movement without rush. A businessman who spends his days there said: "I know that lots of tourists come through the city, but I seldom see one. My business doesn't take me down there."

"Down there" is the area of hotels, restaurants, curio shops, and Zaragoza Plaza, which is almost pure colonial Mexico. The handsome government building stands solidly and the Cathedral's impressive Renaissance bell tower rings out the hours. Beyond, one sees Monterrey's landmark, Saddle Mountain, and the craggy Sierra Oriental range beyond. Venders offer their wares, and strolling musicians, often old or blind, will sing one's favorite tunes. The band plays on Sunday nights, and at any time one can hire an aged victoria drawn by rattle-boned horses. Altogether, the tourist may be comfortable and well served in Monterrey while enjoying the illusion of being in a foreign land.

Monterrey, lacking village crafts of its own, has made a sort of permanent national fair at which one can buy handmade articles from every state. They include the gaudy and tasteless, but much of the offering has been well chosen, and prices are fair. Perhaps the pleasantest shop to visit is that of Humberto Arellano Garza, who lectures on Mexican popular arts at the University of Nuevo León and gathers the best examples of native crafts from every state. His shop, "Carapan," is a pale-blue house opening into a damply fresh patio and cool rooms where wares are displayed as they might be used in a home.

The tourist in Monterrey should be warned that the city, like any dignified hostess, has her standards and expects her guests to live up to them. They are expressed in tidy signs posted at many vantage points: "Monterrey's municipal ordinances prohibit the use of 'shorts' in public, and frown upon any person in scant clothing. Lady tourists are cordially invited to observe the customs of Mexico and avoid embarrassing situations by dressing properly while traveling in our country."

The sign is obeyed. A few police warnings when the ordinance was new solved the problem. Women on Monterrey streets are discreetly clad and tourists are notably well behaved. Men sometimes offend by walking collarless into good restaurants where they are served by men in dinner jackets. Perhaps they do not notice that Monterrey businessmen wear jackets or the *guayabera*, a Norfolk-like cotton jacket, worn without a shirt, that makes them look both cool and well tailored.

Monterrey residents can escape their city's heat without going very far. Saltillo, capital of the neighboring state of Coahuila, is at an altitude of 5,000 feet, which assures cool breezes at night. It manages to retain a restful residential air in spite of its flour mills, textile factories, and leather shops. And one can leave the Monterrey-Saltillo road at several points to drive to mountain resorts or hot springs. I visited Chipinque Mesa, a pine-forested shelf on the mountain, which is only ten miles from Zaragoza Plaza, but 3,000 feet higher. The toll road, rising by breathless zigzags, brought me to a pleasant rustic hotel. Monterrey lay sparkling, seemingly at the cliff's very foot, and beyond it the Laredo road flashed with motor lights. An equally popular resort is La Hostelera de Vista Hermosa (Inn of the Beautiful View), which commands the wide valley south of Monterrey, a continuous orange grove. This little hotel is a happy place with a wide terrace above the valley view and eager servitors who are picking up English. Not many tourists visit these places; they are sustained by week-enders from the city. I encountered a group of students from the University of Nuevo León, boy scouts with bedrolls, and groups of young couples. The young couples account for Monterrey's phenomenal population growth. Every wife was pregnant, and three or four older children had come along. The husbands went off to climb; the wives sat on the porches knitting or playing canasta.

Monterrey citizens are proud of their old families, but they are proud too that their city lacks the tradition of the leisure *hacendado* class. Monterrey's leading men have always worked, still work, and expect to work; in several firms the third generation is showing up regularly, even starting as manual workers to learn the business. This habit and pride of work gave Monterrey a head start on a middle class. Its people gently boast of it. I was told that when Álvaro Obregón was campaigning for president he complained that the citizens gathered to meet him were the well-off; he wished to meet farmers and laborers. "But these," explained Monterrey's campaign managers, "are all the people there are. These are workers in their Sunday suits." Recently Monterrey sent two delegations to Mexico. The workingmen, arriving first, were asked when the laborers would arrive. "And great was their surprise when they learned that the workers of Nuevo León know how to dress like capitalists when they wish to." Monterrey's history sheds light on this situation.

It began in 1597 when the King of Spain granted to a converted Portuguese Jew the lands that now include Texas and the Mexican states of Coahuila, Nuevo León, and Tamaulipas. Monterrey, founded in 1599, was named for the contemporary viceroy. At first it was only a stopover on the long trail to the north, but in the middle of the eighteenth century it became the seat of a bishopric and the north's dominant city. Large and profitable ranches were developed, especially near Matamoros, where several important families got their start. In 1740 the viceroy was advised that the region contained 500,000 head of livestock. But the northern rancher did not lead the easy life of the southern *hacendado*, with his mines and lush plantations. He led a hard life aboard a horse and slept on his arms, as Indians were a constant menace. He ate well and sold enough to buy the luxuries of China and Castile on his infrequent trips to Mexico, but he was developing a type—the tough, self-reliant frontiersman who dominates his environment. These men inevitably played a worthy part in all Mexico's wars, beginning with the War of Independence.

Monterrey's outstanding contribution to that war was a Dominican friar, Fray Servando Teresa de Mier, whose history may be read as typifying freedom of thought as well as action. He had been exiled from Catholic New Spain, as Mexico was then called, and had spent twenty-seven years in Europe. He never ceased writing and working for the independence of all Spain's American colonies, and when Spaniards in London organized to aid Mexico's War of Independence, the friar returned as a soldier. Later he was tried and imprisoned by the Emperor Iturbide, who had little use for revolutionists, but the intrepid friar, one is glad to know, ended his life as one of Monterrey's honored patriots. His statue, erected in 1910, was a gift of the Masonic Lodges of Nuevo León. Masonic emblems look odd under the figure of so Spanish-looking a friar, but the statue may reflect the great influence of Masons in Nuevo León, perhaps in the Republic. Few Mexicans will discuss the matter, but others note that most, if not all, Mexican presidents have been Masons, and that the order has generally been politically influential.

Monterrey was consistently liberal during the nineteenth century. A Monterrey officer, Ignacio Zaragoza, led the Mexican forces in the defense of Puebla which arrested the French invasion—at least temporarily. But Monterrey was most deeply scarred by the war we know as the Mexican War; the Mexicans call it the American Invasion. The story told by Monterrey's historian, Lic. Santiago Roel, is quite different from the one in our schoolbooks. Lic. Roel writes that when one Moses Austin of Missouri was permitted to settle three hundred families along the Nacogdoches River in Texas, he agreed to bring only Roman Catholics, industrious farmers and artisans who would swear allegiance to the Spanish Crown. This was before Mexican independence had been achieved. Later the Texans were allowed to organize militia for their own defense against the Indians and to administer justice in their own settlements. Lic. Roel calls this agreement *la concesión fatal*.

Many United States historians agree with the Mexicans that our government, obsessed to conquer the continent and reach the Pacific, was quick to use border incidents to justify invasion of Mexico. Lic. Roel calls that invasion "the unequal and bloody struggle that ended by depriving us of a great part of the north of our country by means of an unjust and disloyal aggression against a people weakened by internal conflicts."

Monterrey put up a gallant defense, but the Mexicans were outnumbered, and on September 25, 1846, an honorable capitulation was agreed to. The American troops fired a battery salute to the Mexican flag as it fluttered down. But General Zachary Taylor was free to march on south to Mexico City. The scars of this invasion remain. Monterrey's first episcopal residence, El Obispado, had served as a fort during the Wars of Independence, and there General Taylor made his headquarters. It is now a crumbling ruin on a hill that dominates the city, and more beautiful in its devastation than where loving but inexpert hands have tried to restore it. Other and perhaps deeper scars remain in Monterrey's thinking. A young man whose grandmother refuses to receive *norteamericanos* in her home, said: "I shall probably never go to the United States, but if I did I should not go through Texas. My great-grandfather was killed defending his home against the Texas invaders in 1846." Another old lady refuses to go to Nuevo Laredo, the town built on Mexico's side of the Rio Grande when the United States took the original Laredo. So Monterrey, progressive as it is, has its quota of conservative old families who cherish their past and make rather a point of knowing no gringos.

Men in business and public life speak differently. The Chamber of Commerce boasts that Monterrey has no foreign colonies; only the Americans living near a steel mill entertain "out there." Most social and club events reflect a cosmopolitan society; in 1951 the president of the Foreign Club was a Mexican. Non-Spanish names appear often in Monterrey's business directory. The first smelter was established by an Italian, Vicente Ferrara, in partnership with Eugene Kelly from New York, Antonio Besagoiti, a Mexican of Italian origin, and a Frenchman, Leon Signoret. This smelter was served by a railroad bringing coal from Coahuila and iron from Durango, but coke was lacking until General Treviño and a St. Louis lawyer secured loans in New York and brought West Virginia coke by water to Tampico, the port on the Gulf of Mexico. The Guggenheim interests, coming early, were later absorbed by the American Smelting and Refining Company, which, as ASARCO, has played an important part in Mexican affairs. The St. Louis lawyer Joseph Andrew Robertson, deciding to stay in Monterrey, brought in a citrus-grower from California and established the first of the miles of orange and lemon groves south of Monterrey. So the citizens' enterprise has compensated for the lack of a port, a navigable river, and raw materials near by.

Monterrey's model factory that all visitors must see is La Cervecería Cuauhtémoc, the brewery whose Carta Blanca beer is known to thousands of people in the United States. The company now owns a glass factory to produce bottles, a paper mill and print shop to produce labels and wrappers, and a tin factory for bottle tops. Monterrey boasts of Mexico's first law for the protection of workers injured on the job, and the Cervecería conforms fully to the law requiring medical and hospital services free to employees. One passes a large airy clubroom with pool and pingpong tables, and lunches sell in the cafeteria for about eighty-five centavos. A large park offers all sorts of sports fields and swimming-pools for women and children as well as men. The studious may read in a library, attend a theater, or take free courses in office work, dancing, sewing or cooking. Every employee may buy in the company store at wholesale prices or less. La Cervecería and other industries, notably the steel mills, are building workers' colonies with houses blessedly not identical and with garden space. A thousand homes are planned, and six hundred have already been built. Employers, through the Mutual Mercantile Circle, have built a workingman's club no less elegant than the rich man's casino facing it across the Plaza Zaragoza.

Unfortunately this is not the whole picture. In the shadow of the Cervecería and alongside the Pan-American Highway is a huddle of hideous slum dwellings. "Not as bad as those of Chicago or Detroit," my guide reminded me, but bad enough. Board hovels line unpaved streets where plumbing is unknown and annual floods leave puddles to breed malaria and typhoid. Almost every corner has a cantina; prostitution and juvenile delinquency abound; and visitors are warned not to walk alone. The people who live here are not accommodated in the workers' colonies, or work for companies without social vision.

My informant — who warned me that he would lose his job if his employer knew he had talked freely—said: "The companies boast of paying twenty pesos a day; the average is nearer twelve or fourteen. Many get only six. With six pesos you can't even buy bread for a family. . . . One company"—he named it—"that pays six pesos has made millionaires of its owners in four years. . . . No, unions are not strong here. We have two kinds in Monterrey. Company unions with a good spy system. And unions whose leaders have gone into politics, proved traitors to their people."

Monterrey's leaders—thoughtful and public-spirited citizens—are not unaware of these evil conditions and are trying to improve them. They, being both benevolent and despotic, incline rather to benevolent despotism than to anything experimental. They have made an over-all plan for the city which includes damming a mountain stream to increase the water supply, stone and cement work in the city to control the Río Catarina, and an elaborate building project. Hopeful calculators figure on no less than one million inhabitants by 1980. They plan to accommodate this growth by developing seventeen thousand acres of empty land into industrial, commercial, recreational, and residential zones. Homes are to occupy seventy-five per cent of the area. All buildings will be modern in every particular. The spirit of Monterrey is to advance.

The city's architectural pride is one of the most modern churches anywhere. It is the church of La Virgen de la Purísima Concepción (Virgin of the Immaculate Conception), Monterrey's Holy Patroness. Its bell tower, standing apart from the barrel roof, is graceful, and the pointed arches of the entrance are harmonious and impressive. But indoors the effect is dull. Gray cement walls and brown woodwork are little warmed by paintings of the Virgin's life—beautiful as the paintings are—and Biblical quotations in blue block letters suggest a railroad station. The lady in the refreshment stand outside said: "No, we don't really like it, but one can pray anywhere."

The most striking proof of Monterrey's progressive spirit is El Instituto Tecnológico y de Estudios Superiores (Institute of Technology and Advanced Studies). This institution, the best in Mexico, compares favorably with the Massachusetts Institute of Technology, on which it was modeled. The buildings, set against a backdrop of Saddle Mountain and the sierra, are clear in tone and light in construction, with cantilever stairways, airy classrooms, and steel and glass everywhere. The central patio will, in time, be shaded by the bananas, oleanders, palms, and hibiscus, which are growing well. The directors, all wealthy men, meet the annual deficit handsomely and leave academic matters to the president and his faculty, who preside over schools of engineering in all its branches, architecture, and business. Tuition is high, and most of the students come from comfortable families, but about a tenth of them are poor boys on scholarships awarded by the companies. The institute claims 2,000 students and 120 full-time professors who are paid the fabulous monthly salary of a minimum of 2,000 pesos, about $250. It has, besides, about 60 part-time professors.

In sad contrast with this rich man's school is the Universidad de Nuevo León, a state institution hampered by lack of adequate funds. But its rector, Lic. Raúl Rangel Frías, is so active and farsighted that he has inspired his underpaid faculty to make it second in achievement only to the National University. Its schools include the humanities, as well as some sciences, and its students boast, in private talk, that the university produces intellectuals, "not mechanized technicians." Both will be needed to keep their city on its course of continuing advance.

A few frankly gloomy Monterrey citizens believe that its over-all plan will prove too costly; that lack of water in the arid north will finally defeat engineering ingenuity. They even suggest that Monterrey has reached its apogee. Some small businesses have already moved away; larger ones are opening branch offices that could presumably make other cities more important centers than Monterrey. These remarks are unpopular, but they are made. But Monterrey has before now proved that it can break the rules, disregard the probabilities, and win in spite of every disadvantage. The spirit that did that repeatedly shows little sign of having weakened.

PART THREE

Indian Backgrounds

P
A
C
I
F
I
C

32°
28°
24°
20°
16°

116° 112° 108° 104°

La Quemada ■

■ Ixtlán del

O

C

E

MEXICO
Principal Archeological Sites

APPROXIMATE SCALE
100   0   100   200
MILES

DON GREAME KELLEY

116° 112° 108° 104°

100° 96° 92° 88°

32°

28°

24°

MEXICO

GULF OF

20°

El Tajín

Tula

Tenayuca   Teotihuacán
Atzcapotzalco   Texcoco
Tenochtitlán [México]   Tlaxcala
Copilco   Cholula
Cuicuilco   Tepoztreco
Malinalco   Teopanzalco
Xochicalco

Quiotepec

Silacayoapan

MonteAlbán   Mitla

La Venta

Palenque

Uxmal   Chichén-Itzá
Kabah   Tulúm
Zayil   Labna

Yaxchilán

Bonampak

16°

100° 96° 92° 88°

101

XI

MEXICO'S LENGTHENING PAST

⇛ THE PAN AMERICAN Highway rises from sea level
to Mexico's 7,500 feet of altitude and crosses the Sierra
Oriental over steep grades and sharp curves that will test
the driver's motor and his nerve. But the road is so well
graded and banked that any driver able to control his car
and obey road signs need have no fear except of the ubiquitous fool who is a menace anywhere. This highway, 761
miles from Laredo to Mexico, with a shorter arm from
Brownsville to Ciudad Victoria, will continue through Central America to South America. Mexico's part is finished
beyond Tuxtla Gutiérrez in the state of Chiapas, almost to
the Guatemalan border.

Between Monterrey and Ciudad Victoria the desert is
lovely with flowering cactus, but much of it has been
watered into citrus groves and vineyards. South of Ciudad
Victoria the road slides smoothly down into the tropics,
where coffee shrubs grow in the shade of banana plants,
cane fields ripple in pale green, and mangoes shelter tiny
bamboo huts. Near Mante a new highway branches off to
San Luis Potosí and on to the west.

This is the land of the Huasteca Indians, whose villages
of wattled bamboo huts are found throughout the states of
San Luis Potosí, Hidalgo, and northern Vera Cruz. These
Indians are among the most backward in the Republic. One
meets them trotting along the highway, men bent under
burdens upheld by tumplines, women with goods and babies
in carrying-nets. They live in isolated villages, often in

hideous poverty, and practice a few primitive rites that students are trying to relate to the archæology of the region. Schools and other official agencies have scarcely touched the Huasteca villages, but when the people come into modern life along the highway they prove adaptable.

Tom Osuna, when he opened the Hotel Casa Grande at Valles, employed Huastecas. They spoke no Spanish, he no Huasteca. And he proposed a modern well-run hotel! "I got a good housekeeper," he said, "and the two of us set out to teach them the difference between a sheet and a tablecloth, what forks and spoons were for, what we meant by cleanliness. . . . It was a long pull, sometimes funny, more often infuriating. But we won. The people who serve you are the very ones we started with." One is well served in that air-cooled hotel in Valles, from the man with the English greeting who drives the car into the back patio, to the waiters. Even the chambermaids have a few words of English.

The Huasteca region is not yet accessible to tourists, nor would tourists be interested in its archæological finds. Here are no impressive ruins, but only tiny, crude clay figurines and rough stone foundations. But archæologists, with their knowledge of geology, find evidence here that human progress had begun in Mexico as early as 500 B.C., perhaps as long ago as 1000 B.C. Supporting evidence has come to light in other places. In 1945 a worked-obsidian point was found near fossilized elephant bones at Tepexpan, near Mexico City. Two years later, human bones were uncovered in the same geological stratum. This is pushing Mexico's horizons back beyond any date hitherto thought possible. Such finds also dispose of any fairy tales about a Lost Atlantis or about Phœnicians, Egyptians, or even St. Thomas sailing across the Atlantic bringing Old World culture to the New. Every new discovery only makes it more probable that American cultures evolved in the

Americas. This understanding had to wait for the development of modern archæology, which is an interesting story in itself.

Mexican archæology may be said to have begun in 1520, when the Spanish conquered Tenochtitlán, the Aztecs' splendid city on Lake Texcoco, and were told that two overgrown mounds near by covered traces of earlier peoples. These were the famous Pyramids of the Sun and the Moon, said to have been built by the Toltecs, whose cities faced Tenochtitlán across the lake. The Aztecs were the latest comers, arriving in 1325 as a wandering barbarous tribe. They were looking for a sign, and in the Texcoco valley they saw it—an eagle perched on a cactus with a snake in its beak. There they built their city of Tenochtitlán. Their mystic sign is still the emblem of the Republic of Mexico, whose capital still suffers from being built on shifting lake sands.

The Spanish conquerors were not archæologists, but their missionary friars made such excellent studies of their Indian converts that one of them, Fray Bernardino Sahagún, is still considered a first-rate ethnologist. As early as 1640 the University of Mexico offered courses in Nahuatl, the language spoken by the Aztecs. It was needed to decipher old family and property records. But archæology as we know it was a nineteenth-century development.

During that century Europeans ranged North Africa, Asia Minor, and finally the Americas. The most spectacular discoveries in America were the Maya ruins found from Honduras to Yucatán, a region that came to be called Middle America. The oldest Maya date deciphered was A.D. 162. This indicated a high culture long before the Aztecs founded Tenochtitlán, probably before the Toltecs settled on Lake Texcoco. The Maya was now accepted as the mother culture of Middle America.

Archæologists, in Mexico as in other countries, had

founded societies and reviews and were improving their techniques. It was accepted that artifacts found buried under others were older, and that sound conclusions must be based on detailed studies of materials where they were found. Archæologist Ignacio Bernal, my guide in these matters, states that by 1885 archæology was becoming a science.

In 1910 the National Museum of Mexico founded courses in archæology that were later transferred to the university. First as students, later as professors, two of Mexico's most brilliant archæologists, Dr. Manuel Gamio and Dr. Alfonso Caso, worked there. In 1937 these men helped to establish a School of Archæology and, in 1939, an Institute. "For the first time," Arq. Bernal wrote, "Mexico could have career archæologists who did not have to study abroad or teach themselves." These are the men who, working over a vast field and pooling their information, have steadily pushed Mexico's origins back into a misty past.

In 1907 Mrs. Zelia Nuttall, a devoted Mexicanist, found near her home in Coyoacán a few figurines that were neither Aztec nor Toltec. In 1910 Dr. Manuel Gamio, working in the Pedregal, a lava flow south of Mexico City, found traces of human habitation under the lava. This pre-Toltec and pre-Maya era was called the Archaic, and archæologists, continuing to seek the oldest human traces in Mexico, were also trying to establish links among the various cultures. The finds in the Huasteca were very important because they indicate an early connection between those archaic men and tribes developing farther south.

This earliest period has been vaguely dated as prior to 200 B.C. Its traces, found in widely scattered parts of Mexico, reveal people not yet working in stone. They left no monuments, certainly no carved dates, but only tiny clay figurines, and sometimes stones aligned as though for foundations. Certain plants had probably been domesticated, notably maize. No arrows have been found, but an occasional spear point suggests that animals were hunted. This is all that is known of the actual founders of Mexico's great prehistoric cultures.

The second or Formative Period, which lasted perhaps from circa 200 B.C. to A.D. 300, has been gradually coming to light through studies in the tropical jungles of the state of Vera Cruz. Great stone heads had been reported in that area in the middle of the nineteenth century, and in the 1920's Franz Blom of Tulane University had seen one. In 1939 Matthew W. Stirling of the Smithsonian Institution made the most exciting find at Tres Zapotes, a remote spot known only to Indians and oil explorers. He found enough huge heads to bring the total to eight. Then, idly turning over earth piled for a ramp, the workers came upon 480 pieces of jade, the stone prehistoric Mexicans held most sacred. Among them was a jaguar mask carved in the dot-and-dash system attributed to the Maya. But the work was not Maya, and the date, if correctly read, was 31 B.C. Perhaps these people, and not the Maya, invented the system of dating which implies such accurate knowledge of astronomy and mathematics.

This was amazing enough, but Dr. Stirling, working at La Venta, farther south, uncovered a spacious plaza set round with basalt pillars and containing six altars, stelæ, and statues. He also found, in a fine sarcophagus, the first jewel jade ever found in the Americas; it is said to be comparable with Chinese jewel jade. The most vivid account of these wonders is *Mexico South*, by Miguel Covarrubias, who balances the explorer's feverish enthusiasm with the artist's critical appraisal. He writes: "The art of La Venta is unique. It is by no means primitive, nor is it a local style. It is rather the climax of a noble and sensual art, product of a direct but sophisticated spirit and an accomplished technique, and a sober, dignified taste." No wonder its appearance has upset all previous theories.

The casual visitor to Mexico cannot hope to see these glories, which are accessible only by river boat and trail, but it greatly enlarges one's vision of Mexico to know that these highly creative people were producing artists of the first rank at about the beginning of our era. Archæologists now believe that all Mexico's cultures may have grown from this one root in the Isthmus of Tehuantepec, where the country narrows between the Pacific Ocean and the Gulf of Mexico. This mysterious culture is called Olmeca, the Nahuatl word for rubber, which the Aztecs applied to people from the land of the rubber trees.

The peoples of the central plateau seem to have begun their long development quite uninfluenced by these sophisticated Olmecas. They had slowly united into groups and built stone structures, mostly temples set on truncated pyramids. The number of temples and the profusion of statues of gods and priests suggest that the rule was theocratic. Excavations show that several cities were important about A.D. 200–300. Among them are Cuicuilco, buried under the Pedregal's lava, and Cholula, the city of temples near modern Puebla. The greatest and most mysterious city of them all is Teotihuacán, which Dr. Gamio's extensive excavations have established as older than the Toltec culture. The Toltecs were the heirs and not the originators of this great culture of the central plateau. Who developed it is still unknown, but there can be no doubt that its founders were highly intelligent and creative people.

Teotihuacán is unforgettably impressive today, when its stones are dull gray and most of it still lies underground. In its glory, well over a thousand years ago, when it covered seven square miles of land, it must have been lovelier than any modern metropolis. Its stuccoed walls then gleamed like silver above its polished red pavements, and its wall-carvings were pricked out in color. Even in ruins Teotihuacán is proof that it was built by a society able to produce engineers and architects, painters and sculptors, and hordes of workmen powerfully led and directed.

The period A.D. 300–900, known as the Classical, revealed throughout Middle America the development of techniques already known and the lively interchange of styles and methods. Ceramics and carved stones indicate trade from Teotihuacán to the whole Maya region and to the Mixtec and Zapotec tribes in the state of Oaxaca. The city where they all met was Tula, north of Mexico City. Its monuments are impressive only to archæologists, but its significance is great, as it was probably the home of the original Quetzalcoatl.

Tula was founded A.D. 987 by a chief whose son, named Ce-Atl (One Reed) for his birth date, grew up to become chief priest, with the title Quetzalcoatl. This was a title held by many men, and this fact may account for many conflicting beliefs about the culture hero who came to be worshipped as a god and the center of a populous pantheon. He is also credited with the invention of the blood cult that the Aztecs later made so hideous. Bloodletting may originally have been only the pricking of a finger to offer the gods man's most precious gift, his blood. All peoples have given blood mystic symbolism, even to the Catholic Mass. Under the Aztecs, blood sacrifice became a feature of war.

Tula may have been built as an outpost against barbarians who were sweeping in from the north. Perhaps its very cosmopolitanism made it vulnerable. In any case, it fell in 1168, and the dominant tribe of Toltec Chichimec moved on to Lake Texcoco. The Aztecs, one of those barbarous tribes, had served as mercenaries at the sacking of Tula and had then slowly made their way to the lake where they saw the promised sign of the eagle on the cactus with a snake in its beak.

The Aztecs inaugurated even less than the Toltecs, who were artists and intellectuals. Aztecs were builders who magnified, exaggerated, aggrandized everything they touched. Cortés and his soldiers found Tenochtitlán more splendid than Seville; its canals floating with canoes bringing food and flowers from Xochimilco reminded them of Venice; its botanical gardens and zoos indicated a civilized desire for knowledge that was still unknown in Europe. The Spaniards soon learned that the Aztecs were fighters hard to conquer, master organizers who held hundreds of villages subject through tax-gatherers, slave-buyers, and fear. Once they had conquered them, the Spanish found it fairly easy to take over what the Aztecs had done. They employed the same tax-gatherers under the same petty chieftains and replaced the pagan shamans with missionary friars, who built Christian churches on the ruins of pagan temples.

Mexican archæologists have, in less than half a century, widened the horizons of their past by thousands of years and begun to trace the development of Mexican Indian cultures from the crudest work of primitive men. There is no understanding Mexico or Mexican pride in its Indian history and heritage without some knowledge of its archæology. And there are no more fascinating trips anywhere than those to the greatest monuments of peoples whom we know only by what they did. What they wrote remains to be deciphered.

XII

YUCATÁN

⟡ Yucatán, even to the casual traveler, seems a world apart. Coming ashore in Progreso is like landing on an island, though Yucatán is a peninsula extending northward between the Gulf of Mexico and the Caribbean Sea. On its landward side, jungles and distance have isolated it, throughout most of its history, more effectively than the sea ever did. Cuba was always closer to Yucatán than Mexico was, its wealthy families knew Europe, but not their national capital. Airlines are making a difference, as they bring in daily papers, politicians, salesmen, and tourists.

The plane trip from Mexico equally points up Yucatán's remoteness as one is swung around the snowy volcanic peaks of Popocatépetl and Ixtaccíhuatl and past Orizaba's loftier silver cone and so to the Gulf of Mexico. There the plane sails over water mottled with purple cloud shadows and turquoise in the shallows. The shore is mostly muddy lagoons, with now and then a meandering stream. Inland the jungle spreads like a thick mat. The Río Tabasco shows clearly. First named Río Grijalva for its discoverer, it is more important perhaps because on its banks Cortés first saw the peerless Malinche. She was one of twenty slave girls presented to Cortés by a conquered chief, but she soon learned Spanish, became his interpreter, his mistress, and a vital factor in the Conquest.

Mérida, the capital of Yucatán, is fully prepared for tourists. At its busy airport one is taken firmly in hand by a travel agent, usually by "Barbachano's man." In jig time everything is taken care of, and the visitor is speeding over the flat landscape that more than anything marks this land as not Mexico. Mérida, traditionally known as Mexico's white city, has now washed its walls with pastel tints, but it is still fresh and clean. There is no litter, walks and pavements shine, and neither broken pavements nor open manholes trap the unwary. Downstairs windows open, behind their iron grilles, into cool tiled rooms or patios full of freshly sprinkled plants. Upstairs balconies add the lightness of painted iron filigree. Altogether, a gay and peaceful city where life moves leisurely. Among the cars are battered old carriages drawn by tiny horses; they say the breed has not been improved since the conquerors brought the first horses from Cuba. Traffic moves courteously; drivers pause to let a pedestrian pass. A fast or insistent driver is at once recognized as "from Mexico." But there are few out-of-state licenses. No highway yet connects Yucatán with Mexico beyond the jungles.

Mérida's traditional whiteness has yielded to color in dress as well as in architecture. Only older women wear the white mestiza *huipil*, which hangs so awkwardly from shoulder to ankle, and is embroidered with bright flowers. Workmen have abandoned white for khaki or blue, and only gentlemen cling to the *guayabera*.

Mérida has several charming and well-managed hotels and tourist agencies, but the Barbachano Tours have pretty well cornered the business by owning the only hotel at the ruins of Chichén-Itzá. The Yucatán Trails Travel Agency plans to erect a hotel at Pisté in that area. Meanwhile, Doña Victoria, whose personality may compensate for the modesty of her accommodations, receives guests in the house once occupied by the explorer Edward Herbert Thompson, and later by the Carnegie Institution.

The Barbachanos are a charming family. Among the first Yucatecans of ancient lineage to turn from sisal to

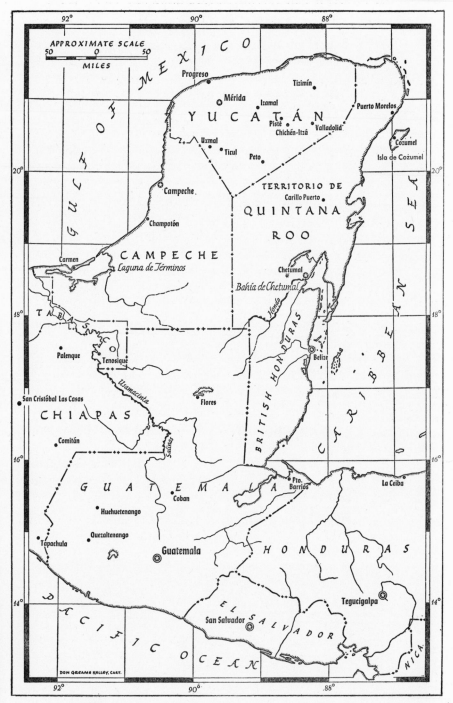

APPROXIMATE SCALE

50   0   50

MILES

GULF OF MEXICO

Progreso

YUCATÁN

Mérida

Izamal

Tizimín

Pisté

Chichén-Itzá

Valladolid

Puerto Morelos

Uxmal

Ticul

Peto

Cozumel

Isla de Cozumel

Campeche

Champotón

Carillo Puerto

TERRITORIO DE

QUINTANA

ROO

CAMPECHE

Laguna de Términos

Chetumal

Bahía de Chetumal

Carmen

TABASCO

Hondo

Palenque

Tenosique

Usumacinta

BRITISH HONDURAS

Belize

San Cristóbal Las Casas

Flores

CHIAPAS

Salinas

Comitán

CARIBBEAN SEA

GUATEMALA

Pto. Barrios

La Ceiba

Coban

Huehuetenango

Quezaltenango

HONDURAS

Tapachula

Guatemala

Tegucigalpa

PACIFIC OCEAN

El SALVADOR

San Salvador

NICA.

DON GREAME KELLEY, CART.

tourists was Don Fernando, whose son is now the active
head of the business. His son, also Fernando, is a Harvard
graduate who has lost none of his Spanish graciousness in
acquiring Yankee definiteness. His son, Fernando, four
years old, is not yet an active partner.

Mérida repays a few days' lingering. Its museum contains
fine examples of massive Maya stonework and of the most
delicately carved jewels. Even more rewarding is a chat
with its director, Dr. Antonio López Cantú, who spices
sound history with puckish humor. The ancient Maya have
been pictured as gentle and peaceful; but Dr. Cantú re-
minds us that Francisco de Montejo, one of Spain's harshest
conquerors, was busy for twenty years subduing the Maya.
Some of them were never conquered; their descendants live
in distant villages where they still practice witchcraft and
refuse to welcome white men. But when the Montejos built
their Mérida palace in 1549, they adorned its façade with
two stern conquerors with mailed feet on the heads of two
crouching Indians. This palace still serves as a home, as
do many ancestral mansions. Wealthy Yucatecans conduct
the city's businesses and raise henequen, dividing their
time between city homes and haciendas. Of pure Spanish or
mixed European heritage, they boast of their Maya background and are proud to speak the language. In Yucatán
one seldom hears derogatory remarks about Indians,
though old families suffered cruelly in the War of the
Castes in 1847 and remember more bitterly the uprisings in
the 1920's when the revolutionary fever reached Yucatán.

The Revolution and all it stood for has come to be personified in Felipe Carrillo Puerto, who, as governor in the
1920's, tried to make land-distribution effective in Yucatán.
Naturally his memory is adored by villagers, workers, and
the Maya generally and damned by conservatives, who considered him a dangerous radical. Objective historians de-
scribe him as a true idealist who perhaps permitted his fol-

lowers too much license. The romantic remember him for *La Peregrina* (The Wanderer), a melting love song sung by all Yucatecans on every occasion.

Felipe Carrillo Puerto looked more Spanish than Maya. His mother was of the aristocratic Solis family, importers of silk from Cuba. His Maya features came from his father, along with some free-thinking ideas that were nourished by the village priest, who read modern books. This was in Motul, the village where Felipe was born in 1872, one of twenty-two children. He had some schooling, but in his teens he went to work as a traveling salesman.

As his cart bumped over forest trails, young Felipe acquired a love for land and a burning resentment against *hacendados*. Once when a planter fenced off a village's only road to town, he protested so violently that he was jailed. Later, as a railroad conductor, he got the workman's point of view. Inevitably he started a newspaper considered dangerously revolutionary and got into a row with the editor of the *hacendados'* paper. By this time the Madero revolution was in full swing, and Felipe became the most influential labor organizer in his state. He was soon in politics, and during the Obregón administration he became governor of Yucatán.

During this period La Peregrina came to Mexico. She was Alma Reed, who went to Yucatán to report for the *New York Times Magazine* on the Carnegie Institution's excavations at Chichén-Itzá. In her native San Francisco, Alma Reed had been an active suffragette and a social worker. So she had two interests in Yucatán—archæology and the reforming governor, Felipe Carrillo Puerto. A Yucatecan *hacendado* had described him for her as "a dangerous red monster with green eyes," a picture that may not have had the effect he hoped.

Alma Reed found the Governor a tall, well-set-up man with a commanding manner and warm green eyes in a brown face. He challenged her admiration at once; later she found him her ideal leader—a visionary with the political skill to realize his ideals. He had appointed women to key posts, and she was a feminist; he had improved prison conditions, and she had seen prisons; he had established the first birth-control clinic in the Americas, and that in a Catholic state where eighty per cent of the babies died within weeks, and Alma Reed had known Margaret Sanger.

One can guess how the eager girl impressed the Yucatecan. Slim and tall, with flowerlike skin and blue eyes, she must have seemed the blond answer to a dream. He was soon her ardent suitor, sending marimba-players to serenade her, bombarding her with orchids, letters, and calls, and finally taking her to visit his mother, which was the Mexican's declaration of intent. He followed her to the States with so many letters that she has hundreds as basis for a biography of Carrillo Puerto. She returned to Mexico for the *New York Times* in 1923. This time she was hesitant. "I was," she recalled thirty years later, "afraid to face my fate; perhaps I had a premonition." The Governor had a message for her at Progreso. If she did not come to Mérida then, he would follow to Mexico on the next steamer. She did not, and he did. In Mexico they became engaged.

Later that autumn Alma Reed returned to Yucatán for a Maya congress of journalists from all the Americas. On a stormy night in the Gulf she heard the marimba and a song. She knew the words; they had been written for her by the Yucatecan poet, Luis Rosada Vega, who said: "I only wrote down what Felipe said." But that night she first heard the haunting melody of *La Peregrina*.

> *Peregrina, Peregrina,*
>
> *Cuando dejes mis palmares,*
>
> *Peregrina del semblante encantador,*

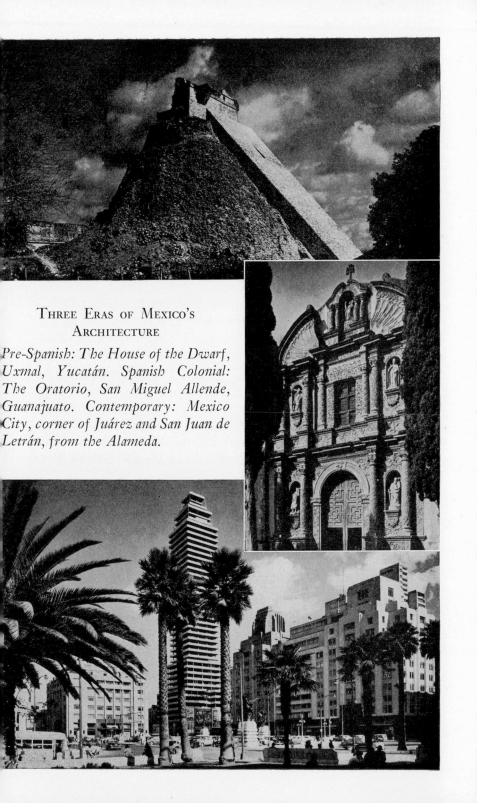

THREE ERAS OF MEXICO'S ARCHITECTURE

Pre-Spanish: The House of the Dwarf, Uxmal, Yucatán. Spanish Colonial: The Oratorio, San Miguel Allende, Guanajuato. Contemporary: Mexico City, corner of Juárez and San Juan de Letrán, from the Alameda.

PULQUE: *tlachiquero about to suck from a maguey the aguamiel (honey-water)*

No te olvides, no te olvides,

De mi tierra, de mi amor.

(Traveler, wanderer,

As you leave these groves of palm,

Enchanting wayfarer,

Forget not, forget not,

My land, my love.)

After that visit in Yucatán, Alma Reed returned to San Francisco to make ready for her wedding. Her clothes filled five trunks, the invitations were out, she was eager as a flame. But instead of a bridegroom in January there came confused news of an uprising in Yucatán. Telegraph wires were cut; only distorted stories came through. Nearly a month later Alma Reed learned through the *New York Times* that Felipe Carrillo Puerto, idealistic revolutionary, the personification of her ideals, had been brutally killed. He had been treacherously led to a spot on the outskirts of Mérida, and there, with ten of his brothers and friends, he had been shot.

Carrillo Puerto might have escaped; any Maya would have given him refuge, even died to save his life. But he would not endanger the people he was dedicated to help. They honor him as their only Maya governor, who lived to serve his people. The anniversary of his death, January 3, 1923, is reverently observed as Carrillo Puerto Day, and Mérida's largest park is dedicated to him.

Outside of Mérida, in any direction, one is impressed by the strangeness of this land. It is flat, with neither hills nor rivers. Thin reddish soil covers a limestone base, which has in places broken into wells from five feet to one hundred feet deep. These *cenotes*, formerly the only sources of water, have been supplemented by windmills whose silvery blades spin ceaselessly. Fortunately a man can raise enough food for his family during the rainy season, and Yucatán's only money crop grows without irrigation.

This is henequen, an agave whose tough yellow fiber is often known as sisal. It grows in long ranks of spiny gray-green clusters that require little care; one sees men moving tiny plants from nurseries to the fields. In drying-sheds the golden fiber hangs in swaying curtains to dry before being run through the cording-machines. Trucks, especially toward Progreso, the henequen port, speed along under bales of fiber and rolls of rope. Some henequen lands have been expropriated and turned into *ejidos*, but as it takes a plant ten years to mature, it is not suited to *ejido* culture. Many plantations are owned by the old families; in others cooperatives have proved successful.

The *hacendado* in his white *guayabera*, dealing in English with a visitor, in Spanish with his family, and in Maya with his workmen, is a charming person. His home, shaded by ceiba and mango trees and flowering vines, is furnished with wicker furniture, straw mats, and hammocks, which are preferred to beds because they make sleep possible on the hottest night. Many such gentlemen have no use for anything that has happened since Don Porfirio's day. They speak of themselves as Yucatecans, not Mexicans.

One of them, now living in Mexico, explained this. "Yucatán never really belonged to the viceroyalty of New Spain, but to the Audiencia of Guatemala. Yucatán was always influenced by British Honduras, and boys were sent to England to school." Of his childhood at the end of the century he said: "Life had no luxury or what you would call comfort. Houses were bare, except for a few wardrobes and stiff chairs. We all slept in hammocks, and doorways were curtained with henequen nets that tempered the light and discouraged the insects without cutting off the breeze. But it was a life of ease such as is unknown today. And it was pure feudalism."

"The master could whip his servants, and did. If he killed one, nobody dared complain. The Indians worked the fields and gardens and served the white family. Until I went to England I never put on my own shoes. But the servants had their rights too, mind you. They could scold the children and even talk back to the grown-ups they had served from infancy. It was a pleasant life for everybody. And food was plentiful. At every meal they served huge platters of rice and meat, including the deer and pheasant Yucatán is famous for, and fish from the sea. And after each meal the surplus food—quantities of it—was set out for the beggars, who came and feasted like lords."

So speaks the master race of any time or place, remembering what a child saw. He knew nothing of the hideous abuse of the Yaqui Indians, who, tricked out of their lands in Sonora, were shipped off in chains to the hardwood forests of Yucatán. There they died off completely, and have been replaced by a hardier breed of mixed Indian and Negro blood. Hardwoods are still important to Yucatán. The administration of Adolfo Ruiz Cortines, dedicated to reclamation and development, hopes to drain swamps and develop enough crops to break the one-crop pattern. Meanwhile, Yucatán is henequen land.

Henequen did not become an export crop until the nineteenth century, though in 1502 Columbus reported meeting canoe loads of Indians whose gear was tied with henequen ropes. The Spaniards, always quick to adopt Indian inventions, were soon also softening the agave fiber in salt water, beating it free, and twisting it into rope and cords to make mats, cloth, and hammocks.

The first commercial load of henequen was shipped abroad in 1811. After that, the trade grew steadily, especially after the invention of cordage machines. A tale, unhappily unverifiable, relates that Cyrus McCormick, idling on the Boston docks one day, noticed some bundles of twine on a ship from the Caribbean. Having just invented a binder, McCormick was looking for a durable cordage that was cheap. He asked what those bundles were. "Henequen," said the skipper, "from Yucatán." Both words were strange, but McCormick, having pulled hard and found the fiber tough, ordered ten thousand bales to be shipped on the next ship.

This overwhelming order, according to legend, roused the leisurely Yucatecans to a business of Yankee proportions. Rich men turned from hardwoods to henequen and made great fortunes until Yankee monopolies, international markets, and finally competition from the Philippines brought on a sad series of crises. Only within the 1950's have organized owners managed a fair degree of stability. But they still need other crops. It is estimated that at mid-century more than half of Yucatán's population, from the man with the hoe to the man with the bank, works with henequen.

XIII

MEXICO'S MAYA RUINS

⌘   THE GREAT ruined city of Chichén-Itzá shows traces of the development and decline of Maya culture from the tenth to the fourteenth century, when those marvelous people were in many ways more advanced than their European contemporaries. The drive out from Mérida, past henequen fields and pretty villages, is too easy to convey any sense of remoteness, but the early explorers had to hack their way through undergrowth if not real jungle. But the first sight of El Castillo could never have been more impressive than today as it looms in stark majesty almost one hundred feet above the earth.

The Barbachanos' hotel Mayaland is just beyond, set in multi-colored foliage like the Maya villages, and built like them in oval shape with pitched palm-leaf roofs. The cabins are named for Maya ruins: Mayapán, Sayil, Labná, Uxmal, Kabáh. And guests are served by Maya people. A short, sturdy, smiling Maya trundled our bags on a cart to Sayil, where we met Remigia. Like all Maya women, she was less than five feet in height, her brown skin was flower soft, her tiny hands and feet were exquisitely made. When she had made us comfortable, she joined another maid, and they fluttered off like big butterflies in their white *huipiles* and with bright ribbons in their hair. Mayas never seem to work hard, so deft are their movements, and so unhurried. They seem a people of another world, giving an impression of fragility in their smallness and immaculateness. Even the men working on a new wing for the hotel were clean, and they sang and whistled all day. Their operation was compounded of prehistoric methods and modern machinery. Men with hundred-pound cans of sand on their heads walked erect up ladders tied together with thongs. But other cans were hoisted by means of a rope attached to a jeep's motor.

The hotel's long red-tiled veranda gave a view, through an arch, of the Caracol (Snail Shell) which archæologists take to be an astronomical observatory. At the other end, the windowless dining-room opened onto a swimming pool, which reflected red and coral bougainvillea, pink oleanders, and lemons like golden globes among the leaves. Just there a quiet Maya gardener was making a *nacimiento* (crèche); he worked slowly, placing the toy images to please his eye. It seemed he would never finish, but by Christmas Eve it was ready.

Every evening the guests were entertained with old and popular songs while moonlight made magic with the Caracol, and waiters and maids finished their kitchen work and slipped in quietly. Gaspar Canul Ku, head waiter, joined in *La Peregrina* and then sang *Farewell to Chichén-Itzá* and ancient battle songs in the Maya tongue. He sang without self-consciousness, his head tilted, his arched nose and full lips just like those carved on the monuments. Then Remigia, laughingly urged, stepped out. She lifted her tender arms to extend her *huipil* into wings and, with the aplomb of a trained performer, she danced. Her babylike feet slipped in and out, but her upper body was still—so still that when a glass of wine was placed on her head, the wine did not even jiggle in the glass. Then it was time for *La Posada*, Mexico's dramatization of Joseph and Mary's search for a place where the Child might be born. All the guests took part with the servants and their families. On Christmas Eve they came to the *nacimiento*, where hallelujas were sung and the Child appeared in Mary's arms. So the

Maya people enacted the sacred drama of another race in the shadow of their ancient temples. But we found them all keenly aware of their antiquity and very proud of their race. It is good to see the ruins with a Maya guide.

Our guide, Martín Dzib, was so Maya that he spoke no Spanish, but he had learned some English while working with archæologists. He took us first to El Castillo which commands the whole city of Chichén-Itzá, which, at its height, covered three square miles of land and had about 300,000 inhabitants. This estimate is based on the number of farmers needed to supply its dignitaries and the number of artisans and artists required to move, dress, erect, and decorate its buildings. The workers lived in perishable huts; the ruins are of the temples and other buildings used by priests and rulers. The Castillo was built in the style of central Mexico with the temple set on a truncated pyramid. The Mexican Quetzalcoatl, known to the Maya as Kulkulcan, appears as the feathered serpent, crawling down the grand stairway's ninety-one steps and ending in wide-jawed heads at the bottom. Archæologists, opening this pyramid, found another inside it, and there they came upon two mosaic discs of jade, coral, and turquoise. Near it was the Red Jaguar, a larger-than-life animal painted red and spotted with real turquoise, and glaring with sharp teeth. Human bones were found there; surely such a fearful god needed much propitiation.

Chichén-Itzá, now a national monument, was excavated by Mexican archæologists and the Carnegie Institute working together in a successful co-operation based on personal friendships and mutual respect. Sylvanus G. Morley, who headed the work for the Carnegie, has left a classic study of the Maya field in *The Ancient Maya*, founded on forty-two years of study. Contemporary records consist of three pre-Hispanic codices, a few later writings, and—by a depressing irony—the report of a narrow bigot. This was

Diego de Landa, Bishop of Yucatán, who, even as he destroyed Maya writings, was so fascinated that he gained a vast knowledge of Maya folklore.

It is the world's great loss that the early missionaries to the New World lacked the appreciation of antique glories which made the Renaissance churchmen such splendid collectors. So they destroyed temples as fine as those of Egypt and Greece, burned books, and deprived a race of its accumulated wisdom. They, in effect, cut off the thinking head, leaving only farm and household lore and the dregs of priestly erudition, which persist as superstitions. So Maya science and art did not enter the stream of European knowledge, but died as old men died and young men became servitors in an alien tongue in alien temples.

Modern engineers marvel at the engineering skill reflected in Maya building which is beautiful and exact without the use of either wheels or metals. Thousands of small sturdy men rolled huge stones over sand ramps and carried heavy timbers for miles. Their obsidian cutting-tools could cut stone as cleanly as modern workmen can cut with steel. It has been accepted that they did not know the keystone arch, but a Massachusetts Institute of Technology engineer said: "I'll never believe that men who understood engineering principles as they did were ignorant of the keystone. There must have been another reason—superstition perhaps." Archæologists bear out this theory; they have actually found a few keystones. All that remains of these magnificent structures is the basic stone; the stucco and paint that covered them originally have worn off except in a few sheltered places, and most of the wood has rotted away.

Martín Dzib showed us a few such traces in the Temple of the Warriors and the Thousand Columns that rise grandly east of the Castillo at Chichén-Itzá. Their excavation and restoration were directed by Earl Morris, whose book, *The Temple of the Warriors*, also shows how archæologists work. "Before" photographs picture an overgrown hill. Careful digging uncovered a few cut stones, but broken, even split to be used again; the entire complex was built in three periods. Morris and his staff sorted out the fallen stones and reassembled them like a jigsaw puzzle. So they rebuilt the pyramid, several temples, and the stately colonnade of the Thousand Columns. Inside the Temple of the Warriors, they found some of the brightest frescoes in the Maya field. One mural pictures a coastal village, with fishermen coming in with a catch, and men and women washing, cooking, and working in the fields.

Chichén-Itzá's great court is inclosed on the north by small temples and theaters decorated with skulls, eagles, and the ubiquitous jaguar. One figure is the Chacmool (Red Claw), which is found widely throughout Mexico and so far is unexplained. It is a human form resting on hips and shoulders with twisted head and a disc on its stomach. It looks bright enough to know the answers, but so far the Chacmool maintains a stony silence.

Chichén-Itzá has seven ball courts; its largest measures four hundred and eighty feet by one hundred and eighty. The Spaniards were much taken with the ball that bounced, but they left no rules of the game, which was played by two teams trying to send the ball through two stone rings in the wall. They used only knees or buttocks—no hands! Betting was so wild that a man might risk his entire fortune or wager himself and his family into slavery. Temples above the court's walls indicate that the game had religious significance too.

The Sacred Well, north of the Castillo, may contain the answer to the question of whether the Maya did or did not practice human sacrifice. In this typical *cenote*, maidens were traditionally sacrificed to the rain god, though it has been said that the girls were tossed in not as sacrifices but

as messengers to the gods. If the victim lived until the midday sun touched the water, she was raised to tell what the
god had prophesied. This well was once dredged by Edward Herbert Thompson, who lived for years at Chichén-
Itzá and sold much material to Harvard's Peabody Museum
and the Field Museum in Chicago. Thompson has no standing with archæologists, and the Mexican government has
charged him with violating his consular privilege to ship
antiques out of the country. But he did bring up from the
Sacred Well many artifacts of clay, copper, gold, and
precious stones.

Martín Dzib led us, one day, through oak and cedar
woods draped with Spanish moss, where it seemed that
every hillock must contain a ruin. Many doubtless do, and
several have been excavated, including the Caracol, whose
astronomical purpose is proved by the fact that its openings are set to catch the sun at its seasonal changes. Maya
astronomers were as accurate as their engineers. A more
beautiful building is known as Las Monjas (the nuns) because its cells reminded the Spaniards of a convent. An archæological vandal once dynamited the west wing to get
out carvings for shipment abroad; but the remaining façades
are extraordinarily beautiful for their perfect proportions
and the lacelike effect of the intricate carvings.

Yucatán is dotted with ruins, some excavated, many not.
Uxmal, easy to reach from Mérida, is one of the most rewarding, both for its quaint legend and for sheer architectural beauty. It lies in the Puuc, Yucatán's only hilly region,
which is so waterless that it lacks even *cenotes*. We stopped
at Kabah to see one of the underground cisterns in which
the ancients captured rain water. There some forgotten
engineer had made a jar-shaped container with a flaring top
to catch the rain; he plastered it so well that it still holds
water for the caretaker's family.

Later our guide, Felipe Castillo, pointed out a crude

stone image of a woman with a snake beside her. It was, he said, the only pagan image he knew which the Indians still pray to. She was the witch mother of El Enano, the Dwarf, who was mystically born from an egg to revenge his parents, the true rulers of Uxmal. As soon as he was strong enough, El Enano went to Uxmal, defied the usurper, and met and defeated him in trials of strength. He proved himself by erecting, in one night, the pyramid topped by a temple which is known as the House of the Dwarf. Except for this Mexican-type temple, Uxmal's buildings are low and heightened only by latticed combs; this was the older Mayan style.

Uxmal's Las Monjas is a noble quadrangle of 200 feet by 250, and so perfectly proportioned that it is easy to believe that only the Dwarf's magic brought it to sight. All four sides are standing on their broken terrace; two are covered with intricate designs of plant, animal, and human forms combined with the Greek fret design. The central theme of one is the dwarf as infant emerging from the egg, as a mature being, as a stern ruler. Maya artists were too fertile of imagination to repeat themselves, so the eastern wing is adorned with geometrical designs and heads carved in the round and as individual as portraits. The south façade repeats the motif the Maya never forgot, the tall-roofed hut.

From there one faces the governor's house, which Morley describes as "the most magnificent, the most spectacular single building ever erected in the Americas before Columbus." Its preservation is remarkable, its general aspect truly regal. Its carvings, unexcelled in the Maya area, carry the sacred serpent motif in filigree that flows like ribbons. This mansion is accepted as the home of the Xiu, a family whose genealogy can be traced since it was first printed in 1557. The contemporary Xiu lives in a thatched hut, but is fully aware of his past.

The Maya area extended far beyond Yucatán, and one

of its finest monuments is Palenque in the state of Chiapas. It is fairly accessible by train from Mexico City or Mérida. Palenque has appeared in the international press since June 1952 when Arq. Alberto Ruz d'Huillier uncovered there the first Maya tomb ever found under a pyramid that was certainly built over it. Dr. Ruz is a modest young man whose natural enthusiasm is well curbed by scientific caution. "It was exciting," he says, "but we do not know what it means."

Palenque exudes a sense of dark mystery; the forest presses close and is so thick that it must be daily hacked back by machetes. Little is known of these ruins; even legend is scarce. The date of the city's founding is unknown, and nothing suggests either time or reason for its abandonment. The earliest date deciphered, A.D. 642, is of the period when Maya sculpture was at its height; and when Cortés passed by on his phenomenal journey to Honduras he heard nothing of it.

The road to the ruins from Palenque village on the railroad passes through heavy woods to the pyramid, where the visitor is asked to register. This is the pyramid Dr. Ruz d'Huillier excavated; it had previously been covered by the jungle's tangle of roots and lianas, which, quite as much as earthquakes and rainfall, has destroyed much prehistoric architecture.

Arq. Ruz's party, clearing the stairway, which rises on eight levels to the temple, found there a portico and inside it a wall tablet covered with 620 undecipherable hieroglyphics. Enough probably to solve the riddle of the temple, if not of Palenque's entire puzzle. Then workmen uncovered a large stone slab in the floor. They raised it, as the Maya must have, by running ropes through holes bored in it. Modern workmen, for all their jacks and wheels, had such difficulty that they only deepened the mystery of how the

Maya, with neither, could have raised such a weight. That one stone weighed eight tons.

A stairway inside the pyramid led down to below ground level. There they came upon a reddened stone, beautifully inscribed with more cryptic symbols. This was the lid of a sarcophagus containing the bones of a chief who must have been potent indeed. Five skeletons indicate that he was accompanied by servitors. Two beautiful stucco heads are unexplained. The ruler himself, a tall man even by modern standards, held or wore marvelous jewels, some of jade as fine as the finest Chinese jade. The face had been hidden by a mosaic mask, which can be reassembled perfectly. All these treasures are in the National Museum in Mexico City.

The other monuments of Palenque are as impressive as their modern names suggest. The Palace, with four patios and a square tower that was doubtless an observatory, measures 300 feet by 250, and is noble enough for any royalty. It contains many carved figures in bas-relief or in the round. Maya sculptors certainly knew human anatomy. All the figures are splendidly attired in woven garments, feathers, and jewelry. The other buildings—the temples of the Sun, the Cross, and the Foliate Cross—are smaller, but as distinctive and beautiful.

Altogether, the Palenque sculptures mark the culmination of Maya art, which was certainly based in true genius, and which was probably animated by religious fanaticism. Happily for the visitor who cannot reach Palenque, much of this beauty may be seen in the National Museum.

XIV

THE VALLEY OF OAXACA

OAXACA, once accessible only by a long train ride, is now a quick flight from Mexico City. The best approach is by car; the motor road offers swift, joltless driving on a highway that sweeps over the Sierra Madre del Sur in long easy ascents with descents into cultivated valleys. This gives Oaxaca the sense of remoteness it should have; its inhabitants are largely Zapotecs and Mixtecs, two vigorous tribes whose art and architecture are quite as impressive as that of the Spaniards who dispossessed them. Most of them still live in mountain villages according to their tribal customs, which are the ethnologist's delight.

The road from Puebla to Oaxaca swings southward over hills whose crests are tufted with conifers and oaks. Indians always seem to live where strong winds ruffle the roof thatch and corn fields threaten to slide downhill. The valley lands are in haciendas that raise sugar cane in the bottoms and cattle on the hills. The trip's high point for unexpected beauty is a view as the road comes down into a valley where earth colors range from ash gray through ocher and terra cotta to the warm brown of turned furrows. There, on a slight rise, stands a noble church with heavy buttresses and a square tower that has unfortunately been topped by a tiled dome. This is Santo Domingo de Yanhuitlán, which the Dominicans built between 1543 and 1568 with six thousand Indians toiling.

Yanhuitlán's cloisters are extremely elegant, with high groined ceilings and narrow arches opening on the patio, where an Italian cypress grows. Its treasures are a colored bas-relief of Santo Domingo and a *Descent from the Cross*, a painted carving of fine-grained native stone. The workmanship is masterly, the feeling at once restrained and emotional. The main church has suffered extreme neglect, though a priest lives there, and it is under government protection as a national monument. The high altar is remarkable in its combination of turquoise and lapis-lazuli blues with watery green. Some stupid decorator has added tawdry ornaments up as far as he could reach.

Beyond one last divide, the road comes quietly down onto the floor of the Valley of Oaxaca, wide between distant blue and purple hills. This is the valley that gave Cortés his title Marqués del Valle; the city was laid out by its conqueror, Pedro de Alvarado, who modified its Zapotec name, Uaxyacac.

Many of Oaxaca's colonial houses, built flush with the streets, still show marks of the six earthquakes that have shaken them, but many have been rebuilt behind their high walls. The streets are lined with jacaranda trees, whose singular grace is to blend their blossom's lilac with shimmering sky blue, deep-indigo paint on walls or doorways, or bougainvillea's magenta. The city's distinctive beauty is its moss-green building-stone that shines like a gem when the rain wets it.

Oaxaca's big plaza is one of the friendliest I know. It is always full of people, strolling, sitting on benches or in the sidewalk cafés, where they take their anis or non-alcoholic *jamaica* or *tamarindo*. True habitués order dominoes also and settle down for hours. A band plays on alternate nights in the central kiosk. Its director is Diego Innes, who has drilled it into one of the country's best. On Sunday mornings Sr. Innes educates his townsmen with classical programs and comment. When the band rests, every other night, a marimba plays such seductive rhythms that even the horses dance. I saw two elegant *charros* who rode nightly, rounding the plaza several times and then going off at a smooth gait. No, they were not of an old aristocratic family; one had made a fortune as a merchant, the other was his intimate; foreigners both. Still, they rode well.

Oaxaca's fertile valley is increasingly productive for a widening market as better agricultural methods are introduced and communications improve. Its climate is favorable to coffee, sugar, tobacco, and many fruits, as well as wheat and corn. And it still exports cochineal, the crimson dye made from a tiny insect; Spain shipped it round the world in the seventeenth century. But Oaxaca is, of all Mexico, most productive of useful and attractive popular arts, which crowd its market and are almost smothered under factory kitchenware and oceans of cotton prints unrolled on the floor. Oaxaca's leather goods, especially boots and saddles, rank among the best; and its steel knives, said to be made by the techniques brought from Spain's Toledo centuries ago, will bend tip to handle. These are Spanish-taught crafts. Indian pottery has evolved into complete dinner sets painted with sprawling flowers or geometric designs from Mitla, and *huipil* patterns are reproduced by the meter for curtains and bedspreads. Oaxaca abounds in small factories that are also shops, and every guide knows where he gets the best commissions.

Certain villages have their specialties, such as Teotitlán del Valle, where men weave stout blankets on foot looms. For the tourist trade they produce hideous fake Indian designs in gaudy colors. For their own use they weave the natural gray, brown, black, and white wool into stripes or large stylized flower patterns; the only dye they use is a warm, rich red.

Other villages specialize in reed flutes or straw toys, cut stones, work clay into dishes or figures, glazed or not, and preserve the methods and designs of their ancestors. Miguel

Covarrubias found traces of cults of Quetzalcoatl in jaguar dances, especially in Tehuantepec, where the Catholic Church rests very lightly. Many village women are known by the *huipil* they wear or by their way with the *rebozo*. The *rebozo* is not Indian; the first Spanish women brought it to Mexico in the sixteenth century. But Oaxaca women have made it fully their own, twisting it into turbans with dangling fringe, folding it out of the way around the hips, or slinging it over the shoulder with the baby's tiny feet sticking out.

Covarrubias suggests that as the conquerors and missionaries crushed out the Indians' fine arts, natural inventiveness burst out in making trivial things for their own use or amusement. The most utilitarian pots, baskets, carryingcloths, and nets show individual skills and styles. Above all, the toys are gay; straw horses and panniered burros, human caricatures, and numberless whistles, bells, and dolls of painted clay. Little shining black angels will bring a girl a lover—if the gift is free and friendly. Candles of fragrant brownish beeswax hang like curtains along the booths or from poles carried on shoulders. You can buy a candle as slender as a baby's finger or as thick as your arm. They are lit in front of images of the saints, where a verger comes along, after a while, to snuff out the flame and save the wax to sell again.

Oaxaca's churches are, by some critics, considered the finest in Mexico. Santo Domingo, built between 1529 and 1608, when the Dominican Order was at its wealthiest and taste most extravagant, is made of Oaxaca's moss-green stone and a wealth of wrought iron. The façade and handsome carved doors bear the motif of rays, which is repeated indoors, giving the whole an unusual unity. The interior glories in fine paintings, statues, and altars and rails washed with gold leaf; it is marred only where French soldiers chipped off the gold when they occupied the city.

The Cathedral is being rebuilt after its almost complete destruction in the last earthquake. And La Soledad, patroness of ships and sailors, is honored in a lovely church, but its treasures of pearls, mother-of-pearl, and other gifts of shipwrecked mariners are no longer shown. The implication is that if the government knew how rich the parish was the jewels would be taken away.

A gentle young Spanish Dominican, with hands folded into his white wool robe, spoke: "Only the Dominicans could have civilized these people. When our order came, they were in complete savagery; we had to teach them to make straw huts." So the white light of faith can blind a man. He could have seen, from his convent's roof, the great city of Monte Albán, built by the ancestors of the Indians the Dominicans used to build their churches; they had been skilled stonemasons for centuries.

Monte Albán tops a mesa within sight of the city. It was probably a ceremonial center; its vast plaza, measuring 1,000 feet by 600, is surrounded by stately stairways and elevated bases for temples. A pyramid rises in the center. Students agree that it was built by the Zapotecs, who, judging by their earliest known work, were far in advance of the peoples of the central plateau. Over two thousand years ago, they were using dot-and-bar hieroglyphics, following an accurate calendar, and building with engineering skill and artistic taste of a high order. Several stone plaques in Monte Albán plaza seem to connect this early period with the culture recently discovered in Tres Zapotes and La Venta in Vera Cruz.

The first systematic study of Monte Albán began in 1931 under Arq. Alfonso Caso, then Director of the National Archæological Institute. He concluded, from his studies of pottery, that Monte Albán dates from before 300 B.C., that the Zapotec age of glory was between the fourth and tenth centuries of our era, that decline began in the tenth century, and that Monte Albán was abandoned in the twelfth. The Mixtecs may have moved in subsequently, but archæologists make no categorical statements. Here as elsewhere they say "so far as we know. . ."

Dr. Caso's excavations turned up pottery vessels, a few jade and shell beads, and obsidian tools. All pretty routine. Then they marked a tomb Number VII and began to dig. As workmen lifted a stone slab, the electric torches caught the gleam of gold, which developed into the greatest treasure ever found in the Americas. It was the archæologists' dream. But it soon turned into a nightmare as they toiled for seven days and nights, afraid to leave their horde for a minute. This treasure, known as the Monte Albán jewels, was taken in a special armored train to the Chicago World's Fair in 1931, to Europe in 1952, and is jealously kept by Oaxaca in its museum. It includes over five hundred pieces of carved bone, obsidian, rock crystal, alabaster, and jade, of wrought gold and silver, and of amber, found here for the first time. There were quantities of mother-of-pearl, of true pearls as large as pigeon's eggs, and of turquoise mosaics.

The workmanship of the Monte Albán jewels indicates that they were made by the Mixtecs, who must have driven the Zapotecs away from their ceremonial city. The Mixtec ascendancy is marked by the most finished work, the most elaborate symbolism, and the finest paintings in deerskin books. This rich period ended with the coming of the Spaniards in 1521. Monte Albán remains one of the most tantalizing archæological fields in Mexico. Other archæologists dream of having Dr. Casco's luck. The natives believe that he had a gnome-like familiar who led him to the hidden jewels.

Mitla, Abode of the Dead, is another ceremonial center that may be as much as one thousand years old. The Zapotecs entered the Valley of Oaxaca about A.D. 100, and

Mitla was built by an earlier people who were powerful enough to handle enormous stones. The Hall of Columns has six monolithic columns with door lintels that weigh thirty tons each. The most remarkable workmanship at Mitla is in the stone friezes, which repeat one motif, a stepped spiral that may be a stylization of the plumed serpent, in twenty variations. These friezes were carved in small bits and set into red stucco like mosaics. Mitla is so close to history that the missionaries heard legends that they could erect into fearsome marvels. They uncovered several tunnels, one so alarming that they closed it forever as the "door to Hell." This tunnel is lost, but others indicate that the Zapotecs believed the spirit world lay underground and was entered through caves. Some of these prehistoric beliefs persist, especially among the modern Zapotecs of Tehuantepec.

The town of Tehuantepec, in southern Oaxaca, has little to attract the eye or the imagination. It lies on the sandy Isthmus of Tehuantepec and on the sluggish brown Tehuantepec River, where the wind seems to blow forever, whirling sand into the eyes. But it also whips out the women's full skirts as they stride along with heavy baskets or trays on their regal heads. Whether one remembers Tehuantepec for its annoying dust or its beautiful women is a good test of whether it is for him or not.

Machine-made goods and ready-made garments are creeping in; factory goods are cheaper than handmade goods, even in Tehuantepec. But most *tehuanas* still prefer the full skirts, which may be Spanish or mid-Victorian, and the Indian straight *huipil*, even if they buy cheap prints in the market and stitch the old designs on the sewing-machine. And they still braid their shining black hair with ribbons tied in bright bows. Only old women wear the *enredo* (wrap-around skirt) that is pictured on the monuments. Most of these are red, dyed with cochineal, and striped with purple; the finest are all purple, with gold stripes. This purple dye is the excretion of snails, like the Tyrian purple of antiquity, which is now produced only for the imperial *tehuanas*.

Tehuantepec is a town of feminists who are so used to independence that they make nothing of it. They carry their beauty with gracious freedom, and they range in type from dark to light, but always with well-cut noses, large brilliant eyes, and full lips.

The statue in Tehuantepec's plaza, as befits a town of women, is of a woman. Doña Juana Cato de Romero sits in rigid bronze on a monument that celebrates her as a patroness of education. But Doña Juana was more than a nice old lady approving education. She was a beautiful candy-seller in the market when Porfirio Díaz was fighting with Juárez's liberals. Juana, alluring and gay, played billiards or threw dice with the conservative officers and lit fires along the river to flash messages to young Porfirio in the hills. More than one successful raid resulted from those flashes. Later Doña Juana kept up with Don Porfirio as he advanced to general, governor of Oaxaca, and president of Mexico, and she became a power in business and politics. She could have men freed from prison or put there. As the richest woman in Tehuantepec, she built a "chalet," where she entertained lavishly whenever Don Porfirio came; and when the railroad reached Tehuantepec, she had its rails laid just outside her garden gate.

If Tehuantepec is for you, you stumble onto a fiesta. I drove around the church of San Blas just as a procession was nearing it. Laughing *chamacos* waved me into a side street, from which I watched as from a theater box. Fourteen heavy wooden carts came creaking behind yoked oxen wreathed with flowers and bearing lovely women with ruffled skirts outspread and heads crowned with white starched haloes framing the face. The fiesta ended, of course, with a dance in an *enramada* (arbor) where a marimba played. The earth floor had been dampened and the sun coming through upright bamboo poles had striped it with light. Women were in their best: old ladies in wrapped skirts, girls in full satin skirts and *huipiles* heavily embroidered with flowers; little girls were dressed like their mothers. Nearly all were barefooted. Most men wore shoes, or at least *huaraches*. Only the oldest wore the heavy felt sombrero, red faded to a soft rose, and heavy enough with silver rope to bend the neck. Men and women danced together, the man cavorting, the lady indifferently moving her feet in the soft dust. They did not touch. The end was to involve a good deal of "taking," so we had been warned with the telling Mexican gesture of a hand lifted to the lips. And as we walked away we passed several *tehuanas*, still dignified, steering their wavering spouses homeward.

XV

CHIAPAS AND THE INDIAN PROBLEM

⊄ THE STATE of Chiapas, which borders on the Pacific Ocean and the Republic of Guatemala, rises out of tropical rain forest to lofty tablelands and soaring peaks with annual snows. Its capital is Tuxtla Gutiérrez, an attractive small city, clean and quiet. I found many new schoolhouses and much paving on main streets, but little moved in the main plaza except shoeshine boys and comfortably dressed gentlemen from offices. Coffee is the state's most important crop, but Chiapas also produces hardwoods, rice, chicle, and some minerals. It is also bidding for the country's most lucrative trade—tourists. New hotels feature separate bungalows, swimming-pools, and dance pavilions. Tuxtla comes alive once a year when the Pan American motor race brings Europeans and Americans from the entire hemisphere to speed dangerously from Tuxtla to Ciudad Juárez. Otherwise, the city lives quietly as a provincial trade center and a taking-off place for jungle and sierra.

The state's fertile soil and fine rivers could, with irrigation, feed all Mexico. This is the boast wherever reclamation projects are proposed. The federal government plans to dam the Río Grijalva, and there is talk of importing labor from the north. But immigration may not be the only solution. Chiapas's own Indians, given Spanish and some training in modern techniques, might share in their state's development.

Chiapas is unaccustomed to considering Indians as citizens. It is the only Mexican state where non-Indians are called *ladinos* or *latinos,* a title implying a knowledge of Spanish. These *ladinos,* the bearers of Spanish culture, have Indian blood, inherited from Aztecs or Tlaxcalans who marched with the conquerors, but they hold themselves apart from Chiapas Indians, who form about one third of the population, live in scattered communities, use the Maya calendar, speak Maya tongues, worship ancestral gods, and wear picturesque dress. But this all overlays lives of ignorance, misery, and ill-health.

Chiapas colonists fought viciously, in the sixteenth century, against the Dominican friars who were trying to enforce the laws prohibiting slavery and the granting of new haciendas. The *hacendados* lost, but slavery was soon replaced by debt peonage, which still exists in the planter's cash advance to Indian workers on the coffee *fincas.* It is said that the colonial *hacendado,* advancing a peso, said: "One I give you, one you owe me, one I mark in the book." So at year's end the illiterate peon owed three pesos on that transaction. Whether this abuse persists or not, Indians arrested for drunkenness or loitering are ninety per cent of the prisoners; they prove useful as street-cleaners. Indians are customarily pushed off sidewalks, refused admission to movies and restaurants, and overcharged in stores.

These Indians naturally pose the state's greatest problem. Advance is impossible without them. How can they be brought into the current of progress? Every American nation faces the same problem; Mexico has perhaps moved most sensibly toward solving it. Its method, inaugurated in the 1920's is a scheme of educating whole communities— children at school, but also adults as farmers, housekeepers, mothers, and future leaders in health and citizenship. They call it "integration."

This is naturally slow work. Trained teachers are too few. The Mexican Congress, like some others, is averse to appropriating money to improve life for the uninfluential.

The work has paid off well in some places and brilliantly in many individual cases. Village Indians have succeeded as physicians, lawyers, educators, and artists, even as congressmen. But a smashing, well-publicized demonstration of "integration" was needed. Chiapas seemed to be the place. Its Indians are intelligent; they live in scattered groups, but within reach of centers; and the state's need for a trained labor force appealed to legislators. So a general program was undertaken in 1951, when Dr. Gonzalo Aguirre Beltrán, for the Instituto Nacional Indigenista, established the Central Coordinador Tzeltal-Tzotzil, named for two linguistic groups near San Cristóbal Las Casas.

The road from Tuxtla Gutiérrez to San Cristóbal Las Casas crosses the rich Grijalva Valley and rises sharply into the sierra. The little town of Chiapa de Corso, whose pride is a red brick bandstand in the form of the Spanish crown, is *ladino;* its Indian population has been long since absorbed. Then one enters the Indian world, where green mountains are punctuated by the gray accents of grass-thatched huts and Indians walk along the road.

These are probably Zinacantecos, a people who number about 7,000 and speak Tzotzil. The ethnologist Julio de la Fuente called them "almost men of the world" for their open manner and readiness to deal with strangers. The men, taller than most Indians, are handsome as they stride along on heavily muscled bare brown legs. They wear white wool jerkins, straw hats fluttering with colored ribbons, and gray cotton squares with bright cerise tassels. These are worn in many ways, from covering the mouth to making a sash. A local joke is that Las Casas is the only place where tourist women look at men's legs. Zinacanteca women are drab as they trot along behind their men; their wrap-around skirts are dull blue, their blouses have been white, and their wraps are dark wool squares.

In Las Casas, where every day is market day, one learns

to recognize other costumes, especially that of the Chamulas, who number about 22,000. Their men wear fringed white wool tunics over white cotton pantaloons. Their women's short skirts and *huipiles* are of black wool. Chamulas are dirtier and mussier than the Zinacantecos, and are found more distrustful and difficult to deal with. Las Casas, despite its swarms of Indians, is *ladino* in spirit, as appears in the disdainful way of market women with Indians.

Las Casas has seen three efforts to civilize the Indians. The great humanitarian Bishop Bartolomé de Las Casas brought in the Dominicans in 1545. They baptized converts and built churches. In time they were succeeded by secular clergy, who, as years and decades passed, came to live in Las Casas, visiting outlying churches only now and then. Dr. Aguirre summed up what he found in 1951. "The priests stayed in the Indian churches only long enough to say Mass, baptize a few babies, collect the fees, and run. They ignored pagan rites that turned the sacred place into a hubbub, the sale of liquor in the church itself. . . . If there ever was a serious campaign of evangelization, not even a memory of it remains." Since 1950 the Church has introduced younger and more vigorous priests, who are trying to restore the Indians' churches to purely religious uses.

The second effort to civilize Chiapas's Indians was made by the government through its regular secular schools. But schooling did not seem to produce education. Many Indians, after five years in school and more as *finca* workers, were unable to speak Spanish and were quite unaware of themselves as Mexicans. If neither churches nor schools were making citizens out of Indians, another approach seemed called for. So the anthropologists were given a chance to try their methods of "integration." They found allies already in the field.

A group of Protestant missionaries had opened a Summer Institute of Linguistics in Las Casas, where they were translating the New Testament into four Indian languages. The Indians called them *"los Cristos"* because of their frequent mention of Christ, and not a few Indians were converted not only to the Baptist faith but to sobriety. This was a signal achievement among people whose every social and religious act involves drinking and where the sale of *aguardiente* is a monopoly protected by powerful politicians. The anthropologists, who co-operate with everybody going their way, find these non-drinking Indians very useful among their own people.

El Centro Coordinador, directed by Dr. Ricardo Pozas A., is employing all the theories, modified by the experience of three generations of work with Indians. Its headquarters, a cluster of buildings freshly painted saffron yellow and laundry blue, was filled with Indians and busy young men. The busiest was Dr. Pozas, who was ready to talk, quick to laugh, full of enthusiasm. The work, he explained, goes on in the Indian communities; the center only co-ordinates. Many new roads were mired by the last rains of summer, but he could send me out to Chamula, the ceremonial center for the largest group of Tzotzil Indians.

Chamula sits in a pocket of the hills where women and children were herding sheep and a few gray thatched roofs indicated homes. We had been warned against the inhospitable Chamulas, so we went first to the clinic. The *ladina* nurse was comforting a Chamula girl whose father had just forbidden her to train as a nurse's aid. The nurse took it calmly. She said the most important part of her job was keeping calm. She then turned to a tall, fine-looking man in immaculate native dress. She handed him some pills from her supply. "Two after each meal," she directed. He repeated: "Two after each meal. Six a day." He was one of the Indian *enfermeros* (nurses) who have been trained in personal cleanliness, the rudiments of hygiene, and in giving inoculations and medicines according to doctors' orders.

They are paid 250 or 300 pesos a month, and enjoy great prestige.

The nurse then took us to call on the new *presidente municipal*, who wore his ceremonial dress of black wool with red and green wool strands across the chest. He was polite, but he did not invite us into his smoky house, where his three wives were busy around a fire. Then we were cleared, it seemed, to visit the church. We crossed a damp open space, still littered with paper wrappings from yesterday's fiesta and with a few drunks still unable to rise. Indians squatted on the church steps, burning copal, the ancient incense with the unforgettable smell. Indoors, people sat on the floor, talking and laughing; a few had candles burning among the pine needles that carpeted the floor. Several men were disrobing an image of the dead Christ and replacing its festival garb with everyday dress. Women watched, giggling, and four harpists and three guitarists played a haunting tune.

A family group was absorbed in the prayers of a *curandero* (medicine man) who knelt beside a glowing pot of copal. He was, the medical director told me later, curing an illness by offering the soul of a chicken that lay before him and whose flesh he would eat later as part of his fee. This rite is based on the belief that every person has a spirit guide, generally a bird or an animal, which can cure ills and evils on the spiritual plane. The Chamulas, who raise sheep, and whose diet is deficient in protein, would not eat mutton; sheep were sacred. This, it developed, was because San Juan, the Chamulas' patron saint, holds a lamb in his arms. Surely it is his sacred guide, and eating it would be a sacrilege. This taboo has been respected, and goats have been introduced to provide meat.

Health work begins with preventive measures. The water supply has been improved in many places by draining pools, covering wells, and piping it from pure sources. Such measures have greatly reduced the incidence of typhoid, typhus, and endemic intestinal diseases. Planned projects will supply 200,000 people with clean water and give them baths and laundries. The Indians have accepted inoculations, probably because the man with the needle is usually their own *enfermero*. Thanks largely to these men, smallpox was eliminated in one year and mumps and whooping-cough were greatly reduced. Many *curanderos* willingly accept modern medicine if doctors meet them with the respect of one professional for another. Often the *curandero*'s prayers help the physician's pills; sometimes, if the *curandero*'s methods fail, he will call the doctor himself.

Work with women moves more slowly, as midwives are most resistant to new ideas. Only two young women have qualified as *enfermeras*, both at worldly-wise Zinacantán. The white nurse there had been called only twice to assist at childbirth. Both times the child had been born before her arrival and the midwife had used no cleanness. Nobody knows how many babies die under such care. Vital statistics are unprocurable. Filth is always the doctor's greatest enemy, but DDT grows in popularity, especially now that it is offered as protection against fleas; fleas lack the social stigma of lice.

The medical men work in the spirit that infuses the entire staff. The agronomist, recently graduated from an agricultural college, operates a small farm where he produces first-rate cocks and swine to breed up the stock and improve the native diet. He meets many problems with his sleeves rolled up, working with the Indians at planting crops in rotation, fertilizing, and pruning, and particularly at contour plowing. Erosion is one of the greatest menaces in the entire area.

Formal schooling is very casual. Children are not forced to attend regularly; their work is too important in the family economy. But thirty-eight schools had enrolled about twelve hundred pupils within two years. Most of them are proud of being in school; people point out the youngsters who can speak Spanish. The teachers are Indians called, like the *enfermeros, promotores culturales,* wear native dress, and teach reading and writing in the native tongues. A bright student—child or adult—can learn to read and write in his own language in about eighteen months, whereas it used to take two or three years to teach Spanish. Spanish is taught as pupils feel the need for it, often in connection with learning a craft. Many teachers have classes in metal, wood, and leather work, even simple book-keeping, and hairdressing. Hair well washed and trimmed does not harbor lice!

The staff anthropologists make important contributions in this program of presenting a new culture without violating the ancient taboos, as in the case of San Juan's lamb. Many Indian traditions can, with understanding, be turned into assets. Each man was expected to serve as an official when called, and this custom helps in recruiting *promotores culturales.* But the Indian official had to celebrate his inauguration with a large and drunken feast, and only abstemious men may serve as *promotores.* The prestige of the new office is slowly replacing the distinction of giving the most drunken fiesta. None of this works with perfect smoothness. One *enfermero,* a convert of the *"Cristos,"* was refusing typhoid shots to all not professing his faith. But he was persuaded that his obligation as a *promotor* was apart from his religion.

All in all, education along many lines tends to free the Indian from his subservience to the *ladino.* An oil, reputed to aid in learning Spanish, sells briskly. An Indian who learns to keep books can replace a *ladino* in the village store. Several communities now have co-operative stores manned entirely by Indians. Fifteen Indians of Chamal formed a company and bought a truck, but with the stipulation that no *ladino* should be permitted to run a rival line into their village. This is learning western capitalism and monopoly with a vengeance!

Certainly the work of El Centro Coordinador Tzeltal-Tzotzil is of far-reaching importance in Mexico, perhaps to other countries as well. Its basic tenets and many of its techniques are applicable to the millions of Indians still unintegrated into the life of the Republic. No worker at the Center will prophesy the outcome exactly, but they are all sure that they are working toward the day when all Mexico's Indians will be Mexican citizens, working out their own salvation along their own lines.

PART FOUR

Conquest from the Gulf

XVI

SPANISH CONQUEST

⊂⊒ MOST travelers from the north enter Mexico by a
back door, whereas history came in from the Gulf of Mexico. The principal Gulf port of Vera Cruz is now a clean
modern city of wide streets freshened by salty sea breezes.
Airy buildings along the waterfront house immigration and
customs offices, international banking-houses, and steamship
lines whose ships fly many flags in the harbor. It is the
busiest port in the nation and one of the most relaxing
spots for lazing indefinitely. On the Plaza de la Constitu-
tión, time is marked only by shifting shadows, by soft-
toned church bells, by the whirr of grackles in the trees at
sunset, and by a waiter suggesting another *apéritif* or plant-
ers' punch. Venders offer clams and shrimps to dip into hot
chile sauce. Others push among the tables with green parrots, soft blue love birds, fuzzy-faced monkeys, and trinkets of seashells and tortoise shell. Family groups happily
whacking their marimbas can sing all night without running out of the songs they know.

Every Vera Cruz restaurant has its specialty, usually fish
or shellfish. *Huauchinango a la veracruzana* is known
throughout Mexico, but it is best where the red snapper
has just been pulled out and a Vera Cruz cook has con-
cocted the sauce. Vera Cruz has its own ways also with
crabs, shrimp, and wild duck from the marshes, and with
the basic foods of corn and beans. Its *tortillas* are hot and
delicate, and they fold into delectable crisp *tacos* filled with
spiced meats. Vera Cruz beans are tiny and black and singu-

larly tasty. Cooked with rice, they are called by the Cuban name, *moros y cristianos*. The state of Vera Cruz produces rice, and its people find only their own coffee good. The state is also rich in tropical fruits. Some, like the custard apple, are as delicious as a prepared dessert as they come from the tree, but the black *zapote* is improved by a squeeze of orange juice, a larger dash of rum, and sugar.

The visitor so inclined finds that Vera Cruz also offers hunting and fishing. The mountains are full of game, including familiar water and land birds and such exotic creatures as alligators, jaguar, and brilliant jungle birds. Northern sportsmen appear as regularly as the seasons, and Vera Cruz has tourist and resort hotels to accommodate them, but the place has never become as fashionable a vacation spot as Acapulco. Perhaps the weight of its history is too heavy. Vera Cruz has a deal of history, long antedating the white man.

Quetzalcoatl, according to ancient legend, sailed away across the blue-green striped sea that sends its breakers curling up against the esplanade. He had promised to return, and belief in this second coming helped the Spaniards in 1519. From the esplanade, one can make out the Isla de los Sacrificios where Cortés and his men first saw evidence of human sacrifice. He made camp near the present city, naming it La Villa Rica de la Vera Cruz. From there he advanced to the conquest of Mexico, surely one of the most daring, dramatic, and romantic exploits of all time. The conquerors were inspired by the purest ideals they knew, loyalty to the Crown and zeal to convert all infidels to the True Faith. Some of their contemporaries, like the Dominican Bartolomé de las Casas, damned them as rapacious and cruel; some Mexicans today make a cult of despising everything Spanish and exalting everything Indian. As others, equally Mexican, hold that all good came from Spain, a deep schism has developed in Mexican thinking.

Indianismo on the one hand; *hispanidad* on the other. Neither belief is incompatible with the fact that the Spaniards were moved by the spirit that was pushing Europeans out of their small peninsula and to the outermost ends of the earth.

Cortés seems to have been a man of his time, capable of deep religious feeling and of extreme cruelty. He was greedy for wealth, avid for power, and unscrupulous. He could enrage his followers by trickery and then win them back by a display of coolness under danger, skill in dealing with Indians, or just sheer charm. A complicated and fascinating character, who with only four hundred armed Spaniards conquered the vast Aztec empire that spread far beyond modern Mexico's southern boundary.

Messengers of the Aztec ruler, Moctezuma, met Cortés when he landed at Vera Cruz. Their skilled artists made pictures of the invaders, some of which have been preserved in museums. They are graphic drawings of the queer bearded men and their astonishing horses, and of one woman with speech ballooning out of her mouth in cartoon style. She was one of twenty slave girls who had been presented to Cortés by a conquered chief in Tabasco. The Spanish priest baptized her Marina, but we know her better as Malinche, a corruption of her Indian name, Malintzin. This girl was one of Cortés's greatest strokes of luck. She was of a tribe that spoke Nahuatl, the language of the Aztecs, and she also knew the Maya tongue of her masters. As Cortés had already rescued a shipwrecked Spanish cleric in Yucatán, he now had a two-span linguistic bridge from Spanish to Nahuatl. But Malinche was not destined for so roundabout an arrangement. She quickly learned Castilian, eliminating the Spanish interpreter, and she soon became Cortés's mistress. She was then known as La Lengua (the tongue) and addressed as Doña Marina. Perhaps her knowledge of Indian psychology and superstitions, her quick wit, and her diplomatic skill had much to do with Cortés's success. But his courage and audacity were his own.

Moctezuma's emissaries had brought gifts of feathers, textiles, mosaics, gold ornaments, and free gold; but they told Cortés that he must come no farther. Cortés replied that as a representative of the world's greatest ruler he must meet Moctezuma face to face. He also mentioned that the Spaniards suffered from an illness that only gold could cure. Cortés was determind to advance, but some of his men were ready to return to Cuba. By typical persuasiveness mixed with guile and gall, Cortés got them to elect him leader, and —lest any disgruntled officers should try to sail for Cuba— he burned his ships on the beach. Now no retreat was possible. Cortés set out for Tenochtitlán through unknown country inhabited by probably hostile Indians, and with an army not altogether loyal to him.

Cortés's route is generally followed by both railroad and highway, and today's traveler can gaze from his comfort down into deep canyons, draped with big-leaved vines, that the conquerors had to cross laboriously, widening trails made for cargo-bearers or Moctezuma's swift runners. The soldiers sweated under their armor, suffering from prickly heat and maddened by insects. Their precious horses bogged down in the swamps that look so beautiful to us with their clouds of yellow butterflies above water hyacinths. The men ate what they could cadge from the Indians, and often it made them sick. They slept on their arms. Cortés prowled the camp at night. Malinche attended the sick, doubtless relieving them with the same herbs Indian women use now. They passed such palm-thatched huts as we see today with naked children at play under ceiba trees and bougainvillea. In the dry season every village is carpeted with vanilla pods drying fragrantly in the sun. Vanilla was new to the Spaniards, as was cacao; both are still important crops. The

Spaniards later introduced coffee and oranges, whose groves bower the lovely little city of Jalapa.

Jalapa, capital of the state of Vera Cruz, is set where warm sea breezes meet the mountain chill and swirl into rainbow mists. It is a dreamlike place of parks and gardens and always scented by day with gardenias and floripondio and at night with the shy *huele de noche* (night jasmine). This city is on one of two highways from Vera Cruz to Mexico City. The other passes through the fruit and coffee center of Córdoba and the textile city of Orizaba, and is at times more spectacular.

The Spaniards had advanced cautiously but without battle, and Moctezuma's spokesmen had met them at every village, begging or demanding that they turn back. But Moctezuma always mistakenly sent gifts, inflaming that Spanish appetite for gold. Cortés was making allies of petty Indian chiefs, many of whom hated the domineering Aztecs, and acquiring porters. The white man was coming into his own. And Cortés was showing his extraordinary gift for playing men, even Indians, off against each other. Here indeed Malinche must have been more than mere interpreter of spoken words. In any case, the Spaniards did not have to fight until they reached Tlaxcala, which has now been dwarfed between Mexico and Puebla.

Tlaxcala was then a proud mountain state that had never surrendered to the Aztecs, and it fought valiantly against the invaders. But fear of men mounted on horses and of mystic powers of these "sons of the sun" led to the defeat of the Tlaxcalans, who became Cortés's most dependable allies. They helped him to overcome the near-by city of Cholula, near modern Puebla, which was the traditional center of the Quetzalcoatl cult. Then the way to Tenochtitlán lay really open.

The Spaniards first saw the lovely Valley of Mexico from

a pass near the town of Amecameca and between the two snow-peaked volcanoes of Popocatépetl and Ixtaccíhuatl. The crossing is now called El Paso de Cortés. It is one of the few spots in Mexico to bear the conqueror's name; Mexico has no monument to him. It has been said that Mexico is his monument.

The conquest of the Aztecs' capital was no easy matter. Their city was as large and splendid as any in Spain, their people were firm in the faith typified for the Spaniards by human sacrifice, their soldiers were a disciplined force. Cortés first won over Moctezuma, audaciously imprisoning him in his own palace. He then toppled the hideous stone idols from their templed pyramids. Moctezuma has been accepted as a weakling or as a superstitious zealot who deferred to the white man as the returning Quetzalcoatl. Modern thinkers suggest that he was a sensitive and civilized man who broke when he saw his faith fail and his gods fall. But Cortés, at the height of his power over Moctezuma, had to return to Vera Cruz.

Cortés had left Cuba against the governor's orders and he had proceeded inland despite instructions to explore the coastline and return. Now he received word that the governor had sent an armed ship after his insubordinate officer. Cortés left Tenochtitlán at once for the harbor, where he staged another of his incredible performances. Winning over the governor's men by lavish promises, he marched that disciplinary force back to Tenochtitlán as reinforcements. He still faced a long and exhausting struggle against Moctezuma's successor and nephew, Cuauhtémoc, who once roundly defeated the Spaniards and drove them out. That was Cortés's lowest hour, *"La noche triste"* (the Sad Night), June 30, 1520. But the man only stiffened in defeat. He held his Indian allies and won others, he made gunpowder and built ships to launch on the lake, he inspired men to the impossible, and he won. On August 3,

Tenochtitlán fell, and the Spaniards began to level its ruins and to build Mexico, City of Palaces.

Cuauhtémoc, the radiantly brave young chief who fought so valiantly against the invaders, was captured, tortured in the belief that he knew where Moctezuma's treasure was hidden, and eventually ignominiously killed. He has become Mexico's hero, the archetype of dash and daring in action and of dauntless courage under torture. Indianists, professing no admiration for Spain, have all but deified Cuauhtémoc, the noble Indian. But Spain was to rule for three centuries.

Vera Cruz was then the busy port through which Spain sent its armies, administrative officers and investigators, high clerics and humble missionaries, new colonists, and orders without end. Fat galleons there unloaded European goods and took on Mexico's jewels and fine gold, and at last the tons of silver bars that made Spain the world's richest country. They also took on cargoes from the Orient which had been landed at Acapulco and brought across the mountains on burros. After Mexico won its independence of Spain, Vera Cruz remained its most important port, though business slacked off as the country struggled through half a century of civil wars. Vera Cruz also saw foreigners sailing in to take over the customs and to collect at least the interest on loans made to the impecunious republic. The British and the Spanish came. The French, under Napoleon III, sent in the feeble, magniloquent Maximilian. And our country misguidedly—as it seems to many impartial historians—twice landed troops in Vera Cruz.

XVII

CONQUEST FROM THE NORTH

⊂⊒ THE FIRST United States landing in Vera Cruz was in 1846 when General Winfield Scott took the city as an incident in the Mexican War. Mexicans refer to this war as "the time when your country robbed us of half our territory." Certainly the war that began in Texas in 1846 and ended with the Treaty of Guadalupe Hidalgo in 1848 added the vast southwest to the United States. Few Mexicans know or remember how little either Spain or Mexico had done for its scattered peoples. President Polk, obsessed to extend his country to California, might have bought the west; wise statesmen might have come to an amicable agreement. But politicians in both countries played politics with the war.

Mexico's flamboyant General Antonio López de Santa Anna, who was in and out of power for twenty-five years, lost to Texas in 1836 and, in 1846, after doing well against General Taylor in the north, failed to stop General Scott at Vera Cruz. There the Yankees are said to have behaved well. The General and his officers, invited to a service in the Cathedral, swallowed their Protestant prejudices and probably endangered their political futures by carrying lighted candles in a saint's procession. They then advanced over the mountains to Mexico City, which Santa Anna, as supreme commander, had ordered evacuated. Only the cadets in the military academy at Chapultepec Castle stood in a classically heroic defense. The last of them, wrapped in the flag, leaped to death rather than surrender. A magnificent monument at the foot of the hill honors these Niños Héroes, and there an annual memorial service is held. Never more impressive than in 1947, when President Truman, placing a wreath, announced that the United States was returning all Mexican flags captured in battle.

Mexicans, betrayed by their leader's pusillanimity, fought with their usual gallantry. When General Anaya surrendered the Churubusco convent, the American commander asked where the ammunition was. "Sir," replied Anaya in words that ring like a bell in Mexican hearts, "if there were any ammunition you would not be here." So the bluecoats marched on into the capital which figures as "the halls of Montezuma" in the Marines' stirring anthem. Naturally the invasion left deep wounds, but Mexicans have much cause for pride too. Perhaps the wounds might have healed in half a century, but by that time the rapacious Yankee was invading again, this time as the hated economic imperialist. This time it was oil, and Mexico's President Díaz was certainly a contributing agent when he encouraged foreign capitalists by exacting neither royalties nor taxes, but only a small stamp duty. British and American oil companies made fabulous fortunes, especially around the Gulf port of Tampico in the state of Tamaulipas.

For two decades Tampico was as lurid as the gold-rush towns of California or Alaska, with the added hazards of tropical insects and diseases. A primitive fishing-village was soon swamped under streets knee-deep in oily mud where people lived in noisome hovels among roaring saloons and dives, and where naked knives flashed readily. A paradise only for fiction-writers. The foreign managers and administrators lived on the breezy hill in modern houses screened against insects and fenced away from Mexicans.

These were the people who gave us such a bad name. They claimed to understand Mexicans, meaning that they knew how to bribe unscrupulous officials and keep underlings in their place. They contributed the ugly phrases about dirty, lazy peons and maintained that educated and trained Mexicans were capable of only ill-paid and inferior jobs. Naturally they bred detestation of the Yankee at every level from the ditch-digging peon to the most sophisticated Mexican. And Washington's handling of our relations with Mexico during the revolutionary years did little to offset such personal resentments.

President Madero was assassinated in 1913, and Victoriano Huerta, trying to be president, faced revolution in every part of the country. The United States, having favored Huerta, refused to recognize him under President Wilson. Altogether, it was an explosive situation easily touched off by what should have been a minor incident. It happened in Tampico when sailors off a United States battleship were arrested by Mexican officers for loading gasoline at a prohibited dock. The Mexican commander promptly released them with apologies, but Admiral Mayo demanded a salute of twenty-one guns, which he agreed to return. Huerta refused. Just then a German ship was approaching Vera Cruz, presumably with arms for Huerta. President Wilson favored Carranza, a general fighting in the north. Admiral Fletcher was ordered to take Vera Cruz, and—presumably in agreement with Huerta's officers—he occupied the port without a shot. But the citizens rose to defend their city, and naval cadets in their academy on the hill barricaded their windows with mattresses and fought gamely. For the second time, the United States was in the position of shooting down Mexican youths pluckily defending their country against invasion.

Mexicans do not forget this episode, but it is comfort for an abashed citizen to know that there were mitigating circumstances. A gentleman who visited Vera Cruz on business during this period said: "Never was that city so clean or so well policed. Those Yankees had laid a sewer and put the *zopilotes* [buzzards] out of the scavenging business. They had almost put a stop to thievery, and merchants were delighted with the steady flow of silver dollars."

Mexicans, proud people, naturally remember invasion and imperialism rather than the invaders' dollars. And Mexicans are rightly proud that they, facing international boycott and poverty, put an end to oil imperialism. Tampico was the center of this independence move, and I went to Tampico.

XVIII

RECONQUEST FOR MEXICO

☙ MY GUIDE in Tampico was a short, heavy-set man with dark skin, gray eyes, and a rich *pochismo* speech acquired in Texas when he was evacuated with all foreigners in 1914. He was Danish-Mexican, he said, and he preferred Mexico to Texas. He took me first, as guides do, to the fine residence district on the hill; it is now occupied by Mexican administrators and directors and foreign oil technicians employed by Mexico's government oil monopoly. We drove along the docks where oil tankers and one small passenger steamer lay among foreign and coastwise cargo ships. Dock workers were manning trucks and cranes; in unionized Tampico no sweaty men walk bent under heavy loads. When I mentioned this, my guide said: "I'll show you how it was under the companies."

We drove then along a muddy, rutted road and across the Río Pánuco, where men were netting crabs that would sell for two pesos a bucket to middlemen who would get six pesos in town. The one, deliciously prepared, that I ate for lunch was eight pesos on the menu. Beyond the bridge, in malarial flats, frame hovels were crowded against miserable small shops, drinking-places, and open dives. Naked children played in the filth, and women walked barefooted carrying cans of water. "They can at least get clean water now," my guide said. "Under the companies the only decent water came from the waste pipes: it had at least been boiled."

In the days when British and American companies controlled ninety-eight per cent of Mexico's oil output, their

workers lived in such foul tropical slums. A population that
was ninety per cent malarial, ridden with intestinal parasites,
and attacked now and again by epidemics severe enough to
attract the attention of the companies' doctors, was doubtless as lazy and unprogressive as reported.

"Now," said my guide, enjoying our tour, "I'll show you
what Mexico has done for the oil workers."

We swung out into the city's suburbs, where oil derricks
rose blackly against the sky, but where the streets were
paved between pleasant small cottages with flowering gardens. Water is now piped into every home. Men were coming off shift in their tin hats, women were marketing in
clean stores, and schoolchildren seemed to be everywhere.
In Ciudad Madero, I noticed a large handsome building
disgorging youngsters ranging in age from tiny to teen-age,
the girls in wine-colored frocks, many of the boys in white.
"A Catholic school?" I asked, sure I was right.

My guide grinned triumphantly. "No. That's a school
financed by the dock workers' union." He exaggerated a
bit. It is maintained by co-operation between the union and
the state and federal governments, a scheme worked out
by President Emilio Portes Gil when he was governor of
Tamaulipas, and extended during his presidency. Here is
a sound solution of the problem of lack of schools which
our country might profitably study.

How this change in living came about is an epic tale,
one that Mexicans glory in as the conquest of Mexico by
and for Mexicans. Its slogan was "Mexico for the Mexicans."

The expropriation of the oil fields which so amazed the
world in 1938 had begun as a labor struggle. In 1935 several
small unions had united and generated enough strength to
strike against the powerful companies. Their demands reflect the conditions then existing in the oil centers. They
included not only the eight-hour day and a raise in wages,

but decent housing, clean drinking-water, schools for both children and adults, double pay for overtime, during vacations, and even during strikes. All this was in line with the Constitution of 1917.

The companies indignantly refused; granting such demands, they said, would ruin them. President Cárdenas appointed a commission which found that, on the companies' own figures, the expense could well be met. The government even offered to place in escrow the difference between its economists' estimate and that of the companies, to insure the companies from loss if the government's figures should prove wrong. Still indignant, the companies went to court and carried the case to the Supreme Court, where Mexico's position was upheld. The companies then appealed to their governments, and the British Ambassador made such inflammatory speeches that Mexico broke relations with Great Britain. Ambassador Daniels, who had ordered the attack on Vera Cruz in 1914, finally won true popularity by remaining smilingly aloof. President Roosevelt declined to act on behalf of United States investors who defied Mexico's laws. Mexicans remember this. Roosevelt is always lauded at the annual oil workers' convention.

It looked like an impasse. Then, on March 18, 1938, President Cárdenas, standing squarely on Mexico's constitution, which declared all sub-soil wealth national property, subject to lease but never to sale, expropriated the oil wells and refineries. This act was the Republic's first vigorous effort to shake free of the economic colonialism that had throttled it since the end of political colonialism. Cárdenas, if he could weather the crisis, would rank with his country's liberators from Hidalgo to Madero.

Private interests in Britain, Holland, and the United States tightened Mexico's credit, and the international press cheerfully prophesied complete economic collapse. But Mexico survived. The President appealed to the people for help, and it came not only in large sums, but in copper coins from the poor. Even the Church, for the first time, supported the Mexican government against foreign interests. Archbishop Luis Martínez endeared himself forever to Mexicans by calling on all Catholics to support their government. Mexico, threatened from all sides, could face the world as a united nation.

A new government agency, Petroleos Mexicanos, was created to control the oil wells and market their product. As expected, the early years were extremely trying. Some politicians saw Pemex as a political sinecure and made spectacular fortunes out of it. The unions took their victory as license to loaf, production fell off, and all direful prophecies seemed likely to come true. Not until President Alemán, taking office in 1946, appointed Antonio Bermúdez director of Petroleos Mexicanos did its possibilities begin to be realized. Bermúdez, who had made a comfortable fortune in his native Ciudad Juárez, brought personal honesty as well as administrative ability to his job. He even ousted an Alemán favorite. He himself was one of the few men from Alemán's administration who was reappointed by Ruiz Cortines.

Expropriation, as Mexico's second declaration of independence, has paid off handsomely. Oil workers are infinitely better off, as any visitor to Tampico or any other oil field can see. Mexico's technicians found themselves quite able to carry on without the gringo boss who used to leave much detail to them while he played politics in the bars. Many former employees of the foreign companies have stayed on to work for Pemex; they have built homes, made Mexican friends, and many have made Mexican marriages. Altogether, Mexico has emerged from what was surely the last exploitation of her as a backward country. The difference is that Mexico is now a forward-moving country, guarding not only its resources, but its people.

PART FIVE

Mexico's Heartland

XIX

SAN LUIS POTOSÍ

⬡ THE STATE of San Luis Potosí seems, on quick view, to lack any beauties or charms to cause heart throbs or tears, but the *potosino* is forever loyal to his cactus-studded hills and his colonial city. The city is beautiful, but his nostalgic song begins with the cactus.

> *Yo soy puro potosino.*
> *Nací bajo de un nopal*
> *Del nopal que está en el centro*
> *Del escudo nacional.*
> (I am pure Potosino,
> Born under a cactus,
> The cactus that centers
> The national coat of arms.)

His state's central position is also a matter of pride to the *potosino;* it touches seven states, and its history offers several important links with the larger history of the Republic.

Long isolated from tourist travel, San Luis Potosí is now crossed by a well-made and almost too flat road that leaves the Pan American Highway at El Mante and meets the Central Highway at Lagos de Moreno. Tourists can now speed across to Guadalajara and the Pacific fishing-resorts, happily missing all the most gorgeous mountain scenery and making time. Beyond El Mante the road rises by long grades along the clear blue stream of El Salto. A few miles off the road one finds El Salto (waterfall) itself, pitching over jagged rocks in foamy froth. Beyond that, the land flattens out to the wide valley around Ciudad Maiz, which produces corn when drought does not kill it. This is *mestizo* country; the only Indians are the primitive Huasteca groups in the state's jungle lowlands.

At Ciudad Maiz, following the rule that truckers always know where to eat, I dined exceptionally well on chicken breast with a rich brown gravy, fluffy rice, *tortillas* hot as pancakes, coffee strong as sin, and crisp *buñuelos* (fritters) in brown sugar syrup. There a state policeman asked if I would take along a friend of his, who, walking in from a distant ranch, had missed the bus. It was he who sang me the *potosinos'* song; he told me how a number of his friends had been tricked out of twenty pesos apiece by a crook who had promised to get them into the United States. He himself was going to Potosí to sign up, but he proposed to do it legally. Why did he wish to go to the United States? "Oh, Señorita, for the money. A man can bring home enough money to start his own little store. You can't imagine how little one can earn in Mexico. . . . Yes, I love my country, but for earning and getting ahead, the United States is better."

The swift road crosses semi-arid land whose only growth is cactus and the tough-looking *ixtle*, known as desert palm for its fanlike top. Cactus gives a deliciously juicy magenta-colored fruit, the tuna, and the people make ropes, bags, and stiff brushes out of *ixtle*, just as their ancestors did.

The capital city of San Luis Potosí reveals its personality at once. Its streets, paved with broad, flat stones probably laid in the seventeenth century, lead to large churches with quiet parks in front of them. The colonial houses are not sad survivals run down into slums; their long iron-barred windows show freshly laundered lace curtains; the brass knockers are polished; and anything as out of character as an electric bell is discreetly unobtrusive. Clearly the citizens love and cherish their city's antiquity; its colonial style has not been preserved as a matter of principle; old families rich enough to live well prefer their ancestral homes.

Such living indicates a conservative society, many churches a Catholic one. Church bells ring the hours; nuns walk the streets not habited, but in black with black veils; convent girls in dark uniforms with white collars appear at closing hours. Catholic and doubtless charitable, San Luis Potosí is notable for the number of its beggars. Two or three a block are usual—old people with scrawny hands, whining children, the blind and lame, the crippled crawling or pushing themselves along on wheels. There seem plenty of opportunities to gain grace by giving alms.

San Luis Potosí, named for the fabulous Andean silver mines, enjoyed, during the colonial era, enough wealth to fill the city with excellent examples of every period's architecture. There is endless pleasure on roaming the streets to make personal discoveries, and *potosinos*, who never lack words, have written several books extolling their city and its artistic beauties. Luis Chessal's book of drypoint etchings with accompanying text is fine; its translation by a student with a Spanish-English dictionary brings into English the poetry of Spanish phrases.

The main plaza, in spite of the Sears Roebuck building and one side of stores, is dominated by the pinkish stone cathedral, which is impressively baroque, by arcaded palaces, and by the government palace. My guide and friend on the plaza was Carlos, a serious fifth-grade student who provided a substitute during school hours, but who personally wiped the windshield daily and fetched water in a bucket to give the car a real wash. He planned to become a motor mechanic. After I visited the government palace, Carlos was ready with a quiz to prove that I had learned my lesson. Benito Juárez was lodged there while Maximilian was lording it in Mexico, and there the President made the hard decision to order the Emperor's execution in Querétaro. Chessal notes in his book that "General Santa Anna visited this place on his way to beat the Texans." Francisco Madero spent some time in San Luis too, but in a private house, where he wrote his "Plan of San Luis Potosí," calling at last for armed insurrection. It was published in San Antonio, Texas, after he had crossed the border disguised as a railroad brakeman.

San Luis Potosí, conservative colonial city, boasts of some modern art. Joaquín Arias, a sculptor whose work is strong in both line and feeling, has made a convincing figure of Morelos on the Alameda, and in the railroad station a sturdy railroad worker in peaked cap. The station, one of the city's finest modern buildings, was decorated by Fernando Leal with two fine frescoes illustrating transportation from the pre-Cortesian Indian bearer to the modern streamlined train.

The city is proudest of its churrigueresque temples with tiled domes. El Carmen's façade, elaborately elegant, seems indeed frozen music. Partly destroyed in 1857 during the Wars of the Reform, it has been restored, but much of its convent garden is occupied by El Teatro de la Paz, a frenchified theater of Don Porfirio's age, now successfully modernized. On the same street is the telegraph office. Unkempt as government buildings often are, this one has a patio overwhelmingly impressive for its stately stairways on flying arches.

The temple and convent of San Francisco, begun in 1640 and repeatedly rebuilt since, is now being used as El Museo Nacional Potosino. The museum's moving spirit was Dr. Antonio de la Masa, who found his avocation more absorbing than his medical profession. Patients waited meekly in his office while the doctor supervised the installation of a fine collection of artifacts from the Huasteca field. The old convent's strong arches and domes have been respected in remodeling, but they have been lightened and freshened with creamy white and soft terra-cotta paint. La Capilla de Aranzazu, at the top of a broad stairway, is a gem of churrigueresque. Its arches, shaped like an imperial crown, rise to a bull's-eye window in the cupola. Behind the altar is a window of pure baroque with plump cherubs as its theme; the colors are clear turquoise blue, rosy terra cotta, delicate cream, and rich gold. The building now occupied by Hacienda (Treasury) is arresting, with its fine façade set cornerwise to the street. Its patio is surrounded by arcades reached by well-proportioned stairways with wrought-iron railing. But its distinction, unique in Mexico, is its bulging iron balconies, which Professor Francisco de la Masa has called "pregnant balconies."

Seeking lodgings, I was presented to Señorita A., a slim lady with tired, resigned eyes, who spoke quietly and moved quickly. Her family home was now filled with shouting students and clamorous children, with servants and vendors demanding her attention. The Señorita's day, after early Mass, included the care of this house, a kindergarten, private students, and another guesthouse, where she offered to accommodate me.

Turning off the wide, shaded Paseo de la Reforma, we entered unpaved streets where poor houses were giving way to modern homes. There Señorita A. had built a house to her plan. A small locked patio gave on a small *sala*, with dining-room on another patio. There were six guest rooms, each with bath. Food from the big house was fetched daily by Chole, who walked several miles with tins and jars in baskets. The other maid was Chavela, and both were chaperoned by old Lupe, who had been a servant in Señorita A.'s family.

Mornings at seven I woke to the splashing of water as Chavela in her bare feet sloshed out the patio. All day she wielded the broom and the long cloth attached to a stick, removing every speck of dust. She made beds, scrubbed bathrooms, washed the roomers' clothes, carried garbage out through the front door when the van came clanging by, and helped in the kitchen. By nine at night, with luck, she was free to go home. On alternate Sundays she could leave after midday dinner; then she would dress herself and the children to walk in the park.

San Luis Potosí, like all Mexico above 5,000 feet, is chilly. Mexicans often ask how we support the terrific winter cold in the States, praising their equable climate. But variations exist in Mexico too. In winter the indoor temperature hovers around freezing, while outdoors is as advertised. This accounts for the difficulty in dressing correctly. Winter clothes for the house, summer for the street is about it. Any sit-down worker will need sweaters and fur-lined boots and an electric heater. When I installed one, it proved to be a wonder. Old Lupe came in to see how it worked, and Chavela came daily to warm her blue-cold feet after washing the patio.

One day she reported that her eldest son, aged three, was sick. He had a temperature and a cough, and her mother had taken him to the hospital, where Chavela might visit him. The Hospital Central, maintained by the national Beneficencia Pública and the state, is a large brick building set cornerwise to catch the sunshine through expansive steel-framed windows. It is the city's pride, evidence of the success of the Revolution's social services.

Chavela's card, marked in red to indicate serious illness, admitted us both. We approached the contagious ward through long halls that had not been swept of late, where dirty rags lay in corners and maltreated brooms leaned or lay where the sweeper had wearied. Floor nurses nodded as we passed; other visitors, poor and troubled people, sat with their sick in small rooms.

Little Pablo lay on a hospital bed covered with a soiled half-sheet. Lightly wrapped in a pink bedspread his grandmother had brought, he was otherwise naked. Yet so resistant is childhood or so potent penicillin that the fever had gone down. Leaving Chavela to clothe him in new warm pajamas, I strolled past an open bathroom, uncleaned and ill-smelling, and paused at a room where a baby lay whimpering pitifully. His tiny hands were filthy, a lace-trimmed dress hung in tatters from his shoulders, his diaper badly needed changing. He had kicked off a thin cotton blanket. Nurses passed, but none looked in. His crying ceased as soon as a friendly hand patted him and covered his icy feet. At last a passing girl not in uniform agreed to change the diaper. She brought a square of colored calico; there were no diapers, she said, but this was clean. When the floor nurse came to take the baby's temperature, I asked what his illness was. She did not know. How long had he been there? Since yesterday. Was there no record? Oh, yes, that was in the office downstairs.

It is only fair to state that, returning to the hospital not to visit a charity case but to interview the manager, I was shown fine laboratories and examination rooms and an operating-theater open to medical students. The manager did not take me to the contagious ward, nor was he disturbed when I mentioned what I had seen there. Diapers, he said, were always stolen by visiting mothers; the people had no blankets at home, why should they here?

This contrast between a well-planned and equipped building manned by competent physicians and its deplorable lack of care might be dismissed scornfully as proof of a hopeless backwardness. It is more profitable to try to understand it, especially as the situation is not peculiar to San Luis Potosí, but exists generally, even in the capital city. Mexicans, speaking frankly, find here only proof that Mexico's progress must perforce be made through its people.

"Remember," a doctor said, "nursing is not yet a profession that a girl of good family would enter. Nurses are considered servants; many are country girls from homes ignorant of sanitation, even of cleanliness. They consider ordinary requirements utter nonsense to be evaded when possible. And we simply have not enough trained people to keep our hospitals clean. . . . But we manage to lower the death rate and the incidence of endemic disease. Give us time." It is Mexico's glory that it has so many men like this doctor.

Chavela's child got well, as he might not have without the doctors and the penicillin. The day he was taken home, Chavela came in, all smiles, to report that her husband was coming home. He had gone *de bracero* to the United States —California, or maybe Texas, she did not know. But now she had a telegram: "tomorrow passed," he would be here. At once she gave up her job and spent her savings on new clothes for herself and the babies. Later she called to say good-by. Her husband had not written because he had been in jail. She did not know why, nor did she seem to care; jail was one of life's vicissitudes, to be accepted stoically. The point was that he had brought dollars; with dollars they could open a *puesto* in their village market. Chavela was a proud matron now with a future.

Friends—a newspaperwoman, a lawyer, a professor—confirming what I had learned at the hospital, took me to see the center of Acción Católica, one of the Church's answers to the government's social program. Decreed by Pope Pius XI as a world-wide organization, Acción Católica reached Mexico in 1929, a year referred to as *pura persecución* (full persecution). The Calles administration was enforcing the anti-clerical laws of the Reform, and some state governors were indeed persecuting the clergy. Acción Católica has, in twenty years, reached every Mexican diocese, organizing men, women (separate, of course), youths, and children.

Its methods are those of modern social work rather than old-style charity. San Luis has perhaps the finest center, in an old Franciscan convent that has been improved with shining cleanliness, repaired plaster, and paint. "It was dreadful when Padre Anaya took it. He has done wonders."

Padre Anaya, tall, handsome, elegantly groomed, gave his hand to the ladies to be kissed, chatted for a few moments in correct English, and left us. In one patio a young men's club was a-building, with pool and ping-pong tables, reading-room, and showers. Street boys, offered classes in reading and writing, religion and morals, had enrolled to the number of eighty. There was a plan to offer homeless ones a place to sleep: on the floor and without covers, "but this is what they are used to."

Clubrooms for young women followed a hierarchical pattern. For factory workers and servants there were practical kitchens and sewing-rooms; store employees and university students were offered a sitting-room and a powder room with frilled dressing-tables; society girls met in a charming little *sala*, with cushions, bookcases, and a radio. Night classes in stenography, bookkeeping, and English had enrolled 250 students; and the center maintained La Casa Universitaria, where college girls might live at cost, and La Casa de Regeneración for girls gone or going wrong.

One patio was given to La Casa de Formación, dedicated to "the moral formation of the country girl . . . and to aid in the Christian restoration of society." Here the Religiosas Misioneras Marianas were training about thirty Huasteca girls in cleanliness, household arts, and religion. Conventual cubicles held each girl's bed, chair, and religious picture or image. The plan is to have at least one girl from every parish who will return as an evangelist as well as a better homemaker. The pupils were marching in to dinner, which was laid on a clean tablecloth with flowers in the center; it was good nourishing stew with beans, *tortillas*, and stewed fruit. Each girl pays an admission fee of ten pesos, and sixty pesos monthly.

San Luis, in spite of the petering-out of its silver mines, is a rich state, producing hardwoods and tropical crops in the lowlands near Valles and cattle in the uplands. It even makes a marketable crop of its desert *ixtle;* among its textile factories are many producing *ixtle* sacks and cordage for export. But the city's biggest business is a smelter.

ASARCO, the American Smelting and Refining Company, employs two thousand men in a model factory that consumes its own smoke and has the nation's best record for workers' safety. The safety engineer showed me his warning and educational signs posted in the workers' restaurant, lounges, and emergency clinic. The primary school, required by law, is supplemented by a night school for men. The manager, preferring not to be named, said that his main concern was developing responsible workers. "We have got to the point where a man will stay on all night for an emergency if I stay with him. I believe we'll soon get to where he will stay alone." The company has a housing program that permits a worker to buy a house by making a company loan and paying it off monthly. One hundred and sixty men bought homes when the plan was inaugurated in 1943; few have failed, most have paid off and borrowed again for improvements. "We are trying," said the manager, "to help make that middle class you talk about. San Luis now has more Cadillacs per square yard than any place, and no Fords or Chevvies. We are trying to build up the small-car class."

The banker, receiving me genially, suggested that he, like the factory workers, was part of the coming middle class. "I was brought up," he said, "to believe that work was degrading. Now I slave here daily. I come punctually, I stay until my desk is clear. And it probably doesn't do me a bit of harm." His bank was founded on *ixtle*. More than a century ago Edgar Meade, of Irish and Mexican parentage, built a thriving export business on *ixtle*. By cannily withholding 1.5 centavos from the price of every kilo, he built up a capital of 500,000 pesos, with which he founded El Banco Ixtlero. It seems too bad that such a descriptive name has been changed to El Banco Central, but by any name it serves citizens of every class.

I watched a woman at the teller's window. A *rebozo* covered hair not combed that day, and her shoes were crooked, but the check she presented for 3,000 pesos was honored, and she stowed small bills away in a woven bag. I spoke to the banker about that negotiation. "Oh, yes. I know her. We have not many like her, but several. She probably buys up chickens or honey or something to ship to Mexico. This woman, and me. We are the coming Mexico. Just watch us!"

XX

QUERÉTARO

◖ QUERÉTARO is so chockful of history that its present is easily overlooked. It was the scene of the beginnings of the Wars of Independence in 1810, of Maximilian's tragic end in 1866, and of the Constitution of 1917. Its plazas and palaces seem alive with important ghosts in period costumes. But Querétaro is important now as the dominant city of El Bajío (Lowlands), which includes the states of Querétaro, Aguascalientes, and Guanajuato, one of the nation's richest areas. Its mountains have produced mineral wealth, its flatlands are covered with grain fields and orchards, and its small cities, once notable for healing springs, miraculous shrines, and the maddest churrigueresque architecture, are growing into industrial towns laced together by heavy trucks on paved highways.

Much of the old remains. San Juan de los Lagos attracts the largest crowds for its religious fiesta in February. Aguascalientes features its hot springs along with its textile factories. And churrigueresque churches flower out with plump angels and cherubs among luscious fruits and riotous foliage. The Bajío also saw architecture's cooling-off when Francisco Eduardo Tresguerras, influenced by Italian neoclassicism, lightened Mexico's churches with clear space and unadorned pillars. The church of El Carmen in his birthplace of Celaya is considered his masterpiece; he also built there a perfect little chapel for his own burial place.

Tresguerras, a sort of Mexican Leonardo da Vinci, was engineer, sculptor, and painter as well as architect. The

road into Querétaro runs for five miles along the arched
aqueduct Tresguerras built, and he designed its stately
Palacio Federal and its loveliest church, Santa Rosa de
Viterbo. These buildings and many others attest Queré-
taro's colonial wealth and importance, but the Federal
Palace was a revolutionary center too.

Any *chamaco* can tell how, in the wonderful year of 1810,
revolutionists met in the palace. The corregidor certainly
winked at meetings of that "literary society" which included
his wife, "La Corregidora," Doña María Ortiz de Domín-
guez, Mexico's revolutionary heroine. Judging by her picture on the five-centavo piece and by her statues, the lady
was no beauty, but she was surely spirited. The corregidor,
behaving as a correct Spanish official, locked his wife into
her room in the palace when he finally had to discover the
conspiracy. Guides there delight to show the keyhole
through which the dauntless lady pushed a twisted note to
a trusted servant, who galloped with it twenty miles to San
Miguel. Captain Ignacio Allende carried the word on to
Padre Hidalgo in Dolores, where the priest rang the bell
and uttered the cry that roused the country. So Mexico's
Independence Day is September 16 instead of December 8,
when the conspirators had planned to take advantage of a
great fiesta at San Juan de los Lagos to start their revolt.

Querétaro is a city of many churches and plazas, and of
palatial homes with balconies. They were all swarming with
the city's inhabitants and country folk for the Christmas
pageant, whose focus was the great church of San Francisco on the plaza. Ladies of the dispossessed great families,
who preside over and lend grace to the museum in San
Francisco's convent, had opened its splendid patio and
arcades to the Caballeros de Colón (Knights of Columbus)
for a kermess with costumed dances and tableaux. Mexico's
girls are beautiful in higher proportion than those of any
other land, and these came of families who could drape

them in priceless shawls and mantillas. The scenes were not memorable, but it was revealing to see how, in this conservative city, girls were heavily chaperoned, and how young men made the most of this chance to court openly.

Outside in the plaza, less elegant citizens were watching the elaborate procession which is Querétaro's proud version of the holiday's old folk-plays. The city's merchants annually finance floats presenting Biblical scenes in colored cardboard with living actors and some excellent lighting effects. I counted thirty floats, whose pace was so slow that the last of them was just swinging onto the plaza at one o'clock in the morning. None of the onlookers had wearied; they all had relatives in the show.

Querétaro, a conservative city, had supported Maximilian, and was the scene of the end of his fantastic empire. Napoleon III, who had beguiled Maximilian into his Mexican adventure, wisely withdrew his support when the Civil War ended in the United States. Carlotta went to Europe to cast herself dramatically at Napoleon's feet and at those of Pope Pius IX. Refused assistance by both, she went mad and lived out a long life in Belgium. Maximilian, reminded of Hapsburg honor in a letter from his mother, did not leave with the French army, but retired to Querétaro. The people shouted greetings, and the best people showered him with flowers from their balconies.

Maximilian's story is most touchingly told in *Maximiliano Íntimo*, by his secretary, José Luis Blasio. Even this adulatory account shows Maximilian a weakling, forever a victim of circumstances. He waited, in Querétaro, for Juárez's army to invest the city; he shuddered when he saw his messengers shot; he nobly ate cat meat with the besieged citizens; he finally refused the liberal general's offer of safe conduct because his Mexican officers were not included. But even in those tragic days he enjoyed dressing in his version of the working *charro*'s tight trousers, short jacket, and sombrero with chin strap.

Juárez's liberal forces were sweeping the country; some of Maximilian's Mexican officers escaped to join them. But Generals Miguel Miramón and Tomás Mejía, remaining faithful, made a last, hopeless stand on El Cerro de las Campanas (Hill of the Bells). The end came on May 15, 1867, when General Escobedo took the city and seized Maximilian and his officers. Pleas for their release came from European rulers and from many Mexicans, especially ladies, and most particularly from the Princess Salm-Salm, a former glamorous circus rider. But President Juárez, remembering that Maximilian had decreed death for all Mexicans taken in arms against his empire, remained adamant. After a correct court-martial, Maximilian, Miramón, and Mejía were shot on the Hill of the Bells. Young Blasio, imprisoned in the Capuchin convent, heard the shots at dawn on June 16, 1867. Blasio, who accompanied the catafalque to Vienna, notes sadly that of all the Mexicans whom Maximilian had enriched and ennobled, not one attended the final rites in the Habsburg royal chapel.

Querétaro, for all its Spanish finery and imperialistic leanings, saw the framing of the constitution that went so far toward making Mexico a land with special privileges for none that it has been variously condemned as socialistic, atheistic, and even communistic.

President Venustiano Carranza had, by 1916, brought some order to Mexico, and—egged on by his liberal advisers—he called a constitutional convention. Carranza himself had little use for either labor or agrarianism, but strong leaders of both had to be reckoned with. Carranza's convention soon got out of his control, and its leaders, largely influenced by Álvaro Obregón, gave Mexico the most socially advanced constitution to that date, 1917.

Three of this constitution's articles deeply affected Mexico's later history and politics. Article 27 declared property rights subordinate to the public good and all sub-soil wealth the inalienable property of the nation, which might grant concessions for its development. This was the basis for the land-expropriations, including the oil-expropriations. Article 23, honored as labor's Bill of Rights, established the eight-hour day, a minimum wage, abolition of child labor, and the right to organize, bargain collectively, strike, and receive many benefits. Article 3, following the lines of legislation of 1857, limited the clergy's right to hold property, and established secular education. Such a constitution was destined to be vigorously fought by both landowners and clergy.

Secular education especially was construed to mean atheistic education. That word is applied, almost forty years later, to government schools that are also accused of shockingly immoral sex education, though apparently no sex education has ever been given; Mexican children still learn —and learn early—about the birds and the bees in the hallowed and unscientific ways.

I was able, in Querétaro, to observe the workings of these articles and their effects on different elements of the population. First I visited a mica factory. Mica comes from Oaxaca, but the factory established there during World War II was later moved to Querétaro, a transportation center. Mica films, of a thinness suitable for use in radio, telephone, or electronics industries, are shipped in quantity to the United States. The work is done by girls, who have been found more apt than men at this delicate work.

The factory, in an old patioed building, was light and airy. Over three hundred girls, most of them under twenty, were operating machines, electrically run but requiring keen eyesight and extraordinary manual dexterity. Each girl receives a small sheet of mica, which she cuts to size or

splits and passes along to her neighbor. So the work pro-
gresses to greater and greater skill as the films become finer
and finer. Industrially this is important as an example of
Mexico's use of its own resources in industry. Its human
aspects are even more suggestive of what is happening in
Mexico.

Most of these girls come from what Mexicans call their
"humble class." Many of them when hired are unshod, un-
combed, poorly dressed, and quite without address or apparent sense, though they must have had at least two years
of schooling. Hired through their union, Unidad Feminina
Queretana, they are paid for a training-period of three or
four weeks and are given all the protections and privileges
required by law. The assistant manager assured me that relations with the union are of the smoothest. "Most of the
leaders we have met are reasonable and understanding. The
stewardesses who direct the girls' work are as a rule co-
operative; most of them have come from the ranks of workers and all are elected delegates of the union. . . . The
necessary discipline of a shop is sure to be forbidding to a
beginner, and the precision required of them is far indeed
from anything they have known. . . . But, come, look at
them."

The girls were of every Mexican type from darkest,
heaviest Indian to delicate magnolia-skinned Spanish. All
were clean, many were groomed even to permanent waves
and colored fingernails. The manager said it took about
three weeks to turn a spiritless creature into a brisk and
efficient young woman. This factory is making not only
mica for precision instruments, but new women for the
middle class.

Similar girls who have not had the advantages of factory
training and union protection work as a rule as maids,
which means that they belong to a past age. Maids throughout Mexico work from dawn until the last member of the

family has gone to bed. Their wage varies from thirty or forty pesos a month in the provinces to ninety or one hundred in the capital. The day off is construed as what remains of a day after the usual work is done at noon or later; many mistresses, in the interests of morals, require the maid to be in before dark. This day off often occurs once every two weeks.

A lady with whom I lived—not in Querétaro—let her maid off for her fortnightly Sunday after the family dinner ended at about four o'clock. When the girl, not returning on Monday, was found to have removed her few belongings, the lady was volubly indignant. "This," she stormed, "is what this socialistic government has done to us. These people have no respect, no responsibility. I now must work like an Indian, and my feet hurt!"

Don Carlos Urquiza, a devout Catholic and a hereditary *hacendado,* gave me the slant of his class on land laws and secular education. Don Carlos, a graduate of the Colorado Agricultural College, where his father had also been educated, cordially invited me to visit his ranch. As we drove along the road between Querétaro and Celaya, he took pains to set me right. "All this," he said, sweeping his arm grandly, "belonged to my father; all was in production— wheat, corn, fruit. Now that we have been robbed of it, just look at it. Empty land, growing up into cactus and mesquite again." The Urquizas had owned some 5,000 acres in this one hacienda. Now that each proprietor is limited by law to 250 acres, the twelve brothers and sisters together own 3,000 acres, which Don Carlos manages as a unit.

He indicated men herding cattle in the fields, "These Indians are like horses. A horse is only as good as his rider. Without good direction the Indian is no good. . . . Look at those houses; they are good houses that we built for my workmen, but do you think they would live there? No. They are now occupied by our top men, those able to accept some responsibility. . . . Remember that there is nothing good in Mexico except what the Spaniards brought, especially the doctrine. Only men with white blood are getting ahead." So Don Carlos expressed his creed in rounded sentences. *Hispanidad*. Catholicism. Anti-Indianism.

As a farmer, Don Carlos was another man. Rancho Mayorazgo raises everything it uses, but is primarily a dairy farm. The cattle were of Holstein-Friesian stock, the only foreign herd registered with the Holstein-Friesian Association of Canada. The Association's standards are so high that it lists as "excellent" only four cows in Canada and two on Rancho Mayorazgo. Many here rate "very good," which is in itself excellent. The herd holds many top ratings, blue ribbons, and gold medals. The ranch sells between fifty and sixty bull calves a year, thus improving the country's dairy herds.

"One day," Don Carlos said, "seven *campesinos* I did not know came to see me. They wished to buy a registered bull calf and they had brought two thousand pesos to pay for it. They wore good shoes, clean clothes. . . . I chose a fine calf for them, and I was so interested that I took time to deliver it myself. . . . You would be interested in what I saw. I'll take you there. There are eleven small communities that belong to owners who bought land so bad the government did not want it for *ejidos*. Each man bought his own. They are good Catholic men, and they did not care to own land that had been stolen by the *agraristas*. They had the luck to find water, and now they irrigate with pumps."

Before reaching the family home, we stopped at San José, a smallish country house where the Urquiza family has established a school operated by a Madre Superior and four other nuns. The gentle sister who met us apologized for the small attendance; only about 20 children out of an enrollment of 147. But yesterday was a holiday. Don Carlos pointed out how many of the children looked white. "We have people here who can learn. We maintain this school at our own expense because, as loyal Mexicans, we wish these children taught the fear of God. Not the Communism taught in government schools. You have only to look at the schoolbooks. No mention of God at all!"

This tour brought us to the dairy, where handsome cows stood in a pavilion still damp from the daily flushing. Each cow's record was in her stall; almost one hundred cows average forty-four pounds of milk daily. Each calf is registered at birth; no royal family has a more accurate genealogy. We visited the separators, where milk is processed to produce butter or powdered milk for shipment. Here we were joined by Don Carlos's son, Jorge, a nine-year-old cotton-top who spoke good English, and who at once constituted himself my guide.

We visited another hacienda, La Labor, whose last owner, a gentleman who lived in Paris, had been despoiled of many acres. Jorge ran me through the patio up to a wide terrace, where he explained the frescoes of French life, including skaters on a pond. He then insisted upon a climb to the heavy stone roof, where he showed me the domed chimney that carried off smoke and charcoal fumes from the kitchen below. The house is empty now, but the family plans a nuns' school there to train country girls as good housekeepers and mothers.

Lunch at the home was served to fourteen people, all members of the family, who stood respectfully while a priest asked a blessing. It was a scene to make one believe in the grace and beauty of life before the revolution, even to believe that if all *hacendado* families had lived as this one does there might have been no revolution.

After lunch we rode out to see the eleven pueblos Don Carlos had praised for their independence of the government. La Luz, the largest, consisted of 103 families; the others ranged in size down to one of only 15 families. Each man owned from a half a hectar to 100 hectares of land; as even half a hectar would support two or three cows, there was no dire poverty. La Luz's daily production of 1,200 liters was processed in a family plant and sold to the Carnation Milk factory near Querétaro.

Our informant was José Martínez, a well-scrubbed, well-set-up man who spoke English. He had worked as *bracero*, he said, on a farm near Indio, California, "for a fine boss." Had he brought home enough money to buy this farm? Well, no, he had inherited the land from his father, but he had been able to invest in stock and many improvements. He pointed out the chapel and the school. Don Carlos drooped a bit when José said that the school was maintained by the government, which also helped with banking and agricultural services. But he felt better when he asked if the villagers owed anybody anything and José answered: "Only God."

In any case, the eleven villages are an excellent example of small proprietorship in action.

Back in his office, Don Carlos pointed to a photograph of his brother. "He was our family's eldest, a noble man and a true Catholic. He was killed by one of our peons who had been corrupted by *agrarianismo*. This man approached my brother at the railroad station, asking for a loan. As my brother reached for his wallet, the man shot him. Dead. He was one of the founders of *sinarquismo* and its first martyr."

Sinarquismo is a coined word meaning "without anarchy" and implying "with order." It was founded by three young lawyers of León, a Bajío city, and José Antonio Urquiza, Don Carlos's brother. The order quickly enlisted many landowners and thousands of peasants, who hoped that *sinarquismo* would bring them all the benefits the Revolution had somehow failed to deliver. Too often they had seen the promised lands gobbled up by corrupt politicians. But the strongest appeal was to devout and simple Catholics to protect their children from secular education and to save freedom of religion, which was not construed as referring to any religion other than the Catholic.

The Unión Nacional Sinarquista spread rapidly from the Bajío throughout Mexico and even into the United States where Mexican Catholics could be reached. At its apogee it claimed almost one million members organized in village units commanded by leaders who gave absolute obedience to their superiors through a hierarchy headed by a layman. Each officer was named by his superior; the retiring head named his successor. There was no pretense of democratic action; members were to be silent and to obey. Much was made of secrecy; village units were frequently called to assemble in silence, making a show of unarmed but highly dramatic force. Only occasionally did *sinarquistas* resort to arms.

Sinarquismo, on its face one more battle in the endless war between church and state, seemed to show traces of Nazi, Fascist, and Falangist influence. Mexican citizens of German extraction, admirers of Franco, and anti-government Catholics welcomed *sinarquismo*'s program of opposition to government and to Communism and Anglo-American culture (lumped as twin evils). It is difficult to learn how vigorously the cult may persist; it appears in political campaigns and is mentioned in private talk as the hope of making Mexico a Catholic country again. Its leadership and its hopes may well reside in El Bajío, which reflects so fully all the nation's conflicting trends.

XXI

SAN MIGUEL ALLENDE

As I DROVE across the hills from Querétaro to San Miguel Allende, I overtook about twenty people straggling dustily along the road and singing off-key. They wore wreaths of flowers, and many carried flower-tipped staves; clearly they were pilgrims going to the shrine of a miraculous saint. This is an authentic Mexican custom; all sorts of people leave home and work to pray for a miracle or to render thanks for a prayer granted. It is Catholic, but it antedates Catholicism in Mexico. It is well known that missionaries built their churches at pagan shrines; who knows —as Anita Brenner suggests in *Idols Behind Altars*—what today's Indian worships at the place that his ancestors revered before the Christians built?

Though the Bajío has no monopoly of holy shrines, it has some notable ones. Its greatest is at San Juan de los Lagos, just across the state line in Jalisco, but still in the Bajío. This is a great popular festival to which simple people come afoot, often increasing their penance with peas in the shoes or cactus spines under the shirt. Here, as in many places, Indians honor the Christian saint with pagan dances. The new monument to El Cristo Rey on El Cerro del Cubilete (Top Hat Hill) near Guanajuato was visited by the National Catholic Confederation of Workers, whose first act was to place a commemorative stone there. Many visitors arrive in handsome cars, make their devotions, and proceed to good hotels in Guanajuato. But the group I saw was going to Atotonilco, the village where Padre Hidalgo took a banner of the Virgin of Guadalupe as his standard. Atotonilco has no wonder-working saint, but it attracts pilgrims all the year. The large convent will house three thousand; they spread their blankets on the floor, hang their bags on pegs, and are provided with stew and beans cooked in mammoth clay pots and *tortillas* that come off a conveyer belt. Sanitary facilities consist of two hundred seats built back to back over running water; as men and women's pilgrimages are separate, no problems of modesty arise. For all this each worshipper pays five pesos a day; each one is required to remain for a week's "spiritual exercises." A maid in San Miguel Allende asked a loan of forty pesos. "My father has to go on pilgrimage to Atotonilco, and he has no money just now. . . . Well, the ranch has to send so many men, and he was chosen."

This strikes the unregenerate as good business for somebody, but the wayfarer on untraveled lanes will encounter pilgrimages infused with folk faith that moves whole villages to such ancient fanes as that of Nuestro Señor de Chalma. They rest in churchyards, cross roadless hills on prehistoric trails, often carry flowers whose freshness on arrival seems a true miracle.

Atotonilco lies between San Miguel Allende and Padre Hidalgo's town of Dolores, where the liberal priest defied the law by planting mulberry trees, vineyards, and olive groves; silk, wine, and oil were Spanish monopolies. He also put people to work in pottery and leather shops. His house is replete with mementos of a man at once reminiscent of sixteenth-century missionaries and a product of his time. To that house Captain Ignacio Allende came galloping with word that the plan for insurrection had been discovered in Querétaro. So on the night of September 15 the cry rang out: *"Viva Nuestra Señora de Guadalupe! Viva la Independencia! Muerte a los gachupines!"* The church bell Padre Hidalgo rang that night was removed to Mexico, where the president rings it every year from the National Palace, giving the cry: *"Libertad e Independencia!"* Padre Hidalgo has been enshrined as the moving spirit of Mexico's ten-year struggle for independence, and his town is now known as Dolores Hidalgo.

San Miguel Allende, however approached, is beautiful with red roofs and church towers against the hills, and streets that pitch down or climb past colonial buildings of the native red stone. "José Mojica," my hostess told me, "saved our town. Before he came, we had all spent thousands of pesos plastering the old stone walls. You can still see some bits of plaster on the walls of old San Francisco. But Mojica, when he lived here, talked about the beauty of the old *cantera*, and now, you see, nearly the whole town is that rose-colored stone you like."

Mojica discovered the town in the thirties when he was a famous opera and motion-picture tenor. He built a fine house at the end of a leafy lane, with the garden overlooking the valley and the blue Guanajuato hills beyond. His home was full of the collections of a successful international career, but its owner was even then a quiet, mystical man, concerned with religion. Finally he entered a monastery in Peru, proposing to end his public career. But as a habited friar he continues to travel constantly, singing over the radio for religious causes.

Mojica also brought Stirling Dickinson to San Miguel Allende. Once when the two men met at a railroad station, Mojica so extolled the old city's charms that Dickinson returned and was convinced. He bought an old tannery near the spring and reroofed the rooms he needed, but left much open to the sky. His garden is a half-wild growth of poinsettias, canna lilies, and the cool blue plumbago that in Mexico is a tall shrub and not a border plant. Orchids grow in sheltered trees.

Dickinson soon found his niche in an art school headed

by Felipe Cossío Pomar, a Peruvian liberal in exile from his own country. The Instituto Allende, housed in an old convent, attracted Mexican and foreign students and distinguished painters as teachers. David Alfaro Siqueiros laid out a mural in the refectory, but before it was finished the school got involved in a political imbroglio, and most of the faculty were exiled to the border. This situation was saved by a student who was also a general and well connected politically. This was the school's low point. Its high was when it was accredited as a G.I. institution and *Life* featured it with pictures of nudes sunning on garden walls. Manager Dickinson then composed a form letter refusing all applications.

Since these hectic days the school has settled down under Don Enrique Fernández Martínez, a former governor of Guanajuato, who finds it one more outlet for his life's dedication to human betterment. The Instituto now occupies a fine old mansion that has been remodeled into class and work rooms where much experimental work goes on with native materials and techniques. The gardens, patios, and large chambers are beautifully shadowed, cool by day, distinctly chilly at night. Here is no pandering to the North American's love of comfort. By day one may sun on open terraces or in fragrant gardens, but there is no fireside comfort for evenings; certainly there are no easy chairs.

My Señora said: "The worst thing these *norteamericanos* have brought us is their love of comfort. They must have soft beds, heat; always they must avoid suffering. Imagine, they do not even like flies! God made the flies, and God meant us to suffer."

San Miguel was founded in 1542 by Franciscans who came seeking a place to settle a group of "reduced" Otomí and Chichimec Indians. One evening their dogs, coming in all wet, led them to a wide, clear spring. There they built. That spring still supplies the town with all the water it can use, and with enough surplus to keep the gutters in the middle of the streets running with fresh water, often grown with watercress and ferns. The plaza is a garden shaded by the Indian laurels that reached Mexico via Cuba. At nightfall they are filled with chattering grackles that come flying in in droves and make sitting in the park hazardous.

Ignacio Allende, whose name was added to that of the town after the Wars of Independence, was born in a house that bears a plaque: *"Hic Natus, Ubique Notus."* Whether he is known everywhere or not, Ignacio Allende was certainly one of the noteworthy leaders of independence, a military man whose disregarded advice might have saved Hidalgo his worst blunders.

Also on the plaza is the palace of the Conde de Canal; its lower corner is occupied by a thoroughly sophisticated shop for guests of the Posada San Francisco; its upper apartments are occupied by the Conde's descendants. The Posada, former home of the Zavala family, retains a monkish austerity in its bedrooms, but its small *sala*, hung with family heirlooms in crucifixes, tapestries, and paintings, panders to the weak gringo with the comfort of a nightly wood fire.

The city's gem is its parish church, rebuilt in 1880 by a local architect who, according to legend, was inspired by a post card from Cologne. Unfortunately his money ran out before he got the central spire as tall as it should have been, and the whole is a bit chunky. Purists often rage, but the church's lacy extravagance is thoroughly Mexican and, seen at sunset from the hill above, the *cantera*'s soft pink takes on an ethereal quality. During Christmas week the parishioners gave there the old folk-play *La Guadalupana*. The parts—Juan Diego, the humble Indian to whom the Virgin appeared, the doubting clerics, and the childlike Virgin in blue—were more artlessly effective than art could have made them. The audience, packed in the atrium, on fences, and on roofs, was devoutly attentive. The missionaries' old art of teaching through morality plays has not been lost.

Just around the corner I came upon a surprise. The store entrance was, as usual, hung with dresses, ropes, hats, and birdcages, and stacked with blue coffins painted with white cherubs. But it bore the name El Arco de Noé and carved into the pink stone above it was the star of David. Curious, I asked a lady standing there with a baby in her arms. She was, she said, la Señora de Isaac Cohen, proprietor of the store, and she invited me in. Upstairs she proudly explained carvings on the cornices. The signs of the zodiac, the tribes of Judah, a statue of Cuauhtémoc, and a less accountable Apache. All were her husband's idea. He had built in the colonial style, but honored his beliefs in décor. Children had appeared, all clean and most mannerly when introduced as Abraham, Esther, Rebecca, Leah, David, Solomon, and Ruth. The baby was Joseph.

"We are Jews from Damascus," Sra. Cohen explained. "My husband came in 1923, and my family brought me in 1926. We came to San Miguel Allende because my husband thought to find good business. And he did. But now our eldest reaches the age of marriage, so we return to Mexico. Even now some of our children wish to be Catholics, and we are Jews." She never tired of talking of her husband's goodness and of his sayings: "Each gathers what he sows" and "When one dies he takes only the good he has done."

Annually on January 6, día de los reyes, when wise men brought gifts to the newborn Jewish Child, Isaac Cohen makes gifts to all comers. He distributes two tons of corn in two-kilo sacks, gives to each woman a warm sweater, and to children garments and candy. So Isaac Cohen expresses gratitude for his success in a Catholic town.

The dominant colonial family was that of Manuel Tomás

de Canal, whose title of Conde was honorary, though he was a Knight of Calatrava. With his equally pious wife, he built for their sepulture a baroque chapel enclosing an exact replica of the Virgin Mary's home in Palestine. A young seminary student told the story with shining eyes. Angels, he said, bore the house from Bethlehem to Italy, and were about to set it down when two brothers began to quarrel about whose land should be so honored. "Imagine," he cried, "disputing about such a thing!" So the angels flew on and placed the house at Loreto, where the count and his lady saw it in 1735 and were moved to have it reproduced at home. They also built the Virgin an exquisite octagonal *camarín* (robing-room) enriched with statues and gold leaf. The Virgin's former great wealth has disappeared. Those who hate the new regime say the government stole it. Padre Solis, whose rheumy old eyes retain a gleam at eighty-six, says that the last Conde de Canal, showing "weak resistance to Hidalgo's call," gave the Virgin's jewels to the cause of independence.

The first Conde de Canal built for his daughter, Doña Josefa, a convent said to have an underground passage to the palace. Doña Josefa refused the usual donor's perquisite of becoming prioress, praying instead to die of a loathsome disease. My devout Señora considered it evidence of great spirituality that she did suffer an affliction so vile that worms came out of her nose. The Casa de Monjas is now inhabited by cloistered nuns, whose low murmuring may be heard behind carved screens. They accept gifts through a revolving door; perhaps they take in washing there.

During the happy days recalled by my Señora, devout gentlemen, wearing medals inscribed *Esclavo del Santo Sacramento*, attended the priest going to administer extreme unction. Each gentleman, attired in high hat and frock coat, served one week as coachman in such eighteenth-century coaches as now exist only in museums; the others bore the sacred vessels. "Now," she sighed, "this awful government has taken all beauty out of life!"

Another story reflects something of what this government is trying to put into life. Once when President Cárdenas was in the Bajío during his land-expropriations, he was informed that the parishioners were hearing anti-government speeches in San Miguel Allende; a new *cristero* uprising was feared. The President characteristically walked straight up to the threat. In San Miguel Allende he dismissed his guard and strode alone through the thronged atrium and into the church. There, as the people began to edge nervously away, he spoke. "No, don't go. This is your church. I have come here to tell you what your government is planning to make your lives easier. Nothing will be done against your church. We speak of land, of farms, of better homes, and of schools." What he said is not so well remembered as is the quiet, courageous man speaking to people in their own simple words.

San Miguel Allende offers whatever you like. Peace and quiet for writing or painting, the stuff of folklore and history, or just a beautiful, quiet town with a good climate for being lazy.

XXII

GUANAJUATO

C⬧ In Guanajuato the *chamaco*, often so annoying, proves himself altogether indispensable. The first one I refused trotted patiently along the narrow twisting streets until I was hopelessly confused. Traffic lights are especially baffling, as cars must stop half a block away from corners too constricted for passing. Guanajuato's streets are exceptionally clean, trash boxes abound, and flat green paving-stones have replaced the original cobbles; they are quite as picturesque and less likely to cause turned ankles or bruised tires. This was the idea of the 1950 mayor, who also diverted a small stream and paved its bed for a street between stone banks that still show the waterline. Guanajuato's plazas are on two or three levels; many lanes are stone steps; one is narrow enough to be called the Lane of the Kiss. The University, topping a stairway, is almost as hard to reach as a pyramid; when the city presented a series of Cervantes's plays, the steps were used as seats and the plaza as a stage.

The *chamaco*, keeping me on the right path, brought me to the Posada de la Presa (Inn of the Dam), where Ricardo, a dignified gentleman of eight years, explained that in his father's absence he could show the rooms. At suppertime I found the sitting-room shut off from the patio by heavy curtains and a brisk fire snapping. Clearly somebody understood the gringo. Two people did, both Manuel Valenzuela, who came in for supper, and his wife, Felícitas. Felícitas, a bit shy about her English, devotes herself to her kitchen, which produces a rare and wonderful combination of Mexican and United States dishes. The rest of the family consists of Gorky, who was visiting his grandmother in Chihuahua, and Yunuén, named for a Tarascan chief, who was more interested in his bottle than in conversation. This was a family to arouse curiosity. I was to learn their story as Manuel guided me through the lovely old city that was a silver center, a revolutionary battlefield, a treasure house of colonial architecture.

South of the city on a high hill stands a rough-hewn statue of the half-naked miner who was the revolutionary hero, Pípila. After Hidalgo's cry had aroused not an army, but a mob of fifty thousand that his trained lieutenants could not control, he led them to Guanajuato, a royalist stronghold. The populace rose against the Spanish army, which, with a few *criollos*, barricaded itself in the Alhóndiga de Granaditas, a huge granary whence they raked the unarmed Indians with artillery fire. The stone building seemed impregnable to such arms as the Mexicans had. Then Pípila appeared. Where he came from nobody knows, nor where he went. His very name, José M. Barojas, has been lost in the nickname. Coming out of nowhere and disappearing into nowhere, he is the archetype of the nameless multitude. What he did was extraordinarily courageous. Flexing his miner's muscles, Pípila lifted onto his shoulders a stone large enough to protect him from gunfire, and, carrying a torch, he advanced to the granary's great door and fired it with a charge of dynamite. So the fortress fell and, in spite of all their officers' protests, the uncontrollable mob slaughtered the Spaniards to the last man. After the royalists had retaken Guanajuato and captured Hidalgo in the north, they brought back the heads of the four leaders —Hidalgo, Allende, Aldama, and Mariano Jiménez—and hung them in cages at the granary's corners. Only years later independent Mexico reverently removed them for burial in the Cathedral in the capital.

Pípila's statue bears the legend: *Aun hay otras alhóndigas para incendiar!* (There are still other granaries to burn.) "Mexico will not be truly free," sighed Manuel, "until we can say: 'There are no more granaries to burn!'"

Across the *barranca* in which Guanajuato lies, and facing Pípila's statue at a distance of a couple of miles, is La Valenciana, the world's deepest and one of its richest silver mines. It made a wealthy man and Conde de Rul of the unlettered miner who found it and who built there a magnificent church dedicated to San Cayetano, but known as La Valenciana. The Conde made every miner a sharer in its building by demanding of each one a nugget from his daily dig. The church is an extreme example of churrigueresque in delicacy and fantasy and in the profusion of flowers, vines, shells, snakes, and cupids that cover it.

Below the city is *La Presa de los Santos*, the dam whose builder adorned it with statues of his twelve children's name saints. Credit is also surprisingly given to "*José Alejandro Durán, maestro de los albañiles*" (master of the masons), who finished the job on November 7, 1778. Down in the *barranca* is El Marfil (Marble), a noble ruin that was mansion as well as silver-smelter. Its present owners have remodeled the home, successfully preserving its style and combining antique furniture with comfort and convenience. The gardens dominate the old smelter, which, like everything in Guanajuato, is remarkable for the colors of its stones—gray, a soft pinkish rose, and the typical green that is almost turquoise and so clear as to suggest paint. No paint was used, but the masons used plenty of artistry in laying stones in patterns of color, and plenty of engineering skill in placing them to uphold arches by their own pressure. Here Manuel Valenzuela, dreaming of possible restoration, showed himself such an artist with such knowledge of Spanish architecture that I begged for his story.

Manuel's grandfather was a redheaded, blue-eyed baby

found on a roadside in Durango by an *arriero*, who raised him, giving him his own surname of Valenzuela. His son, Manuel's father, was a shopkeeper in Chihuahua, who lived for a few years in Ciudad Juárez. When Manuel was sixteen, Mexico was torn by the *cristero* uprisings. Calles, harshly enforcing the anti-clerical laws, had deported almost two hundred priests and nuns who, on order of the Archbishop, had refused to register as the law required of all ministers of all faiths. Devout Catholic laymen staged armed rebellion with the battle cry *"Viva Cristo Rey"* (Christ the King). In several states teachers were killed, and so were priests. Some state governors so mistreated priests as to justify the Catholic term of "persecution." It was a hideous civil war whose repercussions were felt throughout the Republic. It touched Manuel Valenzuela when his uncle, a *cristero*, came fleeing toward the United States.

Manuel was sent across the border on a streetcar to ask aid from a priest in El Paso. The cleric, a United States citizen, arranged through an immigration officer who was a Knight of Columbus to smuggle the uncle across the border. By this time Manuel wished to enlist with the *cristeros;* his parish priest in Ciudad Juárez was recruiting teen-agers. But a mother of one boy went to the padre. "Naturally I wish my son to fight for God and the Church," she said, "but oh, Padre, I cannot bear for him to die in sin. Now if you were to go along, I and all the other mothers would be content to see our boys go." Somehow the padre reconsidered, and the boys were kept at home.

Soon after, Manuel, finding his father domineering, ran away. "I hoboed my way to Los Angeles, where I met lots of discrimination against Mexicans," he said, "but I heard lots of talk about the Franco revolt in Spain with its Moorish army supported by Fascists and Nazis." Surprisingly, considering his Catholic training, the boy enlisted with the Lincoln Brigade and fought with the Loyalists in Spain for two years. This was the greatest experience of Manuel's life. He believed he was fighting for the right; he knew he was fighting against Italians and Germans. In Spain he learned English from "the most wonderful Americans and Englishmen—writers, artists, professors, men who gave us fine lectures, who taught us."

Back in Mexico, Manuel found his country divided between devout Church people, who had been taught that Franco was saving Holy Church and that all who opposed him were both communistic and anti-Christ, and the government, which, accepting Spanish Loyalists as democratic, offered them a refuge in Mexico. Manuel volunteered to work with a refugee colony in Baja California. On his way, as he crossed United States territory, he found immigration officers as harsh against the Loyalists as any Catholic Mexican. "That," he said, "almost broke my heart. I had counted on gringo democracy, freedom of thought, and all that. . . . I guess people are the same everywhere." The colonization project was not a success; Spanish refugees did not take to the land.

Manuel then tried farming in Michoacán, but when a bad season ruined his first crop he went to work at the Hotel El Lago at Pátzcuaro, where he met his fate in two forms. He soon became an expert on Tarascan pottery, and so attracted the attention of Richard Gump, who was seeking Mexican wares for his San Francisco store, deprived of its Oriental supply by the war. Mr. Gump offered Manuel a job in San Francisco. And Manuel met Felícitas.

Felícitas was an orphan, who had inherited her Tarascan father's high cheekbones and her Spanish mother's fine magnolia skin. She reluctantly agreed to marry Manuel by the civil ceremony, but even after their son, Gorky, was born, she yearned for the Church's blessing. Manuel finally consented to the Church service, but he refused confession and communion. "I do not believe," he explained to the padre, "and if I accepted absolution and took communion I should be insulting not only my beliefs but yours."

Happily a wealthy friend arranged a church wedding, not only without the groom's conformity, but with the largest candles procurable. "I think," Manuel smiled, "that Felícitas began to understand as she compared our ornate candles with the tiny tapers held by an Indian couple being married at the same time. 'It was the money made the difference,' she whispered as we left the church."

In San Francisco, Manuel's naturally true taste developed in Gump's store; later he became Gump's window-dresser in Carmel. The child born there was named Richard Gump for the godfather who carried him to the Episcopal altar. Manuel had accepted the fact that all peoples have a naming ceremony. The third son, Yunuén, had a Jewish sponsor, and Manuel wished to have him named in a synagogue. "But the rabbi turned out to be the most intolerant of the lot," cried Manuel.

Finding people the same wherever he went, Manuel had returned to Mexico. It was home. He could help here, perhaps.

PART SIX

Mexico's West

XXIII

¡AY, JALISCO AND GUADALAJARA!

☞ JALISCO and Guadalajara, whose very names sing, have inspired meltingly sentimental songs celebrating beautiful women, fine horses, and tequila. Legends meet one at every step, tradition is honored, old families do not move away, and wealth seems natural in a land that has enjoyed it for ages. But the twentieth century has come to Jalisco too, and the mellow old capital city is hoping—against its dislike of foreigners, the harsh English speech, and push—to become a tourist center.

Tapatíos, as Guadalajara people are called, feel injured because their city is so often discovered by tourists only at the end of their stay in Mexico. They insist that the wonders of the west are quite unknown, though the Sierra Occidental and its seaward slopes are quite as spectacular as anything in the Republic. They count on the new highway and advertising to change that. Meanwhile the highway from San Luis Potosí brings many tourists in over Jalisco's typical rolling hills. They are studded with the gray green spines of the maguey de mescal, whose juice is fermented into tequila, a white and potent drink its devotees consider the equal of vodka. A similar drink made in Puebla or Oaxaca is called mescal. Many tequila haciendas have been abandoned to the distillery, but the one I visited still served the family on week-ends.

We crossed a cobbled patio brilliant with climbing plants and opening on one side into a huge chamber where the tequila was made; on the other side, formal *salas* gave on a well-kept garden. Here was the usual accumulation of many lives lived abroad. Italian statuettes on ebony pedestals, French landscapes with misty trees, elegant uncomfortable furniture, and modern form-fitting chairs. The old-style week-long parties have given way to week-ends, but hostesses cherish old family cookbooks and proudly serve typical dishes. Jalisco has so much hot country that its recipes include pineapple juice, cinnamon, and bananas. It boasts of two fermented drinks aside from tequila—tejuino, made of corn and brown sugar, and the equally potent tepache, of pineapple juice. My hostess said her grandmothers' cookbooks could produce a different *tapatío* recipe for every saint's day in the year.

The highway from the north enters Guadalajara through a busy street between garages and motor-supply houses and traffic that is controlled for motorists but leaves pedestrians free to duck, dodge, jay-walk, or pause to chat at will. Streets are noisy; downtown hotels are noisy; the charm of the city becomes apparent only on closer acquaintance. Guadalajara is suffering acutely from an ill that afflicts all Mexico: modern life and business do not fit comfortably into stone chambers twenty feet high. Fortunately, Guadalajara architects are fully aware of the problem and hard at work trying to solve it.

The moving force in this program was the Presidente Municipal, Ing. Jorge Matute Remos, former Rector of the University of Guadalajara. "Our dream," he said, "is to modernize Guadalajara in every way necessary for living, but without sacrificing its character as a Mexican city." Avenida Juárez, the main shopping-street, tells the tale. Several skyscrapers, built before the program took hold, are out of character, but Sears Roebuck, that Yankee institution, surrounded its store with shaded arcades that are both traditional and functional. Ing. Matute's triumph was moving the telephone building when Avenida Juárez was widened. Telephones must be kept in operation, and the city could not afford to import expensive equipment and even more expensive technicians. Ing. Matute decided to do the job in the oldest, and cheapest way, with Indian arms, back muscle, and know-how. He mobilized contractors, who hired straw bosses, who brought men with poles and ropes. Dirt was moved by machinery, but the supporting pillars were cut through and jacked up, and the whole edifice was swung twenty meters one way, seven another, and all by man power. Not a crack appeared, not a man was injured, not one telephone was put out of order.

Guadalajara, founded in 1535 as the capital of Nueva Galicia, has fine colonial architecture to preserve. Its historic Street of San Francisco has yielded to changing styles, but the church of San Francisco, built in the severe style of 1550, dominates a fine colonial plaza. Its other, lesser temple is the favorite for society weddings, and one can look away from the bus station. La Calle de San Francisco saw all the parades that reflected Mexico's history. Colonial governors and prelates rode along it in their gilded coaches followed by simpler coaches bearing their satins and velvets, their jeweled altar vessels, and their servants. Guadalajara was royal with Spain, imperial with Iturbide, and always devoutly Catholic, and its people greeted dignitaries with flowery arches and jeweled ladies on draped balconies. But when the French General Bazaine rode in, not one arch was erected, not one house adorned. The city watched in somber silence the march of foreign troops and their Mexican allies.

Guadalajara's Cathedral, beyond the other end of the Calle de San Francisco, was begun in 1571 and finished fifty years later. It has been remodeled countless times since into a hodge-podge of styles, but it has treasures of painting and sculpture within. The architects decided to leave the Cathedral untouched, but to give it a worthy setting.

So they landscaped the long narrow plaza between the Cathedral and El Teatro Degollado and restored the arcades that had been shorn off the fine old buildings around it. Happily, three square plazas were so placed that when they were similarly landscaped and restored, the whole gave the stately temple a verdant cruciform setting that was effective from planes in the air and that gave a parklike approach to its every entrance. So Guadalajara's architects were true at once to their city's colonial architecture and to the modern mode of travel.

Modern architecture has overrun the low hills west of the city with homes of glass and tile, but even there most of life's patterns remain unchanged. Life on a quiet residential street begins early when maids appear to sweep the sidewalks and hose them off, often to wash the car. Boys on bicycles leave milk bottles, and others cycle by with baskets of rolls on their heads. My hostess laughed about a gringo who insisted it was not sanitary to buy bread thus exposed. "How silly," she giggled, "I never let the boy touch my bread; I take it out of the basket myself." I watched her do it, turning over the *bolillos* to get the sweet rolls we chose by name—fish, crowns, nuns, or ears of corn. At noon the *tortilla*-woman brought fresh thin *tortillas* covered with a cloth and still warm. They would be reheated before serving. Few Mexican meals lack the hot *tortilla*. Once a week a man strolled down the street ringing a bell; at the signal maids dashed out with garbage pails. In time a truck came along to collect it. Sometimes it was a closed truck opening mechanically; often it was just a wagon that left dribbles of refuse. But the street-sweeper got it before long; our street was very clean.

Often *charros* rode by. In Jalisco the *charro* is not a Sunday rider in parks; he is a working ranchman come to town on business; he wears tight trousers, short jacket, and wide hat because that is his everyday dress, and he rides a good horse because that is his customary mode of locomotion. Calmly he impedes traffic; no cop is bold enough to wave down a man on a horse. Traffic is slowed also by horse-drawn carriages that seem primarily to carry old ladies and huge floral pieces to cemeteries, but that also take tourists sightseeing. Coachmen, like all *tapatíos*, love to show off their city's beauties, and know tales of all its loveliest plazas and stateliest temples. They also know where one had best buy fine leather goods, and pottery from the near-by village of Tlaquepaque. Tlaquepaque offers a dizzying assortment of dishes and ornaments, some fine enough to be called porcelain, some too vulgar to look at, some in atrocious taste. But every tourist must go there.

As a business center, Guadalajara is second in size and importance only to Mexico City. It centers an agricultural area so rich that the state depends little upon imports and has a surplus for export. Its temperate uplands produce grains and fruits, its desert produces maguey, and the pacific littoral gives copra, rice, sugar cane, and pineapples. Jalisco's Department of Economy can boast that there is always work for all, "that only an insignificant number of *braceros* go to the United States, and that those who do go in search of adventure return so disenchanted that the number wishing to go lessens daily." The same authority reports that country men make excellent factory hands as expanding industry and rising wages draw them into the city.

As an industrial center Guadalajara counts three hundred factories that produce leather goods (especially saddles, shoes, and luggage), glass and pottery, oils and soaps, artificial silk, canned milk, rubber goods, and sugar products including soft drinks and alcohol. All but the rubber are native to the Guadalajara area; roads carry an endless procession of trucks supplementing rail transportation. Foreign imports and Mexican petroleum products enter through the port of Manzanillo, which ships out sugar products and peanut oil. Naturally Guadalajara attracts workers from the whole Republic, and it faces a housing problem that its architects are working on.

Arq. Díaz Morales, Director of Guadalajara's Institute of Technology as well as of the Cathedral project, had time for a talk. He rose from his chair to a good six feet of figure too heavy for first youth, but lithe and quick. His chestnut hair had a touch of gray and he had lost a few teeth, but his blue eyes lit with a warm smile. Busy as he was supervising his office force of eight, directing the Institute, and lecturing on architecture, Arq. Díaz himself showed me his pet workman's homes in a factory area. Government has invested three million pesos in houses to sell for about eight thousand pesos with a small down payment and the rest payable as rent. The houses, built with party walls in the old Mexican way, surround a plaza planted with new trees, supplied with bandstand and benches, and closed to motor traffic. An intimate, friendly place where children played on shaded streets that were closed to traffic.

"Everything," said Arq. Morales, "has been planned for better living. Each house, you see, has its patio. We *tapatíos* came from Andalusia; perhaps we have Moorish ideas. A house should be, like a man's wife, an enclosed garden for him alone. Each house has three bedrooms, one for the parents, one for boys, one for girls. This makes for morality. Many of these families have come from slums where they lived in one room with maybe a kitchen, but no plumbing. Here for the same price they have water piped into the kitchen and the bathroom, a patio, and a tiny corral where they may keep chickens as they like to do. They also have a little room open to the street for a little shop." Here was no effort to make over the Mexican life, but one to improve it and to make it safe for children.

At the other end of the city is another effort to improve the lot of poor children. La Ciudad de los Niños, which was frankly modeled on Father Flannagan's Boys' Town, was the first in the Republic; happily, it has since been imitated in Monterrey and in Mexico City. Founded by Padre Cúellar in a vacant lot, it had grown in fifteen years from one shed, where waifs were fed the leftovers from a rich boys' school, to an establishment with over one thousand boys enrolled. "Two hundred are fed," the padre said, "one hundred and fifty sleep, the rest come for the day." All orphans without much other hope, these boys looked husky, happy, and busy, and they met a visitor courteously and went off to find the padre.

Padre Cúellar came from his work in rough clothes, but with joy in his smile and in his bright, almost fanatical eyes. His manner with the boys was easy; often he deferred to one as "knowing more about this than I do." Schoolrooms are overcrowded and not too well lighted, but classes keep abreast of the prescribed course of study, and the boys learn by doing all the work of the place. It is self-governing, with weekly meetings where even the smallest lad has learned to address the chair and is attended to when he speaks. Discipline is in the boys' hands too, under the supervision of one of the priests on the faculty. Punishment usually means deprivation of a trip to town, a treat, a movie —or of half a movie. Padre Cúellar said missing an entire show would be too severe.

Monthly expenses of about fifteen thousand pesos come, the padre said, "from the purse of Providence and the hands of benefactors." Regular contributors are reminded by boyish visitors; associations give benefits; Cantinflas, Mexico's favorite comic, once gave a burlesque bullfight. Padre Cúellar has occasionally not known where the next meal was coming from for hundreds of hungry boys. But the purse of Providence has always opened in time. Once a man drove up at midnight, rousing the padre from his prayer for help, and handed in five thousand pesos. Lesser sums and gifts of food are frequent.

The school's purpose to prepare good citizens for Mexico has proved itself handsomely. None has a police record. Many have gone into industry or farming as trained workers. Two have become priests and work at the Ciudad de los Niños. Three, serving in the armed forces of the United States, sent regular allotments "home."

Guadalajara is equally and justly proud of its orphanage, El Hospicio de los Niños, which was founded by a charitable bishop and later taken over by the state. It is a pleasant place with sunny patios, wide arcades, dormitories with tiny immaculate beds, schoolrooms with small furniture, toys, and well-trained teachers. But one goes there primarily to see the unused chapel that was frescoed by José Clemente Orozco.

Orozco was one of the original artists of Mexico's renaissance of the 1920's, and the only one who never freed himself from the sense of war's horror. One of his typical figures is a Franciscan bending tenderly over a suffering Indian; he has painted bereaved women with gentle pity. Otherwise, his work is replete with harsh scorn, terror, and cataclysmic fury. And such power that many critics consider him the greatest painter of the Americas. McKinley Helm expresses this opinion in his excellent interpretative biography of Orozco, whose subtitle, *Man of Fire*, suggests Orozco's unquenchable flame for righteousness as well as his use of fire as a theme. Helm considers that Orozco's best work is in his native state of Jalisco, in the village of Jiquilpan and in Guadalajara. After the painter's death, his widow gave his home for a permanent gallery of his work. It reflects a pleasant life, but Orozco's frescoes best reveal the man.

His friends say that José Clemente Orozco was a kindly man and gentle with his children, but he apparently gave little thought to the infant mind as he painted the orphanage with his greatest vigor. One stands overawed, against the murmur of children's voices, by the splendor of composition and color. He has placed the conquering Cortés on side panels in quiet tones. His usual blast against the Church depicts Philip II as patron of the Inquisition, and he has again painted his compassionate Franciscan. The dome, filled with four swirling, interlocked figures, represents earth, air, water, and fire. Fire as usual dominates the composition.

When I went to see the Orozco murals in the University, the auditorium was closed, but the porter's wife, continuing to comb her long black hair, obligingly unlocked it. "Horrible!" she cried, pointing to starving figures raising fleshless arms against cynical politicians apparently pointing to Marx's doctrine. Workers and soldiers also appear as oppressors in apelike guise. It appears that to Orozco no good came of Mexico's revolution. A hint of hope is in the man of science, but not much, as genius lies helplessly bound. But even an observer unable to share such despair is overwhelmed by the mural's magnificence. Here Orozco has built his color from cool grays and soft tones on the panels to his typical fiery brilliance in the dome.

In the Palacio de Gobierno, Orozco painted the heroes of the long struggle for freedom. Hidalgo, Morelos, Juárez, and—skipping Madero and Zapata—Carranza. Hidalgo, the dominant figure, is a splendid wild-eyed revolutionist, illumined by a flaming torch and surrounded by figures symbolic of the evils that beset Mexico.

Guadalajara, long before it began to think of foreign tourists, attracted honeymooners to its Lake Chapala, where many Mexicans still maintain country homes. The lake has shrunk more than half a mile from its sedgy shore as its main tributary, the Río Lerma, has been dammed for irrigation. But launches take fishermen out to deep water, and swimming is possible after a brisk walk. Hotels along the shore, as far as the village of Ajijic, offer refuge to retired people and to artists of every persuasion. But one should skip the tourist hotels to sit in the plaza chatting with bootblacks, watching cooks haggle with vendors, and hear the *mariachis* play.

It seems that at any hour of the day or night, music is suddenly in the air, and the *mariachis* have arrived. Fat or slim men in tight trousers, wide sombreros, and black or white blankets woven in red and pink flowers, they play the guitars, violins, and cellos whose soft tones blend so well with Mexico's melancholy love songs. It is said that the French invaders introduced these players at weddings, that the word *mariage* readily became *mariachi*. Fiestas in Jalisco, in addition to the *mariachis*, always include the *jarabe tapatío*, the regional dance that has become national. It is ordinarily performed by a *charro* and a girl in a spangled skirt, but folklorists say that the girl should wear the old-fashioned ranch dress of yellow cotton with magenta yoke and green panels. Her heeled shoes tap the rhythm as her arms weave the *rebozo* around her head with its bright combs and ribbons.

Guadalajara's advertisers, in promoting Jalisco as a tourist state, include the Pacific port of Manzanillo in the state of Colima. A firm of architects has acquired a narrow peninsula there and proposes to develop it as a center for people who own their own homes. It is to be rigidly exclusive, and, as one of the promotors said: "It will make Acapulco look like Jones Beach." In any case, it is a delightful tropical town to visit; its beaches are fine, and its fishing is superlative.

Even the visitor of a few weeks feels the lure of Guadalajara's lovely land, gay and gentle people, so full of song and so ready to dance, and wishes these *tapatíos* well in their effort to make a modern city with all its colonial loveliness retained, and to bring the world to see the wonders of their wide tributary lands. *¡Ay, Jalisco!*

❦ ⊂❦ ❦

XXIV

URUAPAN

⊂❦ THE EASTBOUND road from Guadalajara enters Michoacán, a hilly state with conifers on the highest slopes, and lower hills starred, in the rainy season, with bright red, clear yellow, and delicate violet wild flowers. Michoacán does not become drab, even in the dry season, but takes on the colors of old tapestries. Its soil is often reddish or saffron, its roofs are brownish-red, its houses dusty white, and the lakes azure.

The road to Uruapan leaves the highway at Carapan and runs for forty-five miles through pine and oak woods, varied by small cultivated valleys. Here barefooted men turn the rich soil with yoked oxen; most of their plows are steel, and some *ejidos* own farm machinery, but the effect is still primitively picturesque. Two villages still practice ancient arts. Paracho has many musicians and makers of guitars. They often encrust their instruments with shells or fine woods, and any worker is happy to lay his tools aside to demonstrate his instrument's fine tone and to sing folk songs. In the village of Capácuaro, women sit along the roadside weaving belts on the oldest type of hip-looms and in ancient designs of tiny human and froglike figures.

I caught one brief glimpse of the volcano of Parícutin, a tall spire of smoke spreading along the wind. All activity ceased in 1953. The volcano has announced no future plans.

Uruapan lies in a basin, green and sheltered. The road, dipping into it, passes a lovely wildwood park where the Río Cupatitzio is born in clear springs to go rushing noisily

off over waterfalls and rapids on its way to the Río Balsas
and the Pacific. Facing the park is a fine new hospital, modern in equipment, beautiful architecturally. But woe to the
driver who raises his eyes from the road, which, as soon as
it enters the city, is pocked with large, deep, and dangerous
holes. The worst one is just at the turn toward the plaza
where stand the *chamacos* shouting their English phrases.
"You wanna hotel? I show you. You wanna see the volcano? . . . the park?" Skirting a depression of mud blackened by volcanic ash, one makes the street to the plaza.

Uruapan, though it still bears the scars of Parícutin's
original eruption, is a flower town. Flowery parks, avenues
shaded by flowering jacaranda and flame trees, and patios
as lovely as a florist's window. The countryside, remembered from years ago for moist and shaded roads between
orange and lemon groves, is a near-desert now. Only a few
orchards have been replanted; perhaps, if Parícutin has
really stopped erupting, owners will dare to restore their
groves.

In the central plaza, still marred by marks of the eruption, the church was being rebuilt and small trees were
growing. The *portales,* all but smothered under ugly stands
by day, turned lovely at supper time. Handsome women
then set up their braziers and fan charcoal into a glow
under *cazuelas* (pottery bowls) of spicy, greasy food. They
spread white cloths on long tables and set out bottled
drinks, bowls of the hottest possible chile, and piles of fluffy
lettuce.

Uruapan, at an altitude of 5,500 feet, is between hot and
temperate land. Its markets are filled with coconuts, pineapples, papayas, tomatoes, and the iguanas whose meat is
as delicate as chicken. Its streets have a special charm because of wide whitewashed eaves upheld on carved beams.
The effect is lacy, like mid-Victorian petticoats. Generally
the visitor may look beyond grandmother rocking in the

zaguán to children playing in the patio, which is crowded
with plants. Here are hibiscus, camellias, violets, geraniums, roses, carnations, any flower you care to name, scent-
ing the sun-warmed air.

Because the two hotels named in the guidebooks were
full, I went to the Mansión Tarasca. That was a lucky
break, for it was occupied by Mexican engineers employed
on the great works on the Río Cupatitzio, by traveling-
men, and by a scattering of Mexican families. Modernization was going on, with a new dining-room and baths
that would offer hot water at certain hours. The Señora
was charming, the clerks were attentive, the maids friendly
and willing in Mexico's most endearing way. But for me
the establishment's star was Pedro.

Pedro looked about ten, was fourteen, and was supporting his mother and four younger children by working from
seven in the morning until nine or ten at night. He carried
luggage, often staggering under three or four heavy bags
while the full-grown owner let him strain. He watered the
patios by splashing water about in a bucket; there was a
spigot, but no hose. He swept and washed the *corredores*,
ran errands, bringing in large baskets and bundles from the
market. Pedro was, in short, the *galopín* (runner), the
lowest menial in the establishment, and hence at everybody's call. Always pleasant, quick to respond and to take
a joke, he liked to splash water; when he soaped the tiled
floors, he slid, laughing. But he was always working, always
dependable. What a future citizen for Mexico, given an
education. But for Pedro there is no education. Mexico's
law requiring six years of schooling carries no enforcement
provisions, nor does it provide any way for a family to exist
if its twelve-year-old provider leaves work for school.
Pedro, like millions of Mexico's children, is offered little or
no chance.

Uruapan is also a flower town in its workshops, where

it produces lacquerwork in flower designs. Some say the art was introduced by Chinese junk sailors one thousand years ago; it is produced on Mexico's Pacific slope, where Chinese sailors might have known Indians. Others guess that sixteenth-century clerics brought it from India. But the technique is Mexican enough to make its native development seem likely.

Mexican lacquer is made from sisa, the oil of a wild sage, an oil crushed from a tiny insect, and dolomite. The mixing and cooking of these ingredients is a delicate process, and the resulting lacquer is hard, durable, waterproof, and colorless. The original Uruapan pieces were wooden *bateas* (trays) and *jícaras* (gourd bowls), though many kinds of articles are made now. Each piece is covered with several layers of lacquer and rubbed tirelessly with the palm of the hand. This is the trick, plenty of rubbing. The base color, of natural minerals ground fine, is sprinkled on evenly and polished again. The design may then be painted on; this is the method used at Pátzcuaro. In Uruapan, the design is cut through to the wood, the bit or sliver is lifted out, and the desired color applied and thickened even with the base coat. Often many colors are applied, repeating the operation. This "encrustation" requires endless polishing and great skill.

The oldest pieces were decorated with stylized figures and flowers. In the middle of the nineteenth century, stiff naturalistic bouquets appeared. Ladies were buying lacquer chests and trays. At the turn of the century, the sprawling roses and peonies were introduced by dealers. Lately Uruapan workers are imitating the strings of fruits and amusing birds made of gourds in Olinalá, a remote village in the mountains between Puebla and Guerrero. Olinalá's fragrant wood, *olinalau*, is used only in that village, where they make boxes and hope chests whose scent endures forever. But Uruapan remains the best-known lacquer town.

The engineers living at Mansión Tarasca invited me to a luncheon in honor of the retiring chief engineer of the Río Cupatitzio project. I should see one of the dams that would make a paradise of lower Michoacán; this was one of Cárdenas's dreams, and has been his great interest since he left the presidency. On the drive my guide and companion grew confidential. Mexican girls, he said, had one great fault. Indecision. Now he himself would like to "pretend" to one I should meet at luncheon, but she would not make up her mind. "Such girls are just capricious," he complained, swerving over a high rock and giving my car a knock it did not recover from in months.

At the engineers' camp, I was invited into their dining-pavilion, which was unwalled but screened and set with long tables. The plump, pleasant cook displayed her electric refrigerator and oil stove and then, smiling deprecatingly, the old-fashioned charcoal brazier that she preferred for beans because it kept them simmering all day. *Tortillas* too were made in the old way.

The engineers, as they drifted in, talked eagerly about the Obras de la Cuenca de Tepalcatepec (Works of the Tepalcatepec Basin). This project will harness the swift Río Cupatitzio behind three dams to irrigate 325,000 acres and provide power to electrify farms and homes and, in time, industry. Michoacán has iron ore that could be shipped to the United States or Japan through a port being developed at Playa Azul. They foresaw factories and mills. But these engineers also saw the problem in human terms. They agreed, as I found true throughout the Republic, that the *ejido* allotments were too small. They hoped that as the new project brings wider acreage under cultivation, allotments will be increased enough to make a farmer independent. They also foresaw model communities with co-operative packing-plants for olive oil, citrus fruits, and many vegetables. Southern Michoacán is an Eden that could produce anything, given water.

The most eloquent young man enlarged on the theme of human needs. "These country people," he said, "live in straw huts and wear no shoes. They need knowledge to protect them against malaria and typhoid; they need technical schools." Another engineer, joining us, voiced a doubt heard throughout Mexico. "Can our country really afford this project?" I expected the usual plaint that nothing can be done for Indians, but he said: "All this is for the people, but who will gain are the contractors, many of them men in high government posts. They pay the lowest salaries the law allows and get rich. We, the little people, must ultimately pay the bill in our taxes. . . . We too must learn to control these grasping promoters as you do in your country." I thought of certain newly rich gentlemen in my own state who had made fortunes out of atomic developments. Again I said what must often be said in Mexico: that we face the same problems and are seldom more successful at solving them.

Lunch was a gay affair. Kitchen helpers rushed in with platters and bowls steaming rich fragrances of chile, onion, and garlic. Fluffy rice was followed by pork in a rich sauce and beans refried to crisp delicacy. *Tortillas* came almost too hot to lift out of their napkins. More and more piquant chile sauce was at hand, and down the center of the table marched a row of bottles for every taste from the sweetest soft drinks to the darkest beer. Then it was time for speeches and songs. A veritable orator made the farewell address for the retiring Ing. Sandoval. He made it touching, but he spiced it with humor, and he shortened it himself by bursting into song. Ing. Sandoval's reply was short too; he also could sing. So the feast declined as the sun did into radiant evening.

Uruapan, while it awaits the realization of Michoacán's dream of Eden, is making a very good thing of hauling tourists to its volcano. Its people, who were panicked by the eruptions of 1943, smothered by volcanic ash, and endangered by collapsing roofs, have dug themselves out and cleaned and rebuilt their city. Parícutin is now their most advertised sight, and they have organized taximen to make the trip in turn and for a fixed price. This system does not work too well; tourists are advised to make a deal in advance and with plenty of witnesses.

The drive from the highway to the buried village of Parangaricutiro, the greatest sufferer from the eruption, fully justifies the advice not to take one's own car. The road is rutted all the way, and rocks fly up against the car's underpinnings. Taximen estimate that a set of tires will last three months. Every *barranca* is crossed by a bridge of unanchored poles that roll and creak alarmingly, and dust rises in clouds, first white, then the infernal gray of volcanic ash. Lava that flowed in flaming streams has dried in dark-gray waves and burst bubbles, and trees have been blackened into leafless poles. It looks as though nothing could ever grow here again, but they say the best coffee lands are made of volcanic soil. In time, in time.

This was a lovely green valley, and on the morning of February 20, 1943, women worked quietly in the village and men in the fields. One man, plowing, felt heat underfoot and saw smoke rising. By the time he got to the village mayor, the hole was thirty feet deep, and that night the explosions began. While vulcanologists rushed from all over the world Parícutin began its phenomenal growth to a height of over four thousand feet before 1953, when it suddenly ceased all activity. Among the first outsiders to reach the scene was Dr. Atl, Mexico's oldest living painter, who had for years specialized in volcanoes and who made a remarkable record of this volcano's growth. He has pre-

sented his collection of drawings and oils to the National
Institute of Fine Arts.

Nothing remains of the village except the white church
tower, rising above the lava. The villagers, after the explosions, had found in the ruined church the statue of their
cristo milagroso, whose greatest miracle was this. When
they moved to new lands, given them by the government,
they carried this statue with them in chanting procession.
Now only a few men live near the church to rent horses for
the last steep pull up the volcano.

The driver, as he reaches this camp, shouts: "A horse,"
and a villager leads up a mouselike mount. The tourist,
boosted aboard, is handed a horsehair rope as token rather
than rein; the guide follows the pony, who knows the way;
the rider just sits. The usual group numbers about twenty,
though on holidays they run into hundreds; all reduced to
Churchillian shapes by levis and jumpers provided by the
hotels, and hung with cameras and binoculars.

It was amazing to see green trees rooted in the volcanic
dust along the trail. Pines, obviously older than Parícutin,
have survived the searing heat and come out in fresh green
hope in the midst of such desolation as should never be. We
heard frequent roars like thunder and the sky was gray
with clouds, but the roars were volcanic explosions, not
thunder, and the clouds of volcanic dust bore no rain.

At the lookout, just below the main crater, each guide
handed his charge a serape and offered a log as though it
were a theater seat. Youths from Mexico, with alpenstocks
and sacks, passed on their way to a higher lookout. Their
flashlights marked their progress along the distant trail
when Parícutin's flashes did not blot out everything else.

Those flashes came, as a rule, with terrific rumblings, followed by flares of ruddy flame straight from the crater to
the cloud bank above; in its fiery sheet whirled spots of
pure fire that were rocks as big as a house, burning right of

earth's center. At its most fearful this upsurge of fire was so strong and so fast that it spilled over into torrents of flame that rushed like a fiery waterfall over the cone and down its sides. This is what one had come to see. A volcano in the making, so staged that one could watch it in complete safety.

XXV

PÁTZCUARO AND MORELIA

PÁTZCUARO is a lake that is sedgy around the edges and deep blue in the center, though it is slowly sinking. It is also a town whose every cobbled street is narrowed between close-set houses with wide white eaves. Every street seems to run uphill to a church. On Friday market day the two plazas are full of straw *petates* in corn-colored rolls, coarse blankets, striped ropes laid on the ground, stacks of pottery from many villages, and the tiny silvery transparent lake fish that are Pátzcuaro's greatest delicacy. Many fruits and vegetables are piled symmetrically, and candles of all lengths hang by their wicks. Booths of cheap factory goods have all but eliminated the old dark-blue skirts typical of the lake villages. Unfortunately, cheap cotton is cheaper than fine wool, even in Pátzcuaro.

A political meeting was in progress one evening on the plaza. Trucks trimmed with banana leaves and bamboo stood ready for the orators, a scattering crowd had preempted the plaza benches, and boys were perched on the fountains. Indians were packing their unsold goods to take home. A band played the national anthem, the electrician signaled that the loudspeaker was ready, and the politicians mounted the truck. One was Efraín Gonzáles Luna, a Guadalajara lawyer and candidate for president on the ticket of the Partido Acción Nacional, whose initials spell PAN (bread). He of course could not be heard until several others had spoken, among them a *sinarquista*. The star speaker was a woman. Beautiful and beautifully dressed,

227

she spoke with ease, grace, and a voice that carried without strain. Her theme was that Mexico, the beloved *patria*, must return to the old virtues of the home with woman in it. As the dark drew in, the market women hefting their heavy burdens for the long trot to the dugout canoes on the lake lingered a moment, listening. The speaker was warming up. True Mexican women, she was saying, did not spend their mornings in the beauty parlors and their afternoons playing canasta; they dedicated their lives to their children, their charities, and their church. Few market women remained; only those who were still packing and roping their wares, but they did not seem to listen as the speaker reached her peroration. The true *mexicana* asks no vote, no part in politics; she asks only to remain in her home, to support her husband as the true Veronica did. The last market women slowly trotted off.

After that, the candidate's speech could only be an anti-climax. He began with the holy days of Bishop Quiroga, when every man lived well with fish from the lake and his own craft, and his voice trembled at their present plight, when prices were high and the lake low. He came down hard on the terrible need that took from Michoacán so many strong arms to serve an imperialistic neighbor. He was less explicit about how he and his party proposed to restore the good bishop's good old days. The listeners who had remained until the end applauded.

Pátzcuaro means happy place, and so it seems as one strolls among its old houses and churches with their ancient carved altars and early frescoes, and especially the miraculous image of the Virgin of Health, modeled of a cornstalk paste. Its Museo de Artes Populares, in Bishop Quiroga's first school, is arranged as a series of rooms with the village crafts the good bishop taught his Indians. Santa Clara people still make copper pots as he taught them to do, and every village has its rosary to be worn as a necklace with earrings to match. Pottery is older than the good bishop's day. Tzintzuntzan's black-on-tan ware is balanced and true, the green glazed dishes from Patamba are found nowhere else, and all potters seem to relax making silly toys and fanciful altar ornaments. Both Pátzcuaro and Quiroga make painted ware, like lacquer, and often touched with gold. The outstanding expert on lacquer is Salvador Solchaga, who assembled the museum's extraordinary collection of colonial lacquer. His own ware, using gold, is unexcelled and difficult to come by, as his entire output is snapped up by collectors.

Michoacán has two capitals—colonial Morelia, which is the present seat of government, and Tzintzuntzan (Place of the Hummingbird) on Lake Pátzcuaro. Tarascans are proud that their ancient realm was never conquered by the Aztecs, whose empire was not much larger than theirs. It has left no spectacular monuments, as the region lacks the the lime necessary for enduring buildings. Dr. Daniel Rubín de la Borbolla, who studied Tzintzuntzan from 1938 to 1944, calls it "the most damnably frustrating area in the world. I know," he moans, "where there is a burial probably as rich as any, and we can't get to it. Digging there would loosen some ninety cubic meters of loose stone; or it would cost something like a million pesos." This burial was described by a sixteenth-century friar and again by some nineteenth-century grave-robbers. Altogether, little is known of these mysterious builders; the Tarascans' claim to be their descendants is unproved. But ethnologists find a wealth of legend and such tale-tellers as the Zaldívar family tempt one to relax under the ancient olive trees in the Tzintzuntzan churchyard and believe everything.

Serious historians give some credence to the legends of the last ruler's wealth of palaces, jewels, and hummingbird-feather robes. They perforce recognize the existence of Erendira, a courageous Tarascan princess who, with a white plume in her hair, led the tribe against the Spaniards. They lost, of course, but Erendira has become the Tarascan heroine, as beloved in Michoacán as Cuauhtémoc is in the center. Spanish atrocities were never worse than in Michoacán. The first friars baptized hordes of Tarascans in a monolithic stone font that is still in use, but their leader is said to have thrown idols and gold ornaments into the deepest part of Lake Pátzcuaro. Lay leaders meanwhile were torturing Indians in their search for gold and selling them into slavery.

The Tarascans, after that time of horror, were blessed with the revered Don Vasco de Quiroga, a compassionate priest who was practical enough to establish communal centers on Lake Pátzcuaro and to teach each village the craft for which it is still known. Don Vasco is said to have made the first of the butterfly nets that the fishermen still use. Later he was elevated to be Bishop of Michoacán, and the colony was given a new capital, named Valladolid for that Spanish city. Its site was chosen for the classical virtues of fertility, pleasant climate, good water, and a wood supply. Its name has been changed to Morelia, honoring its most distinguished son, Padre José María Morelos, who led the Wars of Independence after Padre Hidalgo's defeat. But the city remains Spanish and colonial, meaning beautiful and calm.

Bishop Quiroga founded Morelia's College of San Carlos in 1540. More than two centuries later it graduated Miguel Hidalgo as a priest; he, as professor, taught the young Morelos ideas that were not in the religious books. Morelia's school of music, the first in the Americas, attracts students from the entire country to its annual festival, and the summer art school brings foreigners as well. Morelia's museum contains fine collections of Tarascan artifacts and of colonial arts. It has many landscapes of José María Velasco, a nineteenth-century artist who is unequaled in his painting of the luminous quality of Mexico's air. This museum has, as all government buildings must, a revolutionary mural. Alfredo Zalce, an excellent painter in the revolutionary tradition, has depicted the national heroes convincingly, but he let himself be tricked by the current wave of Indianism into painting Malinche, Cortés's brilliant interpreter and lover, as a vulgar street girl in modern dress among the armed conquerors.

Morelia thus reflects the stirring history of Michoacán while keeping its quiet colonial character. Its creamy stone façades and towers, wrought-iron grilles and gates, birds in the plazas and bells in the steeples seem more consonant with the tapestried hills and luminous sunshine than the years of struggle that have made Michoacán one of the most interesting as well as most beautiful of Mexican states. But Morelia, the capital, has yielded again to the lake cities of Páztcuaro and Tzintzuntzan, where the world of tomorrow has taken over.

The traveler approaching the lake sees a rank of brilliant flags. They are the flags of the United Nations, which herald a UNESCO effort to help backward peoples help themselves. President Cárdenas, naming his native Michoacán as a suitable field, gave his Quinta Erendira as headquarters for the Centro Regional de Educación Fundamental en América Latina, popularly known as CREFAL.

Students, named by every Latin American nation except the Dominican Republic and Argentina, come for a two-year course in the education of an entire community—"fundamental education." Mexico has long been the leader in such work, so most of the faculty are Mexicans. UNESCO appropriates about $150,000 a year and Mexico about $175,000 besides buildings and transportation to villages where the work is done. I was permitted to accompany several field trips.

At Juanácuaro we stepped from the launch onto a dock.

"Appreciate this dock," I was told. "We built it ourselves to prove we were not exploiters." This was, in itself, evidence of fundamental education. Many students on arriving were disinclined for manual labor; it took time to eliminate political appointees—and *hidalguía* dies hard. But these students were a working lot who scattered about their concerns.

The Ecuadorian agriculturist's prime project was to get the villagers to collect manure for fertilizer. Even so elementary a farming practice was unknown. The Cuban domestic scientist could show one model kitchen with an adobe oven and a chimney! A returned *bracero*, familiar with modern ways, had built this, but even he demurred at putting in windows. "A man," the professor explained, "feels safer about his women if there are no windows." The Peruvian working on recreation had found that few Indian fathers would let their daughters leave home for community games. Sports were taboo, but a few shy and clumsy girls were taking part in a dance.

Janitzio's problem ran into politics. On that island every man, woman, and child is forever making the butterfly nets that need repair after a month's use and are worn out after three months. The thread, bought in Pátzcuaro's stores, is poor. The economist learned that nylon thread, costing only twice as much, would wear ten times as long. But the gentleman who monopolized the thread market had powerful political connections. This problem was pending.

CREFAL was working in twenty villages, only two of which were classed as *mestizo*. These were proving most responsive; Indians tend to hold back distrustfully, and must be won. These villages doubtless offer most of the problems that will be faced by students returning to their own countries.

The best all-round project is the Tzintzuntzan experiment, which involves various international, United Nations, and Mexican agencies, and is generally supervised by Mexico's Museo Nacional de Artes e Industrias Populares. It was most exciting to hear the work discussed by Dr. Rubín de la Borbolla, director of the museum. He explained that the purpose was to improve living-conditions by developing local crafts, perhaps by introducing new ones. The program was practical—to make production easier, cheaper, and quicker—but it was soundly conceived not to destroy any native artistic values or to force anything on the community. Every proposal was discussed by the Indians as endlessly as Indians like, and its adoption was only by overwhelming majority vote. Happily, the leader in community work was Gabriel Ospina, an anthropologist known and trusted in Tzintzuntzan. His first project—to clean up and improve the neglected cemetery—brought together the rival Church and anti-Church factions and proved that they could work together. Keeping the town's streets clean has become a regular Saturday volunteer effort on the part of people who used only to complain because the government did nothing.

Of the ceramic work Dr. de la Borbolla said: "Men used to bring the clay in in small quantities that women would grind on the metates. Anybody who thinks the metate picturesque should try grinding. Remember that I am a physician. I attended many a woman in Tzintzuntzan and I can tell you that the prolapsed uterus is not the exception; it is the rule. Due to slavery to the metate. We offered to help the people get a grinder for the clay.

"The community agreed, after much talk, to give 350 hours a week to repay the price of the grinder. Now men of the community bring in a year's supply of clay, which is stored to ripen. This gives them the best clay they have ever had. They now own mixing- and glazing-machines

run by diesel engines, and even kilns of local manufacture.
The kilns are perhaps the best example of how our policy
can work.

"We might have bought kiln burners, perhaps cheaper,
but an old Pátzcuaro mechanic said he could make a burner.
He spent several days in Mexico and then reported that
he needed two hundred pesos for materials. What he
bought was junk, just junk. Old steel rods, used gears, nuts,
and bolts. But off he went in our station wagon, and in
time he made a burner that works. It will be patented; he
has a good business; and the potters have their own expert
at hand. If a man wishes to set up his own shop, we offer
technical advice and loans without interest, payable in five
years. The plan always includes the family; many youngsters over five are already at work at the kilns learning
better processes. The old values remain, including pride
of craftsmanship, but potters who were losing money without realizing it now make a decent living."

Tzintzuntzan, never a weaving-center, now boasts cotton and wool looms and two new crafts. This work is considered an experiment, but it too will profit by the sound
practicality and human wisdom of UNESCO's program.
What a curious evidence of a changing world, that a sixteenth-century missionary's work and hope for Indians is
being carried on by an international agency in the twentieth century.

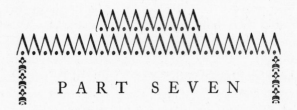

PART SEVEN

South to the Pacific

XXVI

CUERNAVACA

⊟ THE NEW highway from Mexico to Acapulco brings that Pacific port within an easy day's drive of the capital and Cuernavaca within an hour that should be thirty minutes more for safety. Instead of winding through pine forests over the Ajusco range, this four-lane highway sweeps grandly over easy grades to Tres Cumbres (Three Peaks) and comes out above Cuernavaca's soft-hued valley and the stunning cliffs that conceal Tepoztlán. That village, so accessible now, was the ethnologist's archetype of a prehistoric survival where only Nahuatl was spoken.

Today it reveals its changing mores on September 8, day of the Virgin Mary's birth, in a play spoken in Nahuatl but clearly missionary-inspired. The great chief Tepoztécatl, who had been baptized by the Spaniards, was considered a traitor by his people. The play, recounting his story, began with a band of youths, draped like Roman wrestlers, who went leaping around the plaza, armed with bows and arrows and whooping like Apaches. They were seeking the false leader, who was marching up and down on a shaky board pyramid and reciting endless speeches in Nahuatl. His costume, the typical Indian effort to present their ancestors, consisted of a red toga, a feathered headdress, and a spear. He was attended by others similarly garbed, who tried to hold off the attackers. In this confusion of both drama and my own mind, I appealed to a gentleman pointed out as the director.

"I don't understand Nahuatl either," he said, "but the

play ends when all the people are converted to our Holy Church. . . . Tepoztécatl," he concluded with a scholar's certainty, "was the Blessed Virgin's favorite son."

These people, like those of the broken valleys beyond, are descendants of Zapata's men, who came like swift avengers to raid the sugar plantations during the revolution. All around Cuernavaca cane fields shimmer in the sunshine; some plantations are *ejidos*, some are privately owned, some are operated co-operatively. The state of Morelos is today Mexico's leading sugar-producer. The tiny hamlet of Tlaltenango was the site of Cortés's first sugar mill; its church holds a miraculous statue of the Virgin. The road then approaches Cuernavaca downhill and between blue walls with bougainvillea surging over, and now and then a gate opening on a garden of oleanders, lilies, and a shady mango tree.

Cuernavaca's history is split as its terrain is reft by two deep *barrancas*. The first era was that of Cortés, who built his palace and church stout enough to serve as fortresses at need. The second was that of Maximilian, who made a play place of the Borda mansion. The present, dominated by an international colony with sophisticated tastes, so overlays the others that it threatens even to eliminate the *barrancas*.

Cortés's palace is best known for its upper arcade with a fine view of Popocatépetl and Ixtaccíhuatl and the magnificent frescoes that Ambassador Dwight Morrow commissioned Diego Rivera to paint as a gift to the Mexican people. The theme is Mexico's history from the Conquest to the present. The first panel shows the capture of Cuauhnáhuac (a name the Spaniards wrote down as Cuernavaca), which was defended by warriors in quilted armor and fearsome jaguar and eagle headdresses and with obsidian spears that were no protection against firearms.

Cortés on a white horse is depicted looking like the conqueror, athletic and handsome. This was painted before

Rivera got the idea of presenting him as a humpbacked nitwit. Other Spaniards appear as the figures stylized by the revolutionary painters. Mounted soldiers riding down women and children. The overseer working Indians with whips while the *hacendado* lolls rum-sodden in a hammock. The avaricious friar watching the tribute pile up under the cross he holds aloft.

It is told that as he observed the painting of such friars, Ambassador Morrow, always the diplomat, asked: "Diego, did you ever know a good and kind priest?" Rivera said nothing, but later he painted his one kind cleric, Padre Motolinía (ragged one), much beloved by the Indians.

Cortés, having introduced cane from Cuba, built a great sugar mill about fifteen miles south of Cuernavaca. It is now a resort, Vista Hermosa (Beautiful View), where one swims in a blue pool under the mill's ancient arches, dines in a vast groined storeroom, and enjoys every comfort in huge colonial chambers that open on views of four volcanoes. This was the scene of Mexico's first bid for independence from Spain, and the conspirators included two of Cortés's sons—his only legitimate son, Martín, heir of the title Marqués del Valle and of this magnificent property, and his illegitimate son by Malinche, also named Martín. These two plotted with others to free New Spain from the mother country and set up an independent monarchy with the Marqués del Valle as king. The scheme failed due to the illness of the only man strong enough to carry it through. The Marqués got away to Spain, where he founded the family that still bears the title. The true hero of the incident was the *mestizo* Martín, who even under torture steadfastly refused to incriminate his half-brother or the other conspirators. He did not die then; his later life is unknown, but Malinche's son had shown character worthy of both his parents.

An admirer of Mexico's colonial architecture will be disappointed in Cuernavaca. The colonial era left no palaces except the mansion that José de la Borda, finding Taxco unappreciative of his many benefactions there, built for his son, a priest. Either he or his successors made of the Borda Gardens a botanist's joy. Walks and pools are shaded by *ahuehuetes*, Mexico's cedars that live for centuries, and round-topped mangoes. Magnolia, mimosa, orange, and lime blossoms scent the air. Pomegranate, papaya, chico zapote, guava, and the split-leaved anona vine yield richly their fruits. And bougainvillea, hibiscus, oleander, shower of gold make the *barranca* slopes flare with color. There are orchids too, and at night the shy *huele de noche* that scarcely shows by day.

Naturally such a European pleasaunce caught Maximilian's eye, and he restored the graveled walks, shored up the terraces, and furnished the dark *salas* with French gilt and marquetry. It was a perfect setting for Carlotta and her ladies in their hoop skirts. Caretakers like to show the side door to the emperor's quarters through which even a wide hoop skirt could slip sideways. Maximilian also relaxed in the tiny hamlet of Acapantzingo, where old women lately professed to know his India Bonita (Pretty Indian), whose name still graces a few tearooms and curio shops. Her little house, now a ruin, is proposed as a museum—presumably to the emperor's lighter romantic moments.

The Borda Gardens, after Maximilian's day, changed hands several times, and once—during the twenties and thirties—were operated as a charming hotel. This may happen again. Meanwhile, Cuernavaca's architecture has developed along less European lines. Fred Davis and Eduardo Bolio Rendón, who have restored many old houses, agree that during Díaz's time few houses were built there. The town was, after all, only a way station on the road to Mexico City, and, as Don Eduardo says: "Latins never took to country living." The few houses built during the nineteenth century were destroyed in the revolution or deteriorated into slums.

The revolution was particularly destructive in Morelos, where Zapata's men, former serfs on the sugar plantations, looted and burned. Impartial historians remind us that quite as much destruction was caused by the federal troops sent to capture Zapata. Generals enriching themselves out of war did not hope for its end. Zapata was no Villa. A rarity among revolutionary leaders, he remained poor. Mrs. Rosa King, who then owned the Hotel Bella Vista in Cuernavaca, knew him as she knew them all. "Zapata was good," she asserts. "He never committed atrocities himself nor approved what some of his officers did." This Zapata, who has become a legend in folk tale and song, appears in Rivera's murals in Cortés's palace. There he, the Indian revolutionist, is shown with a white horse to balance Cortés as conqueror. Leadership, as typified by the white horse, has swung, in four hundred years, from the white European to the native Mexican. Zapata was foully murdered by a federal officer sent to treat with him, but his influence went marching on.

Even before Zapata was murdered, peace of a sort had been made, and Cuernavaca's caressing air and tempered sunshine were attracting visitors from Mexico's nervous and chilly altitude. A few had built homes in styles no longer approved, but most of the town was a hollow shell. When Fred Davis first knew it, about 1914, nearly all woodwork —door and window frames, floor boards, even beams—had been removed for firewood. But Mr. Davis's trained eye saw possibilities in a dismantled house whose noisy patio was filthy under a shower of gold vine. He remodeled it into the first of six houses which set Cuernavaca's style. Its grace is due to lack of architects with slide rules and rigid ideas. A master mason, a good carpenter, and a knowing gardener—for the garden must come along integrally with the house—would stick in a few stakes, scratch lines on the ground, haul in sand and lime, send to the mountains for poles, hire peons by the hour. Fred says they built in the vernacular.

Such houses were first appreciated by foreigners, who quickly adopted native crafts as furnishings. The British minister, later Sir Edmund Hovey, made a Cuernavaca hideaway to which he once invited Ambassador Morrow and Mrs. Morrow, who decided that this was their paradise too. Mr. Morrow commissioned Fred Davis to remodel a house and Bill Spratling of Taxco to furnish it. Two such distinguished colonists naturally brought followers; now almost any battered door in a high wall may open onto a home and garden with a view of volcanoes across a *barranca*.

Eduardo Bolio Rendón claims that he was the first to discover that Cuernavaca had views. That was in 1925, when he and his English wife were seeking a home. In La Bolsa del Diablo (Devil's Purse) they found a house on the edge of the *barranca*, where an open terrace and a garden could command miles of view. So the house on the *barranca* came to be the approved type. Don Eduardo proposed to the then governor an over-all plan that would have made the town "one of the world's beauty spots." But as governors seldom accept such farsighted ideas, the town was left to grow without regulation into a city of 26,000 people that is, Don Eduardo says, "noisier, dirtier, more crowded than any decent European city of 200,000." Despite the governor, he got a good deal done. Electric lights and paving came largely through his efforts, and during the years he has remodeled fifteen houses, all true to the basic style and all with fine views.

Naturally, with all this going on, Cuernavaca became the favored retreat of the political generals spawned by the revolution. Any house painted pink and plastered like a birthday cake with squiggles and fat cherubs is, ten to one, a general's country home. Some humorist dubbed their avenue, with gardens full of red hot flowers behind iron fences, the Street of the Forty Thieves. The most elaborate home was that of General and President Calles. There he was reading *Mein Kampf* when Cárdenas, the successor he had picked as a biddable henchman, advised him to depart for a long stay in the United States. At once! By a plane that awaited his orders. Calles went. Officials of a later era of extravagance have built at La Palmira, a few miles out of town, but the hills near Cuernavaca continue to be covered with houses of every type of architecture dreamed up since 1920.

There are, naturally, equally elaborate hotels, always with swimming-pools, bright umbrellas, and terraced gardens. The two best known are on the town's two plazas: the Hotel Marik Plaza on Plaza Jardín, which has been repeatedly remodeled until it has achieved a complete California façade, but with charming patios; and the Bella Vista on the Plaza de los Tepetates (straw mats), where Mrs. King sits daily on the *portal* receiving friends and graciously pointing out just where President Madero stood when she raised the British flag and defied the *zapatistas* to advance a single step.

Cuernavaca on every week-end and holiday becomes a kaleidoscopic carnival scene as the capital pours in thousands of seekers after warmth and sun. The plazas, jammed with people, flaunt every color in *rebozo*, dress, basket, and toy, and reverberate with mechanical music. All this is intensified at night under neon lights when wandering musicians make serenade and hotel orchestras warm up for dancing. Especially the Bella Vista is noisy and gay, happy and carefree, with Mexican tourists in peasant blouses, North American escapists in blue jeans, *huaraches*, and woven belts. But with all this, Cuernavaca is not provided with smart night clubs. The people who might patronize them entertain at home.

Don Eduardo Bolio Rendón says that the only time Cuernavaca had a truly sophisticated society was when King Carol and Magda Lupescu took refuge there. Then the place swarmed multilingually with wealthy Europeans who had managed to get out with their money. Many have returned to Europe, but the few who stayed give the town an aura of elegance which has attracted all kinds. A rash of novels, written mostly by unsettled young men, have given the town a scandalous, if not outright vicious, reputation. But if this was ever true, it is so no longer. Like every resort town in a relaxing climate, Cuernavaca has had its share of alcoholics, inverts, and spectacular failures. But they are more obvious than important.

Cuernavaca's all-year residents, generally retired business and professional men, writers, and artists from Mexico and abroad, live quietly behind their high walls, enjoying fragrant gardens and the view of the cool, serene volcanoes beyond the *barranca*.

XXVII

TAXCO

C⬦ TAXCO, lovely mountain-girt mining town, has preserved some quality deeper than the colonial style required
of a national monument. Even a Taxco-lover, warned that
the old town has been spoiled by tourists, still finds there
a serenity too profound to be disturbed by superficial
changes. And there are many. A tempest cut down half the
plaza's Indian laurels, and the new ones scarcely show
among the refreshment booths. Motors now stand where
white sun-shades used to shelter the market, and tourists in
curio-shop garb have replaced natives in white and dull
blue. But the church's rosy towers still rise above the
wrought-iron fence, and Berta's cantina at the corner remains the most respectable spot in town. A silver shop has
not lessened the dignity of the Borda House, built two centuries ago, nor has a modern pharmacy made much change
in its sturdy neighbor. All in all, Taxco shares the stead-
fastness of the hills and the wonder of the sun and clouds
that play variations on them.

Taxco, seen from the air, lies like a pile of jewels in the
tawny velvet hills, which in winter are scattered with gray
leafless shrubs that bear white blossoms or coronas of pink
and yellow flowers. Those same dun hills turn emerald green
in summer when dry water courses leap with waterfalls that
tear loose the roads, every stone is mossy, and every wall
sprouts ferns. Taxco's residents don raincoats or palm-leaf
capes against the daily rains. Otherwise, life goes on much
the same, except that summer's billowing clouds, as silver-

bright as sunshine, darken in the afternoon, are rent by lightning, and pour water like buckets.

Taxco, as the approaching driver sees, climbs the hills, one red-roofed white house topping another up to twenty levels. Miners still live in many of these houses, as their ancestors did when they mined silver for Don José de la Borda. Many work tiny cornfields there or raise fruits for the market. Foreigners have remodeled many old houses with sunny terraces and fragrant patios without spoiling the picture at all. And it is a picture. Taxco is the artist's delight, the post card's best scene. But there is more to Taxco than meets the eye.

Taxco is a growing town of more than 10,000 people, which counts tourists its greatest source of income and changelessness its best asset. It is also an important trade center and its people are Mexican citizens. Taxco's most thoughtful people recognize their dual problem—how to keep the town both picturesque and comfortable for tourists and good for its children. Numberless children overwhelm the visitor where he hesitates on the highway. There the *chamacos* swarm out, shouting: "This is not the entrance. You wanna hotel? I'll show you. I'm a good guide." It is wise to choose one. Getting into Taxco involves a steep, narrow way beset by dragon-like trucks and temptations to stray. A guide will take one to the hotel that pays him best, but many hotels are good and the tourist can insist on his own. In any case, bursting up through that last narrow defile onto the plaza is unforgettable.

From the plaza, silver shops spread in all directions. Taxco's renown as a silver center began when William Spratling opened his shop on the Calle de las Delicias. More than eighty successors have appeared since 1928; they provide work at fair wages, train good workmen, and have produced some superior craftsmen. Hector Águilar, who began as shop manager for Spratling, has a factory equipped with modern machinery in the Borda House. The Castillo family, behind a flowering terrace, turn out prize-winning pieces, and Jorge (Chato) has evolved the art of fusing metals as diverse as nickel and bronze, silver and steel, or silver and gold. He calls it metal painting, and he strives for freedom from both European influence and pure Indianism. Dozens of others who might be named are known to buyers from the States and to tourists.

The organized silversmiths have joined the Comite Pro-Turismo to train registered guides and teach them English, and incidentally to solve the *chamaco* problem. Youngsters were getting out of hand and staying out of school. Many a brat was bringing home more in tips than his father made in a day's work in the mines. So it was decreed that no child should appear on the streets during school hours. Police, armed with long slender switches, soon had things under control. The result is clever youngsters who earn well after school, and a notable lack of beggars. Many a family is kept out of the indigent class by the *centavitos* the boy brings in.

Other problems have been solved in other ways. Catholic charity has always been a part of the town's life, but there remained the questions of health and sanitation, of improving morale as well as morals, and of helping people to use government services they were ignorant of. Dr. Juan Meana, the first to tackle such problems, had a gift with the natives. He could make a busy market listen while he talked about sanitation and child care. He could even convince parents that vaccinations were not witchcraft; as late as 1930 soldiers were bringing screaming children to the doctor with the hypodermic. Mexico's health services soon took over much of this work, but plenty of tragedy remained, especially among children of working mothers. Mexican law, like our law, is helpless to catch the deserting father.

Dr. Meana soon found an able aide in Natalie Scott, who came to Taxco in 1930. She had had social-service experience in New Orleans, she had a seeing eye, and the social grace to slip easily into Mexican life. She invited the Taxco ladies to a tea, where they formed an Asociación de Salud, with Dr. Meana as director. This organization does valuable work, but Natalie kept stumbling on sad cases. A five-year-old boy, left by a working mother to tend his baby sister, shared an unripe mango with her. Both children died in convulsions. "Their father," said Miss Scott, "was a good man who only got drunk Saturdays. He paid for the little blue coffins and the gold paper wings and crowns to turn the little bodies into angels for burial." Another child, splashing in the sudsy water where her mother was washing clothes, took cold. When Miss Scott heard of it, all three doctors had gone to Mexico City and it was too late for home remedies to save the child. She died of double pneumonia. Natalie decided to have another tea. The result was a day nursery, La Guardería de Niños.

A visit there is a joyous experience. One looks from the garden into immaculate rooms with tiny beds, low tables and chairs, and toys on shelves. The children run out, jabbering without shouting, and offering their hands with Mexican courtesy. Miss Scott presents each child by name and makes a little speech about Delfina, the middle-aged woman who keeps thirty children fed, happy, and busy for nine hours a day. Those who are old enough attend kindergarten or school. All go to catechism classes at the church. They have three meals a day, planned by a pediatrician, and treats when visitors bring honey or candy. Each child's mother pays two and a half pesos "if she can." The total expense of nine hundred pesos a month comes from individual and club contributions.

Miss Scott suggested music. The largest girl opened the

phonograph and the children sang nursery songs in English. The girl at the machine had been so mistreated at home that she was rated a low-grade moron. But food and kindness had made her Delfina's best helper, and she was doing well in school. Others danced, one of them a clumsy child recovering from an operation for club feet. Miss Scott's private sideline is taking children to the fine orthopedic hospital in Mexico City. From there they return in fine shape. "Little Pancho," she said, "is out of plaster and all over the place."

Taxco's citizens have also established a hospital. It began when Dr. Alberto Curiel and his wife, María Luisa, a pharmacist, chose Taxco as a quieter place to live than Mexico City. The doctor hoped for wide experience, and he is getting it. Taxco, on the speedy highway, receives many accident victims in addition to the usual quota of Saturday-night stabbings. Once Dr. Curiel sent for Lucy Reyes, a nurse, and owner with her husband of the Hotel Los Arcos. After they had worked all night under a flashlight held in a nervous hand, the doctor said: "Lucy, we need a hospital." "Indeed," agreed Lucy, "we do." Then Lucy had a tea for the wives of Taxco's Rotarians. When they had enough money for a lot, Ingeniero Santiago Arias, owner of the Mina de la Concha (Shell Mine), offered fifty thousand pesos for a hospital in memory of his uncle, the mine's founder, Adolf Prieto. The ladies of his family, the governor of the state, Mexican and foreign visitors have contributed generously. But there is never enough. When Rotary International met in Mexico City, the hospital's one registered nurse, Luz Figueroa, their honored speaker at luncheon, mentioned that the hospital's bank balance stood, that day, at 2.47 pesos. A lacquer bowl, appearing like magic, soon overflowed with two thousand pesos. The hospital meets many needs, and Dr. Curiel has set up a nurses' training-program whose students will take home some knowledge of hygiene even if they do not finish the course.

Another phase of Taxco life the tourist fails to see is an intelligent city government concerned with sanitation. Most Taxco homes now have water piped in or near-by spigots that have replaced wells. But the supply is inadequate to a growing town, and the Federal Department of Hydraulic Resources plans to tap permanent water in the mountains. It will be filtered and safe for everything but drinking. Taxco still recommends its excellent bottled water. Sewage still depends upon the great *barranca* that cuts through the town; summer rains flush it adequately; in winter the unfailing sun disinfects it. Hotels and modern homes have cesspools. One quails before the engineering problem of draining a town built on twenty levels of enduring rock. Taxco, nevertheless, is healthy. It has no typhoid and little malaria. Perhaps nature's ways are enough. Perhaps Santa Prisca has her town under her special care.

The tourist is quite safe drinking bottled water in his hillside hotel where every room is scented with mimosa and roses and every starry night throbs with the music of guitar and song. It also throbs with the non-stop bugling of dogs and the grunting of pigs. Nobody in Taxco is too elegant to have a lowly neighbor. This is, after all, part of the town's imperishable charm.

Any day or night, the walker cautiously feeling his way over Taxco's cobbles may stumble on a serenade or fiesta. Every church honors its titular saint with Masses, Indian dances, and fireworks. Taxco is famous for its *castillos*, skeletal castles built of fireworks that flame and crackle skyward in costly glory. Even more fun is the *torito* (bull), a game between a youth carrying a bull's shape made of pinwheels and crackers, and bullfighters who dash in to dare him and leap laughing away.

Perhaps Taxco's most impressive fiesta is its Holy Week enactment of the Passion, which it presents with the whole town for stage and hundreds of Indians for actors. Every night villagers come glimmering over the hills in candlelit procession bringing their crucifixes to Taxco's church of La Vera Cruz. The play I saw began on Wednesday with the arrest of Jesus, played by a gentle-faced man in white lace gown and brown wig. Roman centurions in modern tin hats led him to the church of San Nicolás where some bystanders said they could hear the clanking of Jesus' chains inside. On Holy Thursday the churchyard of Santa Prisca had been decked with cut boughs and flowers and caged birds. Indoors, crowds awaited the Washing of the Feet while electricians strung wires for the loudspeaker and tested the lights. I scarcely noticed the act of washing because I was so impressed by the sermon of a young Spanish priest, whose theme was the unimportance of ceremonialism. "A man might perform all the rites of the Church and still not be a Christian if he had no love in his heart." His parishioners listened respectfully and then filed out about the many rites they had to perform.

The night's act began in the atrium of the Vera Cruz, where the villagers stood massed under their crucifixes. The empty church was starry with candles, but activity centered at the sacristy door. "The *penitentes*," somebody said. A knot of men came out, in their midst the first penitent.

A man stripped to the waist, hooded in black, with a black skirt hobbling his feet, and a horsehair rope rubbing the skin off his middle. Another rope between his teeth helped to support a large bundle of blackberry thorns laid along his outstretched arms. Solicitous friends kept his two candles alight, now and again eased the weight of the bound thorns. Other penitents followed; we counted thirty-eight. All the crucifixes were borne along by men, followed by women and children carrying candles, some singing. One well-dressed woman limped in unshod agony over the stones; they said she was expiating her husband's sin in betraying her with another woman. They passed for pain-filled hours, each individual reliving the Passion of the Crucified. The *penitentes* left the procession at the Borda House, where they shed their burdens. The bundles, reported to weigh eighty pounds, hefted easily, but the strain of carrying them for hours must have seemed adequate atonement for any sin. Then the procession thinned out as *taxqueños* went home and visitors rolled into their serapes for sleep.

At noon on Good Friday the fair Spanish priest appeared near a loudspeaker in the plaza for the three-hour sermon. He told the tale simply while his parishioners enacted the fourteen stations, each actor stepping out of the crowd to play his part. Later they carried the recumbent and bleeding *cristo* to the Church of San Nicolás. The Passion proper was over, but Sábado de Gloria was still to come.

One of Mexico's best-loved traditions is that of Holy Saturday, Sábado de Gloria. The sacred statues are unveiled, church bells peal joyously, and Judas hangs himself —a macabre episode that has become a comic game with grotesque Judases dangling at every corner, shooting off fireworks and spilling candies and toys. But Pope or Archbishop—nobody in Taxco was sure which—had decreed that such roistering was unseemly while Jesus lay in the tomb. Judas must explode only after Resurrection Day began at midnight. This made Saturday more sad than glorious, with a limp paper Judas hanging in the plaza. By ten o'clock that night the strain had proved too great, and Judas exploded into pinwheels and skyrockets with a truly glorious bang.

Taxco has recently made itself another fiesta, fitting it into a fiestaless week in June. *Día de la Plata* (Silver Day) combines *castillos* and *toritos* with the crowning of a queen and the giving of prizes for the most original and beautiful silverwork. The day ends with a grand ball at the Hotel Borda. Nobody is too poor to go or snobbish enough to stay away. Maids and cooks deck their daughters in nylon net and silver combs; two orchestras come from Mexico City; the resident foreigners make up dinner parties; the state governor and municipal elders greet dignitaries from the capital; and daybreak finds the gaiety at its height. In 1953 the city fathers formally dedicated La Calle de Guillermo Spratling and marked it with a plaque honoring Taxco's favorite gringo and the founder of its silver fame. It is easy to believe that the more Taxco changes, the more it remains the same.

XXVIII

ACAPULCO

⊂ ACAPULCO, touted as Mexico's most glamorous spot, popular with internationally important personages, and visited by three out of five tourists, is actually a true Mexican resort, which was first developed and is most generously patronized by Mexicans. Planes from the capital make it in an hour's flight, and airlines offer special holiday rates. The government has improved the highway and reduced the drive to six hours. Zopilote Canyon remains; its close stone walls still reverberate with furnace-like heat. But the canyon is not long, and the journey is filled with interest. The road crosses the Río Balsas, one of the tropical rivers featured in *la marcha al mar* (march to the sea), which proposes to drain malarial swamps and to irrigate farms of sesame, coconuts, peanuts, and pineapples; even modern dairies are foreseen, with cows bred to withstand tropical heat. All this is in the future; the inhabitants of these lowlands would profit greatly from some health measures, some economic development, and some decent wages. But the villages are picturesque as one drives past.

Chilpancingo, capital of the state of Guerrero, is a quiet little city with dignified buildings around its plaza, an episcopal palace, and a clean, breezy hotel. It is historically important because Padre Morelos called the first constitutional convention here in 1813. This was the first group of Mexicans to propose to limit the power of the landowners by confiscation and of the clergy by abolition of compulsory tithes. Nothing came of it then, but the idea had been planted.

Acapulco is tropical; the visitor being sped from airport to hotel relaxes at once in the softly salt air to the rhythm of a native life wagging along with no concern for him. It is one of the few spots in Mexico hot enough to justify the clothes he bought for the trip. Tourists look comfortable in their Hawaiian shirts, though never as trim as do Mexicans in their *guayaberas*, and women in shorts and halters cause neither comment nor police action. All the year round Acapulco is hot; during the season, from November 20, Day of the Revolution, through the Easter vacation, it is delicious heat fanned by refreshing breezes. Through April and May it is too hot even for its devotees. The summer's rainy months are preferred by only Dolores del Río. "No tourists," she says, "wonderful thunderstorms every afternoon with tropical deluges, and then the most marvelous sunsets over the sea and in the clean, washed air. Then our gardens are heavy with growth, everything blooms, and the egrets shine like snow against the green."

Few people realize that Acapulco has a long pre-history. Little formal excavation has been done, but Lew Riley, working for the Museum of Natural History in New York and the Pennsylvania Museum, uncovered six city sites, finding pottery and carvings as ancient as any yet found in Mexico, and many of the petroglyphs that are found all along the west coast and that have not yet been identified with any culture. They include strange animal forms, cross-legged birds, serpents, and dots and dashes that might relate to the Maya calendar, but that might as well be some fisherman's tally of the day's catch. No fish have come to light, nor any human forms.

The long reach of the Aztecs touched this Pacific bay; at Zihuatanejo, ninety miles up the coast from Acapulco, there are traces of an artificial beach that legend says was made for Moctezuma. It was more likely one of his tax-gatherers who disported there. Better authenticated is the belief that from Zihuatanejo runners carried fresh fish to Tenochtitlán. This would be a shorter run than the better-known one from Vera Cruz. It was tried during the administration of President Alemán, who with his cabinet was building largely in Acapulco. Runners made it to the capital with fish still fresh in damp leaves.

The Spanish lost no time in reaching Acapulco (place where reeds grow). In 1521 Cortés built a fleet there; from there ships sailed to the conquest of the Philippines; and before the end of the century the galleons were putting in regularly with their cargoes of Oriental silks and spices. In the seventeenth century, pirates were such a menace that Spain built the Fort of San Diego at the harbor's mouth. When Spain lost her colony, the new Republic let both town and fort lapse into sleepy forgetfulness.

At the end of the nineteenth century an English and American company planned a railroad to connect with a line already in operation in the state of Michoacán. They dug a tunnel that still forms part of the road to Pié de la Cuesta (Foot of the Cliff), and bought 150 miles along the shore. But the revolution stopped the work. Later Mexico, alarmed at the way foreign capital was buying Mexico, prohibited any foreigner from owning land within ten miles of the coast or twenty of the frontier. This was not caprice; such buyers as Hearst and Doheny, with their empire-size holdings, actually threatened Mexican sovereignty.

Twenty years later, when business seemed stable at last, the railroad interests sent in a clever negotiator to see what could be saved of their investment. The result was a scheme by which investors buy through a bank, which as *fideicomiso* holds the property in trust for the owner, who may renew his contract after thirty years. A new company, including Mexican investors, decided to abandon the shore-line holdings, but to salvage the peninsula whereon Acapulco sits. This company, *La Fraccionadora de Acapulco*, proposed to give Mexico a Riviera of its own.

The revolutionary plutocracy had tended to follow the Porfirian *elegantes* to Biarritz or Cannes. Now they faced gaudy advertisements on billboards, in newspapers and magazines, assuring them that Acapulco had every splendor and amenity of any European resort. La Fraccionadora, lacking capital to build great hotels, and offering lots for private homes, found success where they least expected it. Mexico's little people began making the trying two-day trip in their Fords or by bus and buying lots at four pesos a meter. Acapulco was becoming a popular Mexican resort. In the thirties one stopped at a palm-thatched open-walled hotel just above the breakers on Caleta beach or at El Mirador's series of huts, where Carlos Barnard was proving the perfect host. Between swims it was fun to sit on the dock watching the Negro stevedores loading to the rhythm of their own slow singing. Vendors came along with warm beer and *ceviche*, raw white fish marinated in lemon juice with chopped onions, chile, and tomatoes.

The transformation of that lazy beach town into a sophisticated resort with fifty hotels of unsurpassed elegance has been dizzying. In 1935 Carlos Barnard, taking a chance, bought a lot for 250 pesos. Two years later he sold it to Lew Riley, recently arrived from the States, for 50,000. When the Yacht Club was organized the next year, they bought it from Riley for 250,000. This was unusual, but was becoming typical. During those eight years the Pan American Pacific cruise steamers broke the journey from Panama to San Francisco at Acapulco, bringing ashore hundreds of tourists for a drive, a swim, and lunch with *mariachi* music and native dancers. This brought Acapulco to the notice of tourist agencies, and when the war put an end to cruises, they began to feature Acapulco. Its fame was assured.

Acapulco is now sharply divided between the Mexican resort and that of the tourist. Dozens of hotels offer accommodations and food such as can be found everywhere. Most of them have swimming-pools nearer at hand than the beaches. Many feature huge platters of tropical fruits, marimba or *mariachi* music, and what fish they can get. Fish are all but unprocurable for the simple reason that nobody who lives in Acapulco sees much point in fishing after he has caught his family's daily ration or enough to sell for fireworks, firewater, or some other exigent need. Fishing is hard work, especially as *acapulqueños* paddle their canoes for long sweating days. Lew Riley, who brought the first sailing-boats in for sport, tried to introduce sails or at least *petates* to catch the breeze. But that wild-eyed notion died a-borning.

Lew, however, had fun with his boats, exploring the shore as far as Zihuatenejo and its uninhabited Isla Grande de Iztapan, which he says is like a South Sea Island paradise. He also organized the Yacht Club in 1937, with a membership of ten. It has grown with a largely Mexican membership and a stately clubhouse whose wide terraces fill for the morning anise or tequila, the afternoon cocktails, and dancing at night. Yachting-parties are enormously popular, but sailing as a sport failed to catch the Mexican imagination. "For diversion, yes!" they would say, "but not, for God's sake, to suffer." The self-discipline necessary to handle sails well enough to qualify for international meets strikes the Mexican as suffering. So Lew Riley tried another tack.

El Club Náutico has appealed rather to younger *acapulqueños*, rising young citizens or the sons of prosperous business and professional men. With fifty-four members, about twenty sailboats, no house, and less swank than the Yacht Club, El Club Náutico promises to develop some disciplined sailors who may put Mexico on the international sport map. Their Commodore, Sr. Francisco de la Macorra, owns their largest boat, a sixty-foot ketch.

These imported sports have developed beach boys capable of anything aquatic. Oddly, neither the original Indians nor the later *mestizos* were swimmers. But youths at the Hotel Mirador perform an extraordinary feat of diving 125 feet from a cliff into a pool that is deep enough for only a split second when the wave is high. They surely need the prayer they offer to an image of the Virgin in a niche in the rocks. But fatalities are few. Visitors find good swimming at the long gentle "afternoon beach" of Los Hornos (ovens) or at Caleta's steeper shore with a strong tide. But there one can take a glass-bottomed boat and observe the sea's flora and fauna. Between the beaches, El Puerto Marqués guards the mouth of the Río Papagayo, where a new airport is making new fortunes for property-owners.

Fishing is strictly a sport for gringos, those strange people who make such hard work of all their pleasures. Launches may be hired, and a catch is practically guaranteed at any season. Tuna, sailfish, marlin, and swordfish are the usual catch, some of them of phenomenal size. Giant ray offers good sport to the man with skill with a harpoon. To hold down the take and protect the fish, fishermen have been urged to band a fish and throw it back into the sea. They were even offered stuffed fish with which to be photographed, but the scheme had so little appeal that conservationists fear a depletion of game fish, just as crocodiles were practically exterminated by a company that made them into shoes and bags.

Acapulco remains sharply divided between foreign tourists, week-enders from the capital, flying in on special rates, and property-owners who entertain mostly at home, granting only infrequent appearances at night clubs. Esther Williams has a house, but is never seen swimming. Dolores del Río in her enchanted garden at Roca Seca lazes there in the scantiest beach attire and goes abroad in full skirts and peasant blouses. Cantinflas flies in now and then with guests, or opens the many cottages on his estate to his friends. Ex-President Alemán maintains a yacht in the bay which has been the scene of many political conferences that are whispered about but not reported in the press. Other political figures, enriched by office, make Acapulco their haven.

Acapulco has kept, behind all its glitter of wealth and newsworthy names, much of the character of a small tropical port. Streets that are not seen driving from the airport to the hotel have shuttered balconies that almost meet above stores selling the wonders of the sea—shells and starfish, tortoise-shell combs and boxes, and reptile skins from the jungle. Fruit- and fish-peddlers sing their wares as they lazily push their carts along. These are beautiful people whose skin tones and wavy hair are a reminder that Mexico once knew Negro slavery and that its ships came from the Orient. Away from town, the shoreline is feathered with timber, and several streams flow down from the jungle where a visitor in a motor boat or canoe can see alligators, monkeys, and parrots in their native state. Acapulco has somehow opened its front door to the world while keeping some backwaters inviolate.

PART EIGHT

East to the Gulf

APPROXIMATE SCALE

50   0   50   100   150   200

MILES

DON GREAME KELLEY, CART.

XXIX

PULQUE HACIENDA

A señorita, arranging a visit to her family hacienda, about seventy-five miles northeast of Mexico City and in the state of Hidalgo, put me right on several matters.

"Life on the hacienda is simple, but you will see us as we are, and you will understand Indians better, I think. Please don't idealize them. I have known them all my life and I tell you they have no ambition, no desire to improve. We have to take care of them like children; but very little can be done." How like some southerners speaking out of vast knowledge of Negroes. But the señorita was going on. "Once when I came home from the States full of ideas, I told my father the peons must have warm blankets; it was terrible for them to go shivering like that. But a week later those blankets had been pawned, and all the men were drunk on pulque. . . . You must notice how pulque ruins them. The young ones are alert and bright, but the old ones are dull. . . . No, pulque is not sold on the hacienda, but they get pulque as part of their wage. Also, the peons are given land to till as their own. You will see how much better off they are than the people on the *ejidos*. But they are hopeless. You'll see!

"The younger people are getting badly corrupted by all this government propaganda, but the old ones are still decent, humble people. Last year my grandmother gave them a novena. She was there the whole nine days; the chapel was always filled, and on the last day she allowed them all to come into the dining-room; each one was given something, and they all kissed her hand. . . . It was beautiful!

"Your guide will be Manuel. You will like him; always so respectful and humble. The *administrador* too was born on the place. He is quite young and intelligent and very loyal to our family.

"Write me if you need anything; and remember, the place is yours. The people are there to serve you. Never forget that to the Indians we are gods; we can do no wrong." This promised to be a novel experience to one who had done much wrong and had never felt in the least godlike. In bidding me farewell, the señorita made a request.

"Before you go, will you go to see my grandmother? She is very old, but the hacienda is hers, she loves it, and she was interested to meet you."

The old mistress, living in a house where Carlotta had danced, and attended by two women as aged and frail as she was, received me in a long, almost empty *sala*, and offered a ruby cordial in delicate glass. As I left, she extended a fragile white hand, no larger than a child's.

"That is my hacienda," she said. "I saved money to buy it, denying myself what young people love. I put money there instead of buying extravagantly or traveling abroad, because I loved the land, because I wished to do my duty by the people. Well, my people still love me—those who have not been lied to and tricked away. But now this hideous, irreligious government has taken my hacienda away from me. I, a woman, saved and denied myself for that land. It is mine, and they are taking it, bit by bit. You will see. Think of that when you go there."

She asked me to call on her again, but when I returned from the hacienda she was ill, and then it was too late.

Driving across maguey country, I watched long files of maguey plants wheel stiffly away across rolling hills, green with summer to the ridges and blue with mist in the hollows. Purpling mountains reared against the well-washed sky with the volcano of Malinche outlined against it.

At the gate the *administrador* met me. Tall and swarthy, he showed strong muscles through the tight striped trousers and fresh *guayabera* of the working *charro*. His greeting was formal to freezing until my halting Spanish reassured him and his gray eyes warmed to admit that we might, in time, be friends.

This was not one of the greater haciendas; the old señora's sons had a richer house, he told me. But this was good land; I should see how pulque was made and learn to drink it; and whatever they could do for me would be a pleasure.

"Pulque," he went on to say, "is very good for the health, but it must be taken fresh. And though it is Mexico's cheapest drink, it is so delicate that one gets its best flavor only on a hacienda. Even I, if I carry it to Mexico most carefully, myself holding the jar all the way, its flavor deteriorates before I get there."

The mansion loomed like a fortress with heavy stone walls cornered by watchtowers. Outside the walls huddled the workers' huts, built of adobe and roofed with discarded pieces of corrugated iron or shingles held down by stones. At the gate a man stood respectfully ready to close it. At once the nose was assailed by that unforgettable rotten-apple smell of pulque.

This court was the work center. Dirty children and slovenly women were carrying water from a central fountain, most of them burdened as well with babies slung in their *rebozos*. From a room on one side came a long wailing chant that had no meaning for me; from the other the singsong voices of children learning aloud. The *administrador* presented his señora; the cook, Rita; her assistant, Juana; and the maid, Lupe. Also six-year-old Joaquín, whom he chided for not being in school. His señora explained that he had permission to miss school for the visitor.

Unlike her husband, she was rosy and merry. She showed me through the house, assuring me over and over that it was mine, completely. Little Joaquín tagged along, his big black eyes watching every move.

Only what was necessary to keep the house from falling into utter ruin had been done. The patio's formal flower beds were overgrown in a tangle of roses, bleeding hearts, daisies, mignonette, and one unpruned oleander. We passed room after room, empty but of noble proportions. In the dining-room a table and sideboard of heroic dimensions were reflected in pier glasses set between French doors opening onto a garden. Unkempt too, it had a sunny enchantment even in decay. Lemon verbena and pinks made it fragrant, a half-choked fountain tinkled wistfully, the teahouse had fallen in, and the billiard-room door was gone. Nobody went there now, the señora said.

Between this garden and the peons' comfortless hovels there was no connecting gate. What a perfect schoolroom that deserted billiard room would make, what excellent vegetable plots those untended flower beds! What a perfect human laboratory altogether! and outside in those huts was the unwashed and illiterate human material ready for the experiment. This house was like a tomb from which even the spirit had fled.

Everything had been destroyed in the revolution, the señora said, for this hacienda lay on Villa's march to the capital. What was not ruined, the family had gradually taken to town. They seldom came any more. Only the sons to talk business with the *administrador*, and at long intervals the old señora to hold a novena. It was sad here, so the señora stayed in her own apartments on the outer patio.

Aside from the dining-room, only my bedroom was furnished. The old señora's bed was there, with the Austrian coat-of-arms on the headboard and slender rods to hold a canopy. Instead of a bureau I had a shaving-stand with cut-glass knobs. The washstand was fitted with what remained of a set of Haviland and some pieces of crude pottery. They found an office desk for my typewriter, and I had a bentwood rocker and a straight chair. The room opened on the working-patio, and I was glad of that, for what went on there kept me entertained for all the hours that I was not in the saddle.

Long before dawn I could hear the *tlachiqueros* setting out. Their name comes from *tlachique*, the long gourd used for sucking out the juice of the maguey plant. Among them trotted the burros with bobbing barrels to bring home the sap. Then the clatter of animals began. Sheep's hoofs cracked on the cobbles, punctuating their vacuous bleat. Horses, burros, and mules clumped harder and rattled chains. Cows mooed and calves bawled, milling around, smelling of manure. Dogs barked constantly, urging the animals to the fountain to drink, snapping them away again. When all had drunk, an old man began to sweep with a twig broom, and women and children came with oil cans and jugs for water. They dipped from the central basin; the animals drank from a trough below. The hacienda's only spigot was in the vaulted chamber where they made the pulque.

After Lupe brought my coffee and rolls, tiny Joaquín appeared to sweep off the terrace. He soon came to rest at my window and to report that the Brownies had taken the bread and milk left for them the night before. His cat generally followed him, squeezing through the bars to sun herself on the window sill. Joaquín was an unsmiling child, but bright and eager to learn. When a couple of children's books came from town, he skipped school to read them.

One day the señora told me his story. "A year ago a vagabond came along here. We paid no attention, though my husband knew he was there. The peons let him sleep in their huts, and this boy—he was only four then—went around begging food. I don't know what the man had, but he died and this child was alone.

"He cried so and I felt so sorry that I took him to live with us. He could tell us nothing, not his father's name nor where he came from. For a while he was so frightened he seldom spoke, and now he almost never smiles, you see. Sometimes he speaks of a mother and other children and a city, but when we ask he is silent. Only God knows. He is *simpático* and bright. We unfortunately cannot have a child, so we are keeping him. He will have a good home, an education. By the grace of God, we shall make a good man of that waif."

After Joaquín's sweeping, he would lag along to school, hating it. And no wonder! The government requires every hacienda to maintain a school. This one was a small room lighted only from the open door. The children sat on benches or on the floor. There were no books, no blackboards. The teacher had a small, rickety table. For the required hours I heard her shrill, squalling voice, the spiritless repetition of the youngsters. Her pupils, she told me, were of all the ages required by law, but she made no effort to classify them. There was really no use, for attendance varied from four to thirty; almost no children came regularly. I felt that she was ashamed of a job imposed by a hated government.

"It is impossible," she said, echoing her betters, "to teach these Indians anything. They are stupid, hopeless. Only some of the girls can learn to sew nicely." Her only flash of pride was in the cotton tidies the larger girls were embroidering with pink and red roses.

The school was too sad even to contemplate, but pulque-making was exciting. The master pulque-maker appeared early, stopping to watch men scrubbing the big oxhide vats. Metal cannot be used, as pulque eats it away in no time.

What a tribute to the human stomach! Two old men washed all day, splashing water from the fountain into the vats glowing deep gold and copper in the sun. With stiff brushes they scrubbed and scrubbed, unhurried and thorough. Satisfied at last, each man took off his hat and set the vat, upside down, on his head to carry it indoors.

At mid-morning the first burros brought in the *aguamiel* (honey water), which is pure maguey sap. The master pulque-maker showed me the process in the cool dusky room smelling of fermentation. The fresh sap was added to the mother and then poured from vat to vat until it was prime. It takes eighty days to mature pulque, and part of the process is a secret known only to the *maestro* and perhaps one other. This gives the hacienda's pulque its special flavor. At each pouring the workers burst into a chant: *"Alabo el misterio de la Santa Trinidad."* Pulque-making is a mystery and they chant the greatest mystery they know. Every day's run was shipped at evening to Mexico City, and twice a day Rita served me a tall pitcher of fresh pulque, slightly foamy, rather ropy, and winning me at last to real enjoyment of its pungency. But the *administrador* was right in saying that pulque tastes just right only on the hacienda.

Afternoons I napped or sat in the garden, fragrant of lemon verbena, writing or talking with Joaquín or the señora. When it rained we sat under the *portal*, which was frescoed with Pompeian scenes. At sunset I climbed the pitch-black spiral stairway to the flat roof, Joaquín and his cat attending. We could watch the animals coming in to drink, the milking in the back patio, the train stopping for the pulque; and all around the horizon the draining away of light and the final majestic wonder of the sun going down behind the silver-set sapphire of Malinche.

Evenings I was always welcome to listen to the radio with the *administrador* and his señora. Or we sat outdoors and talked of the old days and the new. I asked about the near by *ejido* village. The *administrador* agreed that I should visit it, but the time never seemed to come. He was a busy man; for days he was occupied with a government engineer, come to advise about a ditch that would drain a marsh to make fertile fields. The *administrador* did not hate the government; he took its advice. Altogether, he was a man who loved land and animals, whose passion was to see things grow. When he was free to ride, he showed me how the new ditch would run, how he was experimenting with rotation of crops, and the fine animals imported for breeding purposes. He was learning constantly. Yet he had not learned to read until he was a grown man. He was born on this hacienda, where there was no school; only after the revolution did he learn to read in a night school. "With reading," he said, "came everything. Then I could learn what I needed."

When I rode with Manuel, he too could not find time to take me to the *ejido* village. Our daily jaunt through the barley and maguey, with side canters to look at a flock of sheep or a bunch of cattle, left only time to get home for dinner. So the *ejido* village became the unattainable goal. But I learned much from Manuel. He talked steadily, proving himself the humble devoted peon the señorita had prophesied. He was grateful for the masters' generosity in giving each peon land to work, for the corn and pulque that supplemented his wage, and above all for the school where his children could learn to read, and without pay! He as a child had had no chance to learn, there being no school. He had begun to work as a sheepherder at ten, "like that boy over there." That one, yes, was of school age, but he was a half-orphan and had to support his mother and the younger children. Then he reverted to his own happy situation. Now, even without the arts of reading and writing, he was *caporal* in charge of all the animals on the place.

Soon we were riding along the border of *ejido* lands. "See," my guide said, pointing proudly, "see how poor this barley is compared with that on the hacienda. It was good land, but the government took it away from the hacienda. A barbarity that was, of truth! And now the villagers try to cultivate it. But how can they, poor things, with no master to advise and help them? . . . And it is sad to see their beasts, so poor. But they cannot afford, poor things, to buy fine bulls and rams as the master does.

"Yes, those fields look better. They were of the *ejido* too, but now they belong to particular men. Men work better their own lands, is it not so? They have their co-operatives now. Maybe they will do better. But it gives me pain that they have no kind master to direct them. . . . Yes, we are better off. When we need seeds, the masters accommodate us. When we are old, they take care of us. My father has seventy-six years now, but he rides out every day and they pay him the same wage. Until he dies they will care for him." Here was indeed the humble peon, the feudal serf next door to the modern world and preferring his bondage.

The *administrador* was a different type. Whenever he found time to chat with me, he spoke freely. "Do you know the meaning of hacienda, señorita? Years ago, they say, a hacienda was expected to give one hundred per cent. '*A cien da, y hasta doscientos!*' And even two hundred!

"And so it was in the days of Don Porfirio. They were all so rich they ate off gold and silver plates, they went covered with jewels, and they never knew where the money came from. Now, having lost so much land, they have to think. We are working hard now to produce as much as we can. Grain grows, you see, between the rows

of maguey. In my position, I have to learn many things.
I study. I read. I ask many questions, and so I have been
able to keep this hacienda paying. So far. But if the government takes what it threatens to take away now, I don't
know. To make less land pay will be practically impossible.

"No, the *ejidos* do not produce as much as they should.
They have let the maguey go. It takes thirty years for a
plant to mature, and then it produces for only a few
months. That requires continuity of ownership, and capital. And these people are ignorant as well as poor. And,
naturally, a few clever men in every village manage to get
the best fields for themselves. Maybe in time, señorita,
they will work it out. I don't know. I hope so. But I cannot
work with them.

"I tried, once. They gave me a job as treasurer—the only
time I ever left this hacienda, and I could not stand it. This
one and that one wanted money, this one and that one
wanted to be excused from his taxes. It was not handling
money for the village; it was using money for the politicians. So I came back to the hacienda. Here I can live.

"I have a good salary, a good home. I can manage these
men well, for most of them still believe they are better off
than those on the *ejidos*. If they do not, others do. But I
make few changes. And here I can see things grow; for me
that is life, señorita; not dealing with politicians.

"And if the masters gain much, that doesn't trouble me.
They put up the capital, they take the risk. And they have
always been kind to me. That they do not come here often
does not trouble me, either. Why should it? If I have come
to a decision by watching closely for months, years, it may
not look reasonable to a man who comes from France for
a few weeks. No, we do very well with the masters away,
and we send them money. But no longer a hundred per
cent!"

At last I went to visit the *ejido* village accompanied by

the señora. Everyone was busy in mid-morning. Weavers sang at their looms. Butchers chatted gaily as they flung about the silvery entrails, sliced heavy red chunks, or stirred the big kettle where hog's fat was rendering. Women passed carrying string bags, cans of water, bundles of faggots, or trays of cakes. Others were washing clothes in the natural basins in the stream's limestone bed. An old one-armed man expertly twirled the wheel on which he made *comales*—those flat clay disks on which *tortillas* are baked. In the ragged plaza a few cows and a few people passed. And from the schoolhouse came a buzzing.

Then bells rang, and the children marched out, boys from one door, in charge of young men, looking well-groomed in white trousers and blue shirts. From another the girls, led by older girls in gay satin blouses, tight skirts, French heels, and shiningly waved hair. Children clean and snappy, stepping quickly in the drill. Arms up and down, feet here and there, turns and bows; and then they scampered off with whoops.

A man in black with a briefcase asked for a ride to the station. The señora acquiesced politely, but with no enthusiasm. He was the school-inspector, taking a train for Mexico City. We chatted politely, impersonally, though I saw his face stiffen and his eyes flash as we rounded the house's high wall with the peons' ragged straw huts against it. Dirty children hung around, many looking ill. When the señora left us for a moment at the store, he spoke quickly, passionately.

"What a barbarity!" he raged. "How pitiful that any children should be so. They must be made clean, educated, given an appreciation of their own value.

"They have doubtless told you that these *ejidos* are not so well worked as the hacienda fields. And that is true; you can see for yourself. It takes more than a few years to turn a slave population into efficient farmers and co-operative workers. It takes, possibly, three generations. And three such discouraging generations, with all the graft, all the confusion. We go slowly, but I believe we go well. And if we can make men and good Mexican citizens out of half-starved peons, that is worth taking three generations to do, isn't it?"

I thought that it was. I thought that my delightful visit on a pulque hacienda had given me the whole picture in brief but telling flashes.

FIESTA IN MEXICO: *a pyrotechnical* castillo *showers the night with sparks*

Lake Pátzcuaro: butterfly net and a dugout

SCENIC MEXICO

The Mexico City-Puebla-Vera Cruz Highway: a valley near Orizaba

XXX

HUEJOTZINGO AND TLAXCALA

❧ THE EASTBOUND highway out of Mexico passes walled haciendas that have been left to crumble or turned into glass-walled factories. On a clear day Popocatépetl's hoary head and the feminine curves of Ixtaccíhuatl are outlined in snow against the sky. Often clouds obscure Mexico's famed sunshine, and people say: "The volcanoes are there; only they cannot be seen. . . . It's that atomic bomb," they explain, "that's ruining our climate."

The road, climbing steadily on excellent grades over a lightly forested range, reaches Río Frío at 11,000 feet of altitude. Masked bandits used it for a hideout once; now it is a double line of Pemex stations and restaurants for the bus lines. Travelers with cultivated tastes and dependable stomachs can lunch very well there on roast goat with chile sauce, *tortillas*, essence of coffee in hot milk, and tequila. Beyond Río Frío the drive is all downhill into a valley that spreads out in tilled fields cut by poplar-lined roads. At San Martín Tezmelucan a side road leads off to Tlaxcala; beyond on the highway is Huejotzingo, whose plaza is all but hidden behind rows of bright serapes hung out to catch the eye.

Huejotzingo's church, built over a destroyed temple, is an excellent example of how Indian craftsmen outsmarted European architects. On the façade are Aztec suns and moons; hieroglyphics adorn the cloister's walls; and in the church itself Quetzalcoatl's emblem, the serpent, entwines a cross. The same diverting confusion marks Huejotzingo's annual fiesta on Shrove Tuesday.

Leaving my car in charge of two helpful highway police-
men, I pushed my way across the plaza jammed with people, milling pointlessly around, munching sweets, tipping
bottles of Coke. The air smelled of frying fat and gunpowder, and every store around the square had opened its
radio to its loudest. It was full fiesta. I presented myself to
the *presidente municipal*, who politely offered me a seat in
his balcony just an arm's reach from the heroine's own.
While we waited, he sent for a manuscript history of the
town. "Guejocingo," it began, "was a republic of 40,000
people who were converted from their gruesome human
sacrifices by Fray Juan de Alameda." In 1553 it was granted
a coat-of-arms by Carlos V; even then it was known as a
center of fine fruit orchards, as it still is. But I was more
interested in the day's drama.

Agustín Lorenzo was a bandit who at the end of the
eighteenth century terrorized all central Mexico, but endeared himself to the poor by his charities. According to
a legend told in Iguala, Agustín, seeing his grandfather
beaten by a majordomo, vowed vengeance, though he was
only a little boy. Aided by a sorcerer, he grew into a strong
man who returned to the hacienda and killed the majordomo. Then he was an outlaw, and he soon became a
famous bandit.

One day, seeing her perhaps at Mass, Agustín the
bandit fell in love with the beautiful daughter of the *cor-*
regidor of Huejotzingo. It seemed hopeless, but Agustín
smuggled letters to his lady love, who agreed to elope with
him. This elopement is the theme of a fiesta which, according to the *presidente*'s manuscript, "has the odor of powder, splendor, rejoicing, and of pleasant memories in the
soul of Huejotzingo people, who, fleeing life's sorrow, enjoy taking part in this carnival fiesta."

The prevailing odor was that of burned powder. I was
told that the people had bought some four tons of gun-

powder at two pesos a kilo, quite an expenditure for sheer noise. Other expenses include costumes, which are worth from fifty to three thousand pesos each, and masks that cost about eighty. Costumes and masks are often heir-looms.

The show's charm lay in its lack of showmanship and in the actors' obvious pleasure in their folk-play. It began raggedly with groups of dancers all jigging to the same thin tune on drum and flute and costumed to represent pre-historic Indians. This meant tall feathered headdresses, but one man, perhaps a clown, though he was not very funny, came wrapped in a deerskin. This fiesta was in-augurated soon after Mexico had driven out the French invaders, so it included figures from that era. *Zapadores* (sappers) danced in red trousers, white tunics, and tall black hats with Mexico's colors in the cockades. *Zaca-poaxtlas*, villagers who fought well against the French, ap-peared in lace-edged pantalettes, bearded pink masks, and blond hair. The *serranos* (mountaineers) came clowning in tatters and carrying stuffed animals as well as machetes and bows and arrows. Even the French appeared. *Zuavos* (Zouaves) wore the correct visored cap with kerchief and knapsacks marked *Viva francia*. These were formerly topped with a loaf of French bread, but that has been sup-planted by Pan Bimbo, Mexico's most-advertised cello-phane-wrapped loaf. At intervals a band passed; ten bands were each earning fifteen hundred pesos. For hours the parade passed in a cloud of blue smoke, gray dust, strong smells, and noise. Photographers impeded every move, de-manding retakes, directing poses.

At last the real drama began. The heroine rode in, at-tended by *charros, chinas poblanas*, and a servitor leading her bony horse. Her pale-lavender dress spread over the horse's haunches, and her wide hat and veil framed a pretty face. Upstairs the *presidente* and the fiesta's director, with

blue bandoliers and unsheathed swords, escorted the elop-
ing maiden to her balcony. Then the bandit's emissary rode
in—a rough mountain Indian in leather kirtle, feathers, and
paint. He held aloft a large piece of paper so that everybody could see. He did it again for the photographers. At
last the lady's attendants dropped a stout rope and hauled
up the paper, recognized as Agustín's promise to come at
midnight. The heroine, perusing it several times for the
photographers, wrote her acceptance with a fountain pen
borrowed from the *presidente* and dropped it to the messenger, who rode away, kicking his horse.

Time now for Agustín Lorenzo. Dressed in silver-
trimmed leather and wide sombrero, he rode smartly in on
a curvetting steed and climbed the rope ladder so expertly
that the photographers accepted the scene. Greeting the
lady formally, he posed with her and let her climb down
the ladder alone. But the lover followed fast, and they
rode off together. The rape was complete. Later the marriage would be solemnized in a brush hut on the plaza,
built to represent the bandit's mountain hideout, where a
priest was in waiting. Meanwhile, it was time for lunch.
Zouaves, *arrieros*, Apaches, and Mexican soldiers, emerging with relief from their stifling masks, made for eating-
booths, *pulquerías*, or home.

It was a good time—as any time is good—to visit Tlaxcala.
The ancient town maintains a remote dignity; the state of
the same name has suffered as gentlemen's pulque haciendas
are taken over by the poor man's *ejidos*. Pre-Cortesian
Tlaxcala was a city state that held out against the conquering Aztecs and later fought the conquering Spaniards.
Curiously, they seem just as proud that after Cortés defeated them they became his most dependable allies. Even
the *chamaco* in the plaza and the *mozo* in the hotel speak
of Tlaxcala's unconquerable spirit and walk proudly for it.

The plaza, before it suffered modernization, was a fine

example of the low-arched sixteenth-century architecture; the Franciscan church on the hill with its stone-walled atrium under ash trees is still impressive. The excessively baroque sanctuary of Ocotlán offers a complete contrast. Its pink-and-white chapel, the acme of the Indian toy-makers' art, is so miraculous that one always finds pilgrims crawling toward it over the stony hillside.

Nothing remains of the city Cortés found so fine. In spite of their promises of friendship and of titles of nobility, the Spanish within a generation had reduced the Tlax-calans to servitude and destroyed their city. Only one small temple, Tizatlán, hints at old glories. The guide there tells the story. A young Tlaxcalan in a dream saw Xicoténcatl, the Tlaxcalan chief, who told him where to dig. There he found worked stones, and government archæologists un-covered paintings and a sacrificial stone that are still clear in outline and bright in color.

Tlaxcala appears on the colonial tax rolls as paying trib-ute in the form of fine textiles. It remained a weaving-center, and at the end of the nineteenth century it was producing striped wool for *charro* pants, tweeds for smart tailors, and lengths of natural white wool for many uses. But the Tlaxcala weavers lost this market to French and German immigrants who opened factories in Orizaba, Puebla, and other cities that now produce textiles of all sorts. This left Tlaxcala only the weaving of serapes; it has developed two distinctive styles. Within the last decade or two, weavers began making black rugs with wreaths of bright flowers reminiscent of Uruapan lacquer or your grandmother's crewelwork. The other style—of blue birds on soft gray or white birds on blue—has a romantic history. A young art teacher from the states, living in a village to paint, married a young weaver. She designed those birds in flight, perhaps as symbolic of happiness. But the young artist too flew away.

The last, and saddest, intervention in Tlaxcala's weaving craft was the dumping of synthetic fibers from the commercial centers at Puebla and Orizaba. Tlaxcala was bitterly poor, its lands eroded away, its crops practically nil. Wool was hard to find and prohibitively expensive for most weavers, but they found the synthetics cheap, easy to work, and quite as salable to most tourists as pure wool. State and federal governments try to maintain pure-wool standards, but the Museum of Fine Arts finds so few worthy examples of Tlaxcala's craft that it seldom shows any.

Synthetics have swamped Tlaxcala's market and the one in neighboring Santa Ana, but the visitor who can disregard the plastic, celluloid, and rayon will find the very goods that Cortés listed for the King. Reed mats for the floor and fans for the charcoal fire; the same pots in the same shapes for cooking the identical foods; the same men's serapes and women's skirts, *huipiles*, and carrying-cloths, the same *ixtle*-fiber bags, nets, and cords and ropes of every thickness and many colors. Fruits and vegetables are neatly piled: many-hued corn and beans, red and green tomatoes, dozens of chiles, fresh and dried. Our familiar fruits are here, as well as tropical pineapples, bananas, chirimoyas, zapotes and sugar cane from Vera Cruz. Long dark vanilla pods mingle their heavy scent with that of herbs and spices, some for cooking, others for curing or bewitching.

A young herb-merchant was pleased to show his wares— forty kinds of dried leaves, seeds, roots, and nameless powders that were guaranteed among them to cure the prevailing diseases of diarrhea, liver complaint, malaria, and tuberculosis. More fascinating were seeds to be put into a faithless lover's ear to make him heed or into a roaming husband's soup to bring him home. The vendor offered a booklet describing procedures. "It is all scientific," he assured me, "nothing of superstition." But Tlaxcala is still famed as a center of witchcraft. Modern healers doubtless augment their potions with mumbo jumbo. And suggestion can cross racial and cultural barriers. A gringa in Mexico City, feeling unaccountably ill, suspected an insolent maid of doping her tea. And on investigation the lady learned that the maid had indeed visited an old witch in Tlaxcala.

XXXI

PUEBLA DE LOS ANGELES

◖ THE VALLEY of Puebla enjoys air so translucent that Popo and Ixta stand against the sky with a clarity seldom seen from Mexico City. East of the city rise Orizaba's pure cone and the lesser one of Malinche, with a small peak near by—as Cortés's son might have followed his mother. This valley's center, in pre-Cortesian days, was the ceremonial city of Cholula. It was dedicated to Quetzalcoatl and doubtless drew pilgrimages from all the world that acknowledged his lordship and prayed for his return bringing beauty and goodness.

Cholula was said to have a temple for every day in the year, each topping a pyramid. Here Cortés, advancing on Tenochtitlán, discovered a trap and in his rage demolished the city completely. The Spaniards then rebuilt the city with a Christian church on the rubble of every destroyed pyramid. Nobody seems to have made an accurate count, but from the highway one sees many tiled domes above the eucalyptus and poplar trees. Highest is the church of Nuestra Señora de los Remedios, which houses the image that Cortés is said to have carried on his saddle horn. Archæologists have tunneled into this pyramid's ruins far enough to establish that it was indeed an important religious site.

Puebla de los Angeles, the city that now dominates the valley, has no Indian tradition except that in 1600 its founder, the Franciscan Motolinía, brought Indians to build a city for conquerors who were ready to retire as moneyed gentlemen. The site was chosen for its beauty and fertility and to break the long journey from Vera Cruz to the capital. The road, dodging a factory section, enters the city through a wealthy residence district of contemporary architecture. Altogether, Puebla, a city of 300,000 inhabitants, and an important industrial center with 20,000 union members and a production of one third of the nation's textiles, manages to appear a quiet city of colonial homes with tiled church domes gleaming among its trees.

Before the end of the century, Spaniards, finding good clays in the hills, brought potters from Spain's Talavera and established a business that is important to the modern city. *Talavera de la Reina*, made precisely as it was in Spain, became *talavera de Puebla* as the original designs of cool blue on white were livened up by Mexican workmen with bright yellows, greens, and terra cotta. Mexicans inevitably added playfulness as well as color, but they have never lost the art of modeling excellent dishes or of glazing them. The city now boasts four glazing-ovens and at least one family —that of Isauro Uriarte—that has operated for over ninety years. All sorts of ceramics are made, from trinkets to complete dinner services and the tiles that floor the houses and cover the domes and many house fronts.

Puebla's other typical craft is the working of onyx, found in the hills as far south as Oaxaca in the natural colors of grayish white and soft buff to brown. Skilled men work it up into boxes, ash trays, a few cups and bowls. Unfortunately, no true artist has seen the possibilities in onyx for either well-balanced dishes or imaginative costume jewelry, and poor taste prevails beyond the routine forms. If fancy does take over, it is capable of producing a lamp base showing Cuauhtémoc's feet burning in reddish onyx flames.

Puebla's laws require the preservation of its colonial aspect, and its narrow streets are lined with tiled façades that hide thoroughly modern interiors. The plaza's arcades are choked with booths and tables where men play dominoes and order food and drink from restaurants and cantinas. A fringe of parked motors does not detract from the leafy quiet of the park. Puebla's laws forbid honking too.

The Cathedral of the Immaculate Conception rises, behind a tall wrought-iron fence, to two imposing towers whose bells ring every hour. This church, one of the largest and richest in the Americas, is of the Spanish episcopal type, with high altar in the center. Its wealth is incalculable in gold leaf, European and Mexican paintings, inlaid statues, and a high altar of onyx carved by Manuel Tolsa, a nineteenth-century architect and sculptor who is one of Mexico's most revered artists. The City Hall, next door, holds one of Mexico's greatest treasures—Bishop Juan Palafox y Mendoza's library, which contains a priceless collection of hand-illumined volumes. Its reading-room, paneled with fine woods and bookcases, is furnished with onyx-topped tables and carved chairs. It dates from 1647; some of its parchment volumes are a century older.

A student of Mexico's colonial art and architecture can revel endlessly in Puebla. Whatever the preferred period, Puebla has a fine well-preserved building, often fully furnished. The Museo Bello, gift of the Bello family, is a dignified nineteenth-century home with the family's living-rooms completely furnished. The original Bello, as a lad in Vera Cruz, fought against the Yankee invasion of 1846; as a man he fought against the French; and, as a Mexican, he declined for his wife the honor of serving as lady-in-waiting to Carlota. "She," wrote the stout old patriot, "who is queen and mistress of a home need not be a maid in anybody's house."

La Casa Alfeñique (almond-cake house) is a pink-and-white confectioner's delight, churrigueresque gone to sugar. Its museum contains some fine Aztec paintings of Cortés's march. Its top floor has been restored as a colonial palace worthy to house a viceroy. Dozens of churches give the city as many charming small parks; their tiled domes make it look, from the hills, like a basket of Easter eggs.

A small house is shown as the *china poblana*'s home, and a stone in the church of La Compañía de Jesús dates her burial in 1688. The *china poblana* (Chinese Pueblan) was a Chinese girl captured in Asiatic waters by pirates, rescued, and carried to Acapulco, where a charitable Puebla gentleman befriended her and took her home to his wife. Baptized Catarina, the girl grew in grace and was known for her charities. She wore a full red skirt with green yoke and the customary white blouse and dark *rebozo*. This is the basis of the heavily spangled skirt, richly embroidered blouse, and silk *rebozo* that Mexican dancers wear.

Puebla's "Hidden Convent," Santa Mónica, is secret no longer. All nunneries were closed by the Juárez reforms, but Santa Mónica went on for seventy-seven years. Surrounded by busy streets, girls there took the veil and lived out long lives in cells and cloisters opening on patios grown with orange trees and flowering vines. The place, now a national museum, is entered stupidly through a door; visitors used to go in as the police went, and that was more exciting.

An alert policeman, stationed across the street, noticed that a great amount of food was going into what appeared to be a poor apartment house. He called, and was received by a lady sewing on a machine near a wall cupboard. The officer, chatting, spied an electric bell under a dusty paper wreath. Quickly he pushed the button, and the back of the cupboard slid aside, revealing the startled face of a nun. He acted fast, but the officers were not quick enough to catch the fifty-two nuns, who escaped through the woodbox in the Mother Superior's bathroom, the only item of comfort in the house. The sisters had passed through the latticed choir, from which they had been accustomed to hear Mass, and into the church. Friends gave them black shawls, and so they slipped unnoticed through the streets to homes where they were protected. Doubtless many of them still live so.

Much of the convent has been preserved and given verisimilitude with wax figures of kneeling nuns. In an underground chapel knotted scourges hang over each nun's chair, and hair shirts and other penitential articles are displayed. No nun ever left the convent; inscriptions in the burial crypt show that most of them lived to be eighty or ninety years old. Only one stone marks the pitiful end of a girl of twenty, who apparently died by her own hand. The cells, left for years as the nuns used them, contained their handiwork—tiny settings for miniature saints of the kitchen or the farm, exquisite garments for the Infant Jesus or for Saint Elizabeth, who was a queen. Recently these touching exhibits have been removed to a museum in Mexico.

A gayer convent is that of Santa Rosa, whose big tiled kitchens are famous for the concoction of *mole poblano*, Mexico's superlative festival dish. Salazar Monroy, in *La Típica Cocina Poblana*, tells that when a colonial viceroy visited Puebla, all the convents vied to entertain him suitably. The Mother Superior of Santa Rosa charged Sor Andrea de la Asunción, mistress extraordinary of cookery, to outdo herself. Sor Andrea put a turkey to simmer and assembled all her sharpest chiles, subtlest spices, and most savory herbs, grinding them with almonds and peanuts. She toasted bread crumbs and fried bananas to thicken the gravy and added bitter black chocolate to darken it. So, by testing and tasting and by sheer genius, Sor Andrea made *mole poblano de guajalote* (turkey). The Viceroy and the Bishop, who was his host, were enchanted, and all the other convents begged for the recipe.

Srta. Chuchita, a mistress of cookery herself, said that Sor Andrea's secret lay in the toasting and frying. She added sadly that no perfect *mole* could ever be made in the

United States, as that country lacks most of the necessary ingredients. It would be best, she thought, to start with a good canned *mole* sauce and add spices to taste. Srta. Chuchita was a slender, stooped little body, always bustling off with the maid to Puebla's excellent market. She never seemed to eat; she was always planning food for others. Afternoons she taught fine cookery to ladies whose husbands disapproved of their leaving their own kitchens even for a cooking-school.

Srta. Chuchita's mornings, from nine to two, were spent in the government pawn shop, where she dealt with people asking loans on sewing-machines, bicycles, electric motors, even jewelry and fine furniture. Sometimes only the price of breakfast was asked. Loans are seldom refused, interest is low, articles are kept in clean, well-ventilated lofts, and many families are kept afloat during hard times.

Srta. Chuchita was the eldest of three sisters who permitted me to share their home. Daughters of a Tlaxcalan *hacendado*, they had seen the maguey fields turned into *ejidos;* a half-brother lived in the mansion, but the gently bred sisters had had to go to work. Their simple living in a small apartment was a triumph of aristocratic tradition over working hours and small pay. Each sister held more than one job and made her own clothes. But they maintained old friendships and appeared at social affairs as smartly turned out as their affluent friends.

Social life in conservative Puebla follows the Church calendar, which determines many family festivals. The infant at baptism is held by his godparents, who will share his entire life. Parents and godparents are *compadres* (co-parents), a religious relationship that explains much in Mexican life. Inconceivable that one could fail to assist—or to protect—a *compadre!* Children are confirmed in infancy, and the first communion, often given before a child is ten, is marked by social affairs in honor of the tots in white.

Mexico's traditional time for gifts is not Christmas, but *diá de los reyes*, Twelfth Night. Advertising has given Mexican youngsters the idea of demanding Christmas trees and presents in December, but they still write letters to the Wise Men and set shoes outside the door for Twelfth Night.

A girl's fifteenth birthday marks her coming-out. She attends Mass with her parents and godparents and a flock of maidens as beruffled as bridesmaids. I was a guest at such a ceremony and at breakfast in an old garden. Long tables were laid with cold meats, jellies, and salads, and white-coated waiters offered steaming platters of fluffy rice with shrimps or clams. Young men, callow students or softly mustached young lawyers and doctors, danced with the girls; while older gentlemen presided over a table where wines shared honors with the sparkling cider from Puebla's orchards. Weddings are marked by two old customs we do not know. Special godparents of the marriage are quite as important as young attendants, and during the service a silver chain or white ribbon is laid across the couple's shoulders; sometimes the symbolism includes momentarily covering the groom with the bride's veil.

Carnival in Puebla, as in all Catholic cities, is a gay time, but in conservative Puebla Lent has cast its shadows before, and even Carnival menus feature Lent's special dishes of fish, mushrooms, and eggs. Pueblans manage to eat well even when fasting, and every holiday has its traditional dish. On the *día del Carmen* in August every girl named María del Carmen is feted with *buñuelos de rodilla* (knee fritters). These should be bought from street vendors near the church of El Carmen, where women do indeed shape *buñuelos* over the bare knee, made sanitary with a clean napkin. These fritters, flavored with anise, crisped in deep fat, and served with sugar syrup, are a real delicacy.

Puebla, like all Mexico, observes the *día de los muertos*, November 2, with prayer and visits to the graves. But even the sophisticated buy buns marked with crossbones and delight children with jiggling skeletons, candy skulls, and funeral processions that turn with a crank to move paper priests with chick-pea heads and blue coffins with cadavers on top. Simple families lay a table with the best cloth, wax candles in black pottery holders, and the dear departed's preferred food, whose spirit will be absorbed by the ghosts. Only the best of everything will do. Pawn shops notice a sharp rise in loans, and merchants make fortunes by cornering the wax market; tallow tapers are considered too cheap for the beloved dead.

Puebla celebrates national holidays too, particularly the Cinco de Mayo, Fifth of May, the anniversary of the day in 1867 when poorly armed Mexicans here withstood trained French troops. The French General Laurencez had incautiously written Napoleon III that defeating this undisciplined rabble would be no trouble at all. The caretaker's son at Fort Guadalupe, where the battle was fought, loves to show that letter because there France's famous Zouaves were roundly trounced by General Zaragoza's forces. A young officer named Porfirio Díaz distinguished himself there too. The battle was only a setback for the invaders, but Mexicans celebrate it as an example of magnificent bravery against overwhelming odds.

Early on the Fifth of May Puebla's streets were jammed with people. We finally ceased pushing in front of the Church of La Compañía, where any further movement was impossible anyway.

The procession, when it belatedly appeared, consisted mostly of schoolchildren drilled and uniformed, if only with bits of insignia. They moved in step with their drum corps; some younger groups wearied, but all kept on for three full hours. Indeed, the Mexican's unconquerable spirit showed well in that crowd that day. Police tried to hold back the people who surged into the street, impeding the parade. They were like water; pushed back with guns, besought with words, they seeped out again. An officer came along, haranguing the crowd, begging space for the marchers. Nobody gave him any attention. When he halted a well-dressed woman, she waved a paper. When he insisted, she stood. What dignified officer would be caught dragging off a lady with a paper? He desisted. The crowd was amused. If Mexico is ever again threatened with invasion, it need only mass its frontiers with fiesta crowds.

Children were followed by the military, well turned out, smartly drilled, and well equipped. Trucks and tanks, a brigade of messengers on bicycles, a Red Cross unit, a medical corps. Zacapoaxtla Indians, famous for their stand against the French, wore an adaptation of their native dress, but their arms were of the best; their pride was manifest in every haughty head and every military stride.

Puebla is proud of its Zacapoaxtlas, who dance at all its fiestas, and Indians are a part of the city as they roam the streets with things to sell. But Puebla is unalterably a white man's city whose Spanish tradition has been reinforced by immigration from Spain. Some Spaniards came with wealth, some acquired it, others brought culture that has enriched the city and its university. Pueblans do not go in for Indianism. They accept culture without isms and support many societies dedicated to the arts. Puebla de los Angeles has somehow managed to remain a Spanish and Catholic city while becoming patriotically Mexican too.

PART NINE

Capital and Center

XXXII

MEXICO, THE CAPITAL

◖ MEXICO, the capital, is the apex, the heart of the Republic; its every throb reaches somehow the remotest hamlet and the most primitive Indian. All roads lead to Mexico, distances throughout the country are figured from its Zócalo. The city of Mexico lies in the Distrito Federal as our Washington in the District of Columbia; but Mexico not only is the center of government, but also of industry, the arts, and religion. Descendants of all the people who have made its long history throng streets whose architecture is of every style from Cortés's time to our own. Mexico is consequently one of the world's most beautiful and thrilling capitals.

The city, set in a wide valley 7,439 feet above sea level, is dominated on clear days by its stupendous volcanoes, Popocatépetl and Ixtaccíhuatl; on dull days by the smoky cloud of its industrial plants. Travelers by air land at a modern airport where a solicitous tourist bureau has provided English-speaking aides and dependable taxi-drivers. Motorists from the north, as most approach the city, come in over a low eminence to see Mexico spread out in muted color or flashing lights. The tourist bureau is there too with maps and guide service. The prudent newcomer will demand credentials, as clever crooks also flash official-looking cards.

The highway which bisects the city from north to south, the Avenida Insurgentes, keeps the same name all the way, a gratifying peculiarity in a city where most streets change their names every few blocks. At once the driver is engulfed in Mexico's traffic, which will test his skill, however good he may be elsewhere. No stranger will ever match the sure eye and quick co-ordination of the Mexican driver, who silently—honking is against the law—swoops past with infinitesimal leeway. A miss is as good as a mile, and much more fun. Cars and buses crowd each other, passing on right or left, dodging from lane to lane, turning right from the left lane and left from the right with never a hand signal. Among them skim the bicycles, pedaled by boys with sidecars or with baskets on their heads, or the more terrifying motorcycles.

Traffic is regulated; oh, yes. At busy corners are traffic lights—sometimes low, sometimes high, sometimes in the middle. Then, as one has become habituated to lights, there is no light, but a cop on a box. He faces traffic or turns his back to stop it; his whistle may mean stop or go or just that he feels like blowing. At night his red light describes parabolas rather than a line to follow. It is safest to follow other drivers, letting the most daring run interference. These traffic officers are always polite; they will often hold up traffic to permit a greenhorn to make a wrong turn. But they never try to regulate the pedestrian, who is an untrammeled citizen edging between fenders, dashing through every break in the line. Vendors work among the cars at every corner, offering chamois skins, fruits and vegetables, brooms and feather dusters, and, in season, *gusanos de maguey* (maguey worms), which are as great a delicacy in Mexico as snails in France.

The city's east-west axis, while changing its name several times, is for most of its length El Paseo de la Reforma. It also tells the longest story. It starts at the Zócalo, though before reaching that splendid plaza the traveler from the east will have passed through many crowded streets of sixteenth-century palaces. Here are old churches with markets in their laps, the ancient home of the Inquisition, and magnificent old buildings formerly occupied by the University's scattered schools. The Zócalo is a noble square bounded by four-lane avenues and surrounded by magnificent buildings. The Spaniards erected their Cathedral on the site of the Aztec *teocalli* (temple), whose human sacrifices had filled them with horror. Begun in 1573 and completed in 1815, this largest religious building in the Americas is of many styles. The National Palace, which houses the federal executive offices, stands where Moctezuma's palace was. Soldiers guard its wide entrances, Diego Rivera has painted Mexico's history on its patio walls, and it reaches back to the National Museum, bursting with ancient arts. The wealth, energy, and skills of the Spanish are best revealed in these sixteenth- and seventeenth-century buildings.

Three streets lead westward from the Zócalo: 16 de Septiembre, 5 de Mayo, and the central one, Francisco I. Madero. This last, formerly called Calle de los Plateros, then Avenida San Francisco, clearly reflects Mexico's architectural history. The heavy colonial style near the Zócalo is succeeded by the more sumptuous taste of the Palacio Iturbide and the eighteenth-century House of Tiles. Churches have been crowded as their convents were preempted for business, and show windows have replaced iron grilles. The House of Tiles was grandest as the Jockey Club of Don Porfirio's day. In time it occurred to the Sanborn brothers that a drugstore there might do well. It did, and, as drugstores will, it has expanded into a restaurant, a curio store, and the tourists' favorite hangout.

Avenida Francisco Madero ends where it is crossed by Avenida San Juan de Letrán, a street that Mexico widened into a much-needed traffic artery by demolishing some of its finest colonial buildings. Roaring with traffic, it now passes between tall new buildings whose shining gray, black, chromium and glass functionalism marks the end of the "City of Palaces," as Mexico was called.

Before leaving the Avenida Madero, the pedestrian must shove his way through a crowded planked passage. This masks the forty-five-story steel skeleton of Mexico's tallest skyscraper, defiant evidence of the city's determination to be a modern metropolis the equal of any, and its disregard of its own peculiarities. Before walls began to cover the girders, work was suspended with the explanation that re-financing was necessary. Rumors insisted that as the weight increased, the foundations had begun to sink, endangering its neighbors. So it remains a looming question mark.

Mexico, the magnificent city, is set on sand. When the conquerors destroyed Tenochtitlán, they drained the lake and built on its sandy bottom. In time, the heavy buildings began to sink. This is most evident in Díaz's Carrara marble Opera House, which now houses El Instituto Nacional de Bellas Artes. It has sunk a couple of feet, as have many other buildings; walls crack, windows and doors list, plumbing-fixtures leave the walls. Engineers explain that the original base of wet sand, which tended to float the city, has been pumped dry by the three thousand wells that supply the city with water. Proposed solutions of the problem range from stopping all the wells and bringing water from the mountains, to displacing enough of the underlying mud to compensate for the weight of the building above. The National Lottery Building, most successful at maintaining its equilibrium, rests on concrete pillars. No sure solution has been found, but the Ruiz Cortines administration began a program of clearing sludge out of sewers and enlarging the sewer system; this alleviates some distressing features of the annual rains.

The main thoroughfare, beyond the Palacio de Bellas Artes, becomes Avenida Juárez, which is twice as wide as Avenida Madero. It runs for four blocks along the Alameda, which, beginning as a bull ring and cockpit, was later Frenchified into the pretty park it is now. Children frolic there, Indians rest their burdens, and during the long lunch hour young lovers moon there in the unselfconscious Mexican way. At midday, too, certain benches are regularly filled by a group of Chinese, mostly old, always vociferous and argumentative.

Avenida Juárez does not go far. It ends at the equestrian statue of Carlos IV, which Mexicans call *El Caballito* (The Little Horse); as Avenida del Ejido it continues to the Monument of the Revolution. This is a triumphal arch topped by chunky Indian figures such as were popular when the exaltation of the aborigine was at its height. But as though symbolic of Mexico's actual development, traffic veers southwestward to follow the beautiful six-lane boulevard of the Paseo de la Reforma to Chapultepec Park and Castle. The Paseo shows traces of all its history; one era's taste even planted the central parkway with desert cactus, though the circles known as *glorietas* (leafy spots) still flourish their palms above thick shrubbery. Many of them are adorned with statues: Columbus, Cuauhtémoc, the golden angel of independence on a tall column, Diana, and Bolívar. Statues of heroes adorn the walks where groups of schoolchildren play on holidays, apartment-dwellers walk their dogs at night, and the highest-class prostitutes stroll in haughty disregard of any man not driving a superior car. Their methods are obvious; their bargaining is open.

Along the Paseo are some of Mexico's smartest hotels and restaurants, some modern business buildings, and a few solid-glass apartment houses. Among them stand the mansions, with mansard roofs, double stairways, and French windows, which were built in the period when Mexico was most slavishly aping the French. Some have sunk in the social scale to see gardens used as parking-lots, houses as cheap rooming-houses. But, happily, appreciative architects have remodeled old houses into smart shops, galleries, and restaurants without destroying their grace or style. "Just like the rue de la Paix," said a Francophile.

The Paseo de la Reforma enters Chapultepec Park at the statue of Bolívar and, leaving the Park, turns left and climbs a gradual hill to Las Lomas de Chapultepec, one of the city's wealthiest districts. It too recalls Mexico's history. A few houses are French; many are built with porches like United States homes or in California's Spanish style. But the newer homes are modern in style and materials. Mexicans, in this land of sunshine and light, have at last permitted both to enter their homes. Few new home have patios; they run to lawns set with outdoor furniture, but they are still protected by iron fences and locked gates in the Spanish-Moorish way.

Chapultepec Park is still shaded by the majestic *ahue-huetes* (cedars) that Moctezuma knew; lesser growth under them shimmers with moving sunflecks and shadows. One can explore these woods for hours and find new fountains, tiled benches, and statues hidden in leafy coves around the lake. Bridle paths are kept clear for horsemen, many of them members of the *charro* associations that keep alive Mexico's tradition of superior horsemanship. Few are too haughty to pose for tourists' cameras. Horse-lovers will find, just beyond the park, Sunday exhibitions of riding and roping at El Rancho de Charro, and excellent racing and high betting at El Hipódromo de las Américas.

Chapultepec Park on Sunday is an entrancing scene of Mexican family life. A few young couples drift in rowboats on the lake, and old people sit on benches to hear the band concert. But most of the people come in family groups. Fathers proudly lead small boys in long trousers and rakish hats and tiny girls in ruffled dresses and big hair bows. This must be when Mother is "giving light" to another baby; many a mother with two or three children under school age is clearly expecting another. Youngsters ride ponies and merry-go-rounds, clamber over playground equipment, and recover at soft-drink booths.

Chapultepec Castle, built in 1783 for a viceroy's red-haired bride, was neglected during the Wars of Independence, but in the nineteenth century it housed the national Military Academy. This was the hilltop castle that the Boy Heroes so nobly defended in 1846. Maximilian later refurbished the castle and made its gardens look like the Bois de Boulogne. Mexico's presidents lived in the castle during the revolutionary years, and then it was converted into a museum. The Ruiz Cortines administration has made it a military academy again, depriving visitors of one of the finest views of the city.

The southbound visitor will see more of growing Mexico. Avenida Insurgentes, after crossing La Reforma at Cuauhtémoc's statue, becomes busier and noisier with every block until it emerges from the city as highway again. It was once a fashionable thoroughfare between country homes, and one may still turn up leafy streets into tranquil plazas. But most new homes are the *multifamiliares*, huge hives of low-rental apartments for federal employees. Insurgentes, dazzling with neon lights and jittery with moving advertisements, grows more modern yearly as outmoded architecture yields to glass towers and horizontal lines. Here the Mexican love of color has had free and often beautiful play in department stores, motor showroom, theaters, and supermarkets.

Avenida Insurgentes calms down a bit, beyond all that, where it has a central parkway and carries only suburbanites to their homes in San Ángel, now Ciudad Bolívar, Coyoacán, and other ancient pueblos. Traffic even here is dizzy on Sundays when the bullfight or football crowds pour into it, or when the Insurgentes Theater is offering a popular show. This theater's bulging front flaunts Rivera's most posterish mural of the history of Mexican drama. It runs from Indian rites to movie queens, with Cantinflas in the middle turning his back on wealth to serve the poor. Indoors, the theater is a triumph of designing for sight and sound, charming in décor.

Insurgentes leaves the city between Mexico's two grandest architectural achievements—La Ciudad Universitaria, planned as hemispheric as well as national cultural center, and Los Jardines del Pedregal, a private venture in turning a lava flow into the city's smartest residential district. The Pedregal, one thousand acres of lava congealed in rough waves, was considered a worthless, snake-infested wasteland until Luis Barragán, engineer and architect, had a vision of homes and gardens there. He saw that the land's contour would give every house a wide view and that the lava's dull grays and brownish blacks would make a strong background for plants. The lava held pockets of rich virgin soil, and there was ample underground water.

The start was difficult, even for a rich man with an enthusiastic partner. Nobody would invest in such desolation, so the partners decided to turn desolation into paradise. They laid a pink cement driveway from the highway to their lofty gate of orange slats set off by tall jets of water falling into a blue pool. They laid out streets planted with native cactus, yucca, maguey, and *colorín*, a naked plant that bears coral blossoms in winter and green leaves in summer. They softened all this angularity with pepper trees, also native to the lava. Their pride was a garden of a beauty that catches the breath of visitors from every country on earth. An orange gravel path winds around the jutting lava, where lawns seem greener than natural and brilliant flowers riot in dissonances that are cooled by white lilies and blue plumbago.

Such a garden naturally attracted visitors and comment,

but buyers came slowly. The partners had to sell 300,000 square meters at less than cost to tempt a few builders. But persistence won. Prices, beginning at thirty-five centavos a square meter, soared to seventy-five pesos, and the Pedregal became the most fashionable place to live. It is a restricted area, where builders must agree to surround their lots with stone walls, build with flat roofs and without the tiled roofs known scornfully as "California style." Palms are also taboo, as are *frontón* courts and screened windows. How fly-hating foreigners will make out is not revealed, but many are buying there. The effect of all those stone walls is not as prisonlike as one might fear; many entrances are gay with plants, pools, or fountains, and louvered gates and fences permit entrancing glimpses of houses and gardens.

La Ciudad Universitaria is even more overwhelming. Here Mexican architects have combined modern materials and techniques with typically Mexican form and decoration. Mexico being short of steel, they have used *ferroconcreto* (iron-braced concrete) and native stone in many colors. The directing architect, Carlos Lazo, made effective use of contour by hollowing out of the lava the magnificent sweep of the Olympic stadium. Its décor is a frieze of painted stones designed by Diego Rivera to illustrate Mexico's sports under the traditional Olympic torch.

The administration building provides the highest accent as it rises in glass to skyscraper height where there seems little reason to scrape the sky. It is adorned by scenes of youth serving Mexico with knowledge, painted by David Siqueiros in his favorite medium of Duco. The Tower of Science balances the administration building with flat yellow walls, and between them stands the library. This gracious and harmonious building was designed by Juan O'Gorman and decorated with stone mosaics whose muted colors are repeated in windows of Puebla onyx, which also provides soft reading-light indoors. These massive structures are partly balanced by solidly built academic buildings made of native stone, brick, and concrete. But many rooflines are low and odd, as they follow tiered seats inside or bulge into beehive skylights. The whole seems to lack unity of style or effect.

The only motor road circles the entire campus, passing playing-fields for every sport and swimming-pools large enough for hundreds of swimmers. The inner courts and buildings are connected by arcades into departmental units. The over-all plan includes dormitories for both men and women, separate houses and apartment dwellings for professors, a shopping-center, lecture halls, and auditoriums. There is even a Catholic church, with priest's house and clubrooms. This is privately owned, though built on government land.

Mexico's University, founded in 1553, began as a theological school for favored youths. The revolution changed that, and within this century students of all classes came to crowd the old convents where lecture rooms were badly lighted, laboratories were inadequate, and libraries—often filled with priceless tomes—offered few facilities for modern study. Overcrowding became acute. Ten thousand students in 1910 had become 29,000 in 1950. There was no campus, and there were no dormitories; students, who often lived in slum conditions, gathered in *pulquerías* or rioted through the streets. Professors, paid too little to give full time to their courses, practiced their professions, lecturing only a few hours weekly. Many of these problems remain unsolved, especially that of adequate pay for professors. But La Ciudad Universitaria stands as the realization of the educators' dream of a proper plant in which to prepare young Mexicans to take their place in the modern world.

XXXIII

FOLK ART BECOMES BIG BUSINESS

⊂₿ Fred Davis, whose first name seems a title, likes to entertain at breakfast. His guest, entering the *zaguán*, faces a dizzy little bar in the old carriage house across the patio. The host, a mild gentleman with youthful face, retreating fair hair, and well-kept hands, resembles a city banker in an exclusive club. Breakfast is served in the sunny corner of a *sala* lined with books on Mexico, many autographed to the friend who helped in their making. All the rooms are filled with pictures, statues, carvings, and tapestries— all the beauties that came from Europe and the Orient—and with Mexican Indian handiwork. "Really good pieces of Mexican popular arts," says Fred Davis, "are so fine in design and so exquisite in color that they will fit into any environment." Naturally such a man is the final authority on both colonial and folk art. Collectors ask his judgment and artisans bring him their handiwork, knowing that if it is good he will buy it. If he refuses a piece, he often suggests how to make a better one.

Fred Davis dislikes talking about himself, but he talks freely of the growing appreciation of Mexican Indian crafts, and that is largely the story of Fred Davis in Mexico. He began selling Indians trinkets along with newspapers and chewing-gum on Southern Pacific trains. When the Sonora News Company expanded to a store in Mexico, young Fred went along to the new place in the Palacio Iturbide on Avenide San Francisco. There he sold antiques to such buyers as Edward Doheny and William Randolph Hearst, who arrived in private cars. The antiques, after 1910, came on the market in a flood of family treasures, sometimes openly sold as collections, sometimes brought in secret by family servants.

Among the European articles were some that were made on the haciendas by native craftsmen. Every *hacendado* had valued his wool serape, woven in zigzags and stripes, satin-soft, and firm enough to hold water. These were the original Saltillos. Every lady had drawnwork linen handkerchiefs, tablecloths, and napkins, and every church owned drawnwork altar cloths. The Sonora News, supplying skilled women with Belfast linen, shipped thousands of dollars' worth of drawnwork to Marshall Field and Carson Pirie Scott in Chicago. This is one of the lost arts, due to the difficulty in getting materials, and the deft fingers that made it are now producing crude embroidery on coarse cotton.

Silver and some gold filigree had been made for people who could not afford fine jewels; bracelets, necklaces and earrings sold well in the United States. These articles were produced by Indians for the upper twenty per cent of the population. What Indians made for themselves was quite unknown; no Mexican hidalgo, with his scorn of the Indian, could have seen merit in his crafts. Only a person with the taste to recognize beauty in alien arts could penetrate that fog. Fred Davis was that person.

Living in rooms over the store, Fred Davis quietly surrounded himself with what he liked. The Indians' straw hats, leather sandals, and woolen blankets; the women's skirts, tunics, and *rebozos*. He used the pottery they used for cooking, their floor mats, and carrying-baskets. And he found true artistry in the saints they carved, the toys and flowers they made for their fiestas. "I just bought what I liked," he explains, "and sometimes I liked things so well

I wouldn't sell them." This by way of explaining that he is not really a collector, just a merchant.

As a merchant, Fred Davis made a double contribution. By demanding the best, he upheld standards. As a seller, he managed to give many customers a taste for good work. "I could, you see, explain to a clerk why I had refused a piece of sloppy work. Then it would be easier to sell something good to a customer who just happened to overhear what I said."

Fred Davis is quick to point out that he was not alone in trying to save the Indians' ancient arts. Many Mexicans shared his enthusiasm. Ernesto Cervantes of Oaxaca went into the blanket business to save the Indian weavers from merchants who were selling them aniline dyes and promoting hideous designs. "No self-respecting Indian would buy one," said Sr. Cervantes, who, by buying what the Indians liked, has built up a successful business in Oaxaca and on Avenida Juárez in Mexico City.

World War I helped this development as people cut off from Europe discovered Mexico. Artists and writers furnished peasant houses with what their neighbors made; tourists saw, admired, and bought. But the real job of dignifying the Mexican crafts was done by Mexicans after the revolution. Painters, through their frescoes, gave the Indian a sense of his own worth, and educators, headed by José Vasconcelos, Manuel Gamio, and Moisés Sáenz, included crafts in their enlightened educational program. Moisés Sáenz took the practical step of opening a shop in Mexico whose high standards reinforced the work of Fred Davis and Ernesto Cervantes. And about this time Fred Davis hired a salesman who was perhaps the most picturesque invader since the conquest. This was René d'Harnoncourt.

He was an Austrian count who had been too young to

serve in the war, had been refused admission to the United States, and was so broke on landing at Vera Cruz that he borrowed the fifty-peso landing-fee from a shipboard acquaintance. He was six feet six inches tall and he wore a black bowler, riding-boots, and a checked coat obviously not tailored to his measure. But his ready smile and keen bright eyes were winning, and the monocle dangling from a black ribbon was most diverting. René knew five or six languages, including a Gypsy dialect, but neither Spanish nor English. He had, however, the essentials for doing well in a new land. He meant to get on; he was adaptable and friendly and quick to recognize worth and beauty anywhere. The going was hard. The young aristocrat hung around the bull ring making sketches to sell to tourists. He bought Indian idols for William Green, an oil man with a taste for ancient art. He learned dozens of new words and songs daily. His first break came when Fred Davis gave him a job in the Sonora News, where he was soon making sales in both Spanish and English and dazzling tourists with his courtly manners and monocle. He was soon offering tea—or tequila, which came at one peso a bottle—to likely customers in his penthouse. He had furnished the washer-woman's shelter on a roof with straw mats, serapes, bean pots, and maguey chairs, and he had a magnificent view of the mountains.

René's real talent appeared when he went out to buy for the shop. Astride tiny horses with his knees knocking his chin, he rode rocky trails to wherever good workmen were making things. Every village had its specialty. Gourd birds or straw toys. Lava corn-grinders. Heavy cotton in double weave. Painted jars. René's unfailing selection of the best pieces, and his courteous request for more, inspired good workmen and actually revived several arts. He asked to be taught how the old dyes were made and offered to buy any weavings so colored. His best persuader was his

The Engineering Building

UNIVERSITY CITY

The Olympic Stadium (it seats more than 100,000 spectators), with mural-in-depth by Diego Rivera

The Pedregal: *an exclusive, fashionable suburb in the great lava field*

readiness to buy. So he returned to the Sonora News leading caravans of men and burros loaded with entrancing articles such as had never been offered for sale before.

So far, dealers were buying what Indians made for themselves. The idea of teaching them to make articles for modern homes was due to William Spratling of Taxco. He might have become notable as a writer on Mexico—his *Little Mexico* is one of the most sensitive studies of the people—but chance turned him to silver-making. Naturally he furnished his own home with Mexican crafts; often he designed furniture, rugs, and tinware, such articles as are sold widely now. Spratling was among the advisers of Ambassador and Mrs. Morrow when they built and furnished a home in Cuernavaca, and he helped Mrs. Morrow collect an exhibition for the Carnegie Institute to send to the United States. Mrs. Morrow's choice of René d'Harnoncourt to travel with the show was inspired. He was more acceptable to Mexicans than any gringo, and his unique charm, wide knowledge, and cultivated taste helped to make the show a success. This led indirectly to his later work as government consultant in primitive arts of the Americas and his appointment finally as Director of the Museum of Modern Art in New York.

The Mexican government had never lost interest in the development of Indian arts. The National Indian Institute had, in 1922, sent an exhibition of Mexican arts and crafts to Los Angeles and later to Argentina and Brazil. Its organizers—the painters Dr. Atl, Roberto Montenegro, Miguel Covarrubias, and Rufino Tamayo and the anthropologists Alfonso Caso and Miguel O. de Mendizábal—had made studies of the basic æsthetics of Indian art, but they went no further. The idea seemed to have spent itself. Then, in 1940, delegates from several American nations met as the First Indian Congress at Pátzcuaro. Mexico, always the leader, presented a resolution calling for the protection of Indian arts. The notion struck most delegates as too arty, and little came of it in the other countries. But Mexico, having taken a stand, proceeded with it; in 1940 it sent a magnificent show—*Twenty Centuries of Mexican Art*—to the Museum of Modern Art in New York.

The government, in 1948, established a board for the practical purpose of preserving the native arts while developing them as a business. Alfonso Caso and Ignacio Marquina, archæologists; Jorge Enciso and Miguel Covarrubias, anthropologists; Alfonso Best-Maugard, painter; and Fred Davis were appointed to the board of directors, which will be self-perpetuating and hence free of politics. They made their executive secretary Dr. Daniel Rubín de la Borbolla, Director of the National Anthropological Institute. He also serves as Director of the Museo de Industrias y Artes Populares on Avenida Juárez.

This institution exhibits rare examples of the best popular arts, but it is also a shop. Dusty Indians from the sierra brush past students of design, buyers from smart city shops, and tourists. The director is modest in his claims. "It is an experiment," he said, "no more. We need time, maybe even to get rid of some of our own false ideas. Maybe we are too sentimental. But we are learning. And broadening as we constantly run into national problems. Our workers must be supplied with wool, wood, leather, metals. We are forever fighting off synthetic materials, which are often cheaper, but which tend to debase the work."

The Museum's field workers visit the villages and the workers who may be using inferior materials and doing sloppy work. They then ascertain the price of materials and how much it costs a family to make an article if several work at it; this estimate includes living-expenses and the demands of the corn patch and the stock. On that basis the Museum computes its prices.

They then ask the best craftsman, usually a man much

respected; if he can make something like a superior sample offered. Not a copy, but something like it. Indeed he can. He then shows his best work, which he has made for his *feria*, the regional fair, where it will compete with the best work of his compeers. The notion of making his best for sale is often new. But the Indian's craft and good taste have not been lost. "On this foundation," says Dr. de la Borbolla, "anything can be built."

It is often necessary to finance a family during the work, to provide materials, even to give advice and social service. "We may give technical advice," says Dr. de la Borbolla, "but never æsthetic direction. We buy only what is good, but the Indian recognizes that as well as we do. Any true craftsman prefers to do his best, but if anyone likes to turn out shoddy work for other markets, he is naturally free to do so. We put our stamp on approved work, whether we sell it or not; we aim at no exclusiveness. And most merchants, once they understand that, are glad to get better work."

Villagers are more distrustful than merchants. Above all, they distrust paper. Old men have painful memories of being tricked out of lands, into the army, or defrauded of wages just by marking a cross where a white man indicated. Anyway, they won't sign. One old man said: "My word has been good for sixty years. I won't shame my word by putting my mark on paper." This fear of fraud is general, so the Museum does not insist upon written contracts. It has lent thousands of pesos throughout the country without signature or security, and in only one case has the borrower failed to pay. Surely this is a record worthy of any people at any stage of development.

What is the result of this work? It is estimated that some 2,000,000 people, out of the population of 24,000,000, live wholly or in part as craft workers. The Museum certainly does not reach them all, but its influence is not negligible, and it is educating buyers as well as workers. Salesmen in the shop say that buyers are more conscious of good materials than of good taste, but that on the whole they prefer good things. And the Museum staff agree that all poor taste is not gringo. "You can see Mexicans in any market," says Dr. de la Borbolla, "buying hideous horrors." But Mexicans too are beginning to appreciate peasant crafts.

Fred Davis says that years ago Mexican ladies in his shop used to burble *"Que precioso!"* over something made in their own village market. They never went near a market. Now they are making Mexican rooms in their modern homes. "They are as stylish," he says, "as Turkish corners were when I was a kid."

This Museum makes no effort to indicate how Indian crafts may be used in a modern home, but a clever buyer soon discovers that she can acquire stout furniture of native wood or bamboo with cane or leather seats, reed floor or table mats, and complete dinner service of fine Tlaquepaque or Puebla ware or the cruder pottery from Oaxaca or other places. She can buy glass in blue, green, mauve, or amber and complete her color scheme with fine cotton tablecloths and napkins. She can choose silver tableware and jewelry of silver, gold, or copper set with native jade, azurite, amethyst, and opal. And if her fancy runs free, she can indulge in painted wood or plaster altar ornaments or toys, tiny horsehair trinkets, or bits of featherwork, all that remains of Moctezuma's sweeping capes.

The Museum is a self-supporting business with a fair profit to invest in materials, tools, and workers. The social program is vital. De la Borbolla says: "The persistence of popular arts depends upon women and children. Men take a job in town or go as *braceros*, but women and children stay at home and keep their fingers busy. They often need help or advice." He chuckled. "So do we. The only one of us who knows merchandising is Fred Davis, but he is generous with his advice."

The Museum has stepped into a growing business, which has expanded, since Fred Davis came to Mexico, into one of the country's greatest sources of income, ranking close to oil and mines. Popular arts altogether bring in over one hundred million pesos a year, of which perhaps twenty-five million goes to the artisans. Not a negligible addition to the farm income.

The Museum has no detailed plans for developing new crafts or reviving old ones, though it has done so at Tzintzuntzan. The directors hope that individuals will take the lead; they believe that filigree work may be revived with the adoption of certain Italian and Portuguese techniques brought in by refugees. Mexico may even in time spin that #300 cotton thread that made the lovely old *rebozos* soft enough to pull through a finger ring. The Instituto Allende is studying old dyes; and people who are frankly commercial are experimenting with silkworms and flax. Designers are using Mexican materials and designs in smart clothes that have been successfully shown in New York and Paris.

Altogether, Daniel Rubín de la Borbolla refuses to admit that there are any lost arts in Mexico, though a few may have been temporarily mislaid. Nor will he or his associates admit that there are any limits to what Mexicans can do with this government project standing by to help.

XXXIV

PEOPLE OF THE CAPITAL

⏚ THE CAPITAL's three million inhabitants are drawn from all the human elements that compose the Republic. One meets them all on the streets. "Unintegrated" village Indians timidly follow a leader among busy people in city dress. More tragic Indians, wretchedly dirty, sit on the pavements begging "for the love of God." Often they are despairing refugees from eroded districts; here they only increase the numbers of the miserable poor who form a human base as unstable as the moist sand on which the city rests.

Their plight and its importance are fully recognized by informed leaders. President Ruiz Cortines, in his 1953 report to the nation, spoke at length on national misery. A congress of social workers reported that of 442,500 children between thirteen and eighteen in the capital, 49,368 were in school and the same number working. If half the rest of them were girls and at home, many boys were left adrift to become delinquents. Government films, widely shown, picture life in the "sand mines," dug into the *barrancas* just below the wealthy Lomas de Chapultepec. A mother, standing in her hovel's sack-hung doorway, handed her son a cup of herb tea—all she could give him for breakfast. It showed the boy at school later, too listless to learn or to play.

I went with a buyer to the home of a mask-maker. We crossed a sixteenth-century patio where filthy children played among the refuse and a privy door hung on rusty hinges. In a dusky room four adults were painting bulls' heads and devils' faces and three grimy children hung around a frowzy woman cooking over a bed of charcoal on the floor. When the rancid lard sputtered, she stirred in garlic and a bowl of rice. Then she added a crushed tomato, some chiles, and water. Finally she poured in a cupful of broth. This was the midday meal for the whole family. The scene was quiet except for the buyer's insistence that the price for masks was too high.

Such quarters produce the beggars, banned from the center but still sneaking about with hand out, a deformity exposed, the inevitable skinny child. The more vigorous or healthy find some form of work or peculation; nothing is too small or unlikely to be stolen. Bits of metal off a car, food exposed on stands, anything left on a doorstep. Pickpockets are well organized; each works his beat—concerts, movies, bullfights, churches—without invading another's field.

Most people try, however feebly, to make a living. Police aides who direct the parking of your car and guard it well, *chamacos* at filling-stations, women mending stockings in dim and drafty doorways, whole families living in tiny stores, and numberless street vendors, especially of lottery tickets. Four or five at each corner seems average. "A million pesos!" they cry, poking a sheaf of tickets at you. "It plays today! Try your luck! This is the last one!"

More than two thousand street vendors work out of two hundred centers which theoretically give the vendor 7 per cent of the 10-per-cent commission. This is not checked, but the National Lottery commands general respect for integrity and its contribution to charity. Operating expenses take about 15 per cent of the ticket sale, 65 per cent goes to prizes, and the remaining 20 per cent is given to Beneficencia Pública, the government welfare agency. It maintains hospitals, orphanages, and asylums, and operates the Green Cross ambulances that appear throughout the city.

All Mexicans play the lottery and refuse to find any evil in it. The well-off find it a game; the poor man, risking a peso or less, hopes for miraculous relief from a hard life. People pray to certain saints for luck; one man crawled on his knees to touch an image with his ticket. He did not win, but there is always the next time. The big prize may be as much as three million pesos, but, as tickets are usually divided, almost nobody wins so much. The average five-peso ticket could win twenty-five thousand pesos, a nice take for anybody. Naturally everybody knows of a friend's friend who won a fortune.

Beneficencia Pública, which the lottery helps, and the Health Department are the federal agencies closest to the miserable poor. The Health Department goes to people on jobs, on pilgrimages, in prison, wherever they are, with vaccination, inoculations, lung- and heart-examinations. It has eliminated smallpox and greatly cut down other scourges. Tuberculosis, venereal disease, and undernourishment remain the greatest threats. Beneficencia Pública patrols the streets nightly to collect homeless boys and take them to centers where they are bathed, fed, given medical care. Pro-Nutrición, headed by Mexico's First Lady, gives hot breakfasts to some ten thousand needy children without the stigma of charity. But official figures show that about ninety thousand youngsters go to school underfed.

Many private agencies supplement these efforts, notably the Mexican Red Cross, which does not limit itself to war and disaster work. "All Mexican life is an emergency," they say, and so they maintain six emergency hospitals with six resident physicians and eleven ambulances. A reporter in one night saw 150 cases rushed in on blood-soaked stretchers that were rushed out immediately on the next call. Other doctors work as volunteers, as do office workers, hospital visitors, and the collectors, whose semi-annual drive nets some 200,000 pesos a year.

The greatest private agencies are those of the Catholic Church, organized through the parishes, which support orphanages, day nurseries, centers where mothers may wash and sew, food depots. Volunteer ladies recondition clothing and make layettes. Doctors man dispensaries and clinics without pay. About sixty young women have been trained as nurses' aides. And Acción Católica, which I had observed in San Luis Potosí, leads in social work. Its leader, Padre Pedro Velásquez, is an earnest young man whose book, *La Miseria de México*, is a devastating study of what he calls "the most backward of civilized countries." Padre Velásquez is deeply interested in labor relations: Acción Católica emphasizes duties rather than rights—"the duty of the employer to respect his workers and of the workers to accept responsibility." Asked about the general attitude of the clergy, Padre Velásquez smiled ruefully. "The priesthood," he said, "has lost much of its early apostolic impulse without gaining an understanding of modern social problems."

I found that getting lost in unpaved districts was a good way to see how Mexico's people live. Where old houses have run down into slums or new workers' shacks have been built, children laugh and splash in the gutters, men and women in cantinas or refreshment booths chatter gaily, boys whoop at play in vacant lots. Most houses, even here, have a touch of beauty in a vine or a potted plant. Radios are everywhere. Every ward has its fiesta; if you miss it you will see cut paper still hanging on the houses and a scattering of used-up fireworks. The busiest spot is the market, sometimes well housed, often uncovered on the sidewalk. There is laughter there, but tough bargaining too. It takes sharp buying to feed a family on what a man can earn.

A man of thirty, married and with three children, earns

850 pesos a month, working both day and night. As supervisor in a tire factory, he is classed as *empleado* (employee) and not *obrero* (workman), so he is not a union member. By day he works as foreman on a sewer, where he earns less than the unionized diggers; he believes this is due to a deal between union leaders and politicians. This man's expenses include rent of 165 pesos for two rooms and a patio kitchen; about 350 pesos for food; and 10 pesos each for cooking-oil and electricity. His Social Security payments are three per cent of his wage, a sum matched by his employer. This leaves less than 200 pesos for clothing, emergencies, amusements, and what his mother—a cook who gave me this data—calls his vices: he smokes and attends American football games.

A foreigner's slant on the Mexican wage scale came from a young mechanic sent down from the United States to speed up production in a factory. "Here comes my boss," he growled, "a Mexican citizen all right, but a Yank from Chicago, yelling that our production isn't up to standard. Well, I tell him, neither are our workers. How can you pay eight pesos a day and get the production of men in the States who are paid fifteen *dollars*? You pay a decent wage, I tell him, let me hire the workers, and I'll produce the goods. . . . But nobody listens to me; they just yell for more work and go on paying sub-standard wages."

A large part of Mexico's difficulty is a shortage of schools. Mexico City, building thirty new primary schools a year, each accommodating six hundred children in two daily shifts and three hundred adults at night, is barely keeping abreast of the city's population, which almost doubled between 1940 and 1950. The secondary schools lag even further behind, though they offer what Mexico needs so much—technical training. Specialization begins after two years of general studies; the student may then take up normal or commercial training, or household arts. Students aiming for the professions, including teaching in secondary schools or colleges, must finish six years of secondary school and take the *bachillerato* as preparatory to the University's professional schools. Education is federal, secular, and without religious training. The government accepts the Catholic schools as welcome aids, but they—like all private schools—must follow the official course of study and give the prescribed examinations.

The Mexican worker, whatever his education, is entitled to Social Security, which offers him and his family complete health protection and many related services. Twelve clinics in the Federal District maintain specialists and visiting nurses and social workers. Four large hospitals are planned, and one—Hospital de la Raza—has been erected. It is a splendid building, fully equipped and duly adorned with frescoes. Many employers welcome Social Security, which they find costs them less than caring for their employees. Others resent and try to evade it. Employees likewise require supervision on the part of the social workers. Railroad men, for instance, were registering families at both terminals and even at way stations. Complete proof of marriage is now demanded.

Mexicans have a word for this dual-family situation: *machismo. Macho* means male. Mexican psychiatrists seem agreed that the Mexican needs proof of virility. *La casa chica*, where the mistress lives, is not the prerogative of the rich, but a general pattern that even wives accept either with religious resignation or pure cynicism. Many Mexicans believe this attitude will change, with consequent change in the customs, as more women become wage-earners.

Women workers put up a gallant front. Even those from the dreariest slums appear at work brightly dressed and made-up and full of chatter. One meets them in the stores, where they handle four or five customers at once, efficiently and with speed. State what you want, pay for it, and begone, seems to be the idea. Laws for the protection of women are frequently and easily evaded. Only the bilingual secretaries, who may command as much as 1,800 pesos a month, make a fair living. Most secretaries earn about 1,000; store clerks make from 300 to 600 pesos a month. Such pay is cited as the reason that some working girls live in some *casa chica* or spend their evenings in houses of assignation. Other informants heatedly deny these charges; they say the Mexican mother still rules her daughters, who report at home immediately after work.

Mexican workers are unionized. In 1953, 327,286 men and women belonged to 712 unions in the Federal District. The majority are affiliated with La Confederación de Trabajadores de México, CTM; but important groups, such as federal employees, many teachers, and some service workers, are not. CTM succeeded, in 1953, in getting the minimum wage raised to 8 pesos a day; it had asked 12.50. Its critics, including many workers, believe that CTM, which works closely with the government, often sells them out to politicians or employers. They rally to the left-wing Confederación de Trabajadores de la América Latina, CTAL, which is headed by the brilliant attorney Vicente Lombardo Toledano. He is generally accepted as a Communist, though his friends deny it.

Lombardo Toledano founded La Universidad Obrera, which claims an enrollment of some 500 working people studying to become leaders in the "economic, cultural, and social development of Mexico." Its leaders believe that they alone are training women to make intelligent use of the vote they acquired in 1953. "The women who will fail to vote are the comfortable women, and they don't matter. . . . Do you know how sewing women and domestic servants are exploited by these women? how children are overworked in their homes? The rights of women will

be protected by working women. They will vote, and
they will know what for."

Whatever the right and wrong of these matters, Mexico
is clearly in ferment, and Mexicans are forging rapidly
ahead. They are hard-working and ambitious without—
gracias a Dios!—losing their love of color and fun, of fiesta.
In any group, somebody plays the guitar and others sing;
every special day is celebrated. Teachers, postmen, masons,
garbage-collectors all have their day when gifts are in order. Mexicans are also honest. Much is said of graft in high
places, perhaps with truth, and crime and petty thievery
exist. But the people you deal with daily in hotel or home,
in garage or shop, exhibit a high degree of integrity and a
friendly interest and willingness to serve that is truly Mexican. I could illustrate every point with many stories, but
the most important relate how Mexicans are getting ahead.

Victor, after two years of secondary education, joined
up with a man who had a parking-lot and repair shop. Soon
Victor was meeting the thousand peso monthly rent, the
light bill, and taxes while his partner had become a hopeless drunk. He even found himself liable for twenty-two
hundred pesos in back taxes, delinquent before he joined
the business. But he prospered and began buying government bonds. One day he gave a thousand pesos to a client
whom he knew as a representative of the National Savings
Bank, taking a receipt. But the man proved to be a de-
faulter. The bank agreed to reimburse him, but a year later
had not done so. This and an illness at home wiped out
Victor's savings, but he began again. When I knew him,
Victor, still living in a poor district, had bought furniture,
a gas stove, and a radio, all from Sears Roebuck, where he
had a charge account. He boasted that his were the only
children in the neighborhood who wore shoes to school.
His wife was well dressed, but she lacked her husband's

vision of a higher social scale. Victor's ambition was clear; he wanted a good business. The men in his shop teased him for a weakling. He did not drink or whore; he kept fit riding a bicycle to work and playing soccer on Sundays. And he was always a cheerful person, trying to learn English, trying to be as much as possible like those to-be-admired North American mechanics.

Victor called himself an Aztec, said his father was completely Indian in his ways. But Victor is Mexican and, as a citizen of a free country, free to go as far as his talents and opportunities will permit. Mexico may be said to have won its Revolution in that its racial problem has been solved. The nation is *mestizo* and proud of it. However snobbish individuals may be, Mexican life and laws accept the fact that Mexicans are the heirs of two cultures, and they move easily from one social group to another. Enrique, a man mentally better endowed than Victor, illustrated the point.

Enrique was the youngest son of a peon family, the kind that had no chance in the Díaz days. After the turbulent years, his older brothers opened a small shop in the village and prospered. They, uneducated themselves, sent the youngest to the Law School of the University in Mexico. There Enrique, living as poor students did, managed—as all Mexicans do!—to buy lottery tickets. One day he won, and dutifully sent his brothers twenty-five thousand pesos. They invested in an agency which, after twenty years, had made them the leaders of the town's business and social life. They married advantageously, sent their children to good schools, and even bought the hacienda where their father had worked as a peon. Enrique meanwhile had graduated with honors, married a "well-related" girl, and set up an office in one of the city's finest buildings.

Such cases, multiplied a thousandfold, are remaking Mexico. This pattern, so common in our country, is just becoming common as Mexico's people are surging up against the barriers that formerly kept them in the "humble classes" while the "upper classes" dominated their country's life. The upper classes still exist; many of them are important, productive, and creative people who must be considered in any over-all picture of Mexico.

XXXV

MEXICO MOVES ON

☒ THE VISITOR finds Mexico a brilliant, cosmopolitan capital which offers whatever he seeks. He may dine well on an international cuisine in elegant restaurants frescoed by Mexico's best painters. Little places specialize in Mexico's many regional dishes and many from other lands. Tourist agencies conduct parties to supper clubs where Indians dance in costume; to gay night clubs with name performers; and perhaps to the famous Salon México, where guests are requested not to drop lighted cigarettes, which may burn the ladies' bare feet. The venturesome may go farther and fare worse, though it is fun to visit Las Tenampas, where *mariachis* congregate to play in noisy competition, hoping to win employment elsewhere.

The Palace of Fine Arts offers seasons of opera, symphony concerts, and ballet—often with foreign conductors and stars—many exhibitions of the plastic arts, and serious lectures. People who understand Spanish will find amusing variety shows and more sober theaters that give plays from Spain and all the Americas. Cinemas are as numerous as in any city, and many excellent pictures are Mexican-made. Dozens of private galleries show the work of Mexican and foreign artists, who generally grace their openings. Mexico offers all the sports known elsewhere, plus bullfights on Sunday afternoons and *frontón* on most nights. Many clubs offer cards to visitors; one may look up his university club or leave cards at his embassy. All this is easy. It is not easy to know Mexico's *alta sociedad*, the high society, which is

324

one of the most exclusive aristocracies in the world. Few
foreigners know it, or even suspect its existence, but it is
important not only as a gracious survival, but because many
of its younger members, heirs of brains and the habit of
leadership, are prominent in the city's business and cultural
life.

The grace is preserved by old ladies, a few of whom still
live in ancestral palaces with their heirlooms, with autographed photographs of a pope, Spain's Alfonso XIII, and
always Porfirio Díaz. These ladies move easily through
several languages; as the daughters and wives of diplomats,
they were educated abroad and lived in several capitals.
They receive, theoretically, only Mexicans of high lineage
and they uphold rigid standards. Ardently Catholic, they
refuse to receive divorcees "unless," as my informant said,
"they are rich or titled." My informant is a composite of
several people, born into the inner circle but able to discuss
it with a touch of humor.

High society currently uses titles, though they are out-
lawed in the Republic. A few families can trace a pure
Spanish heritage back to the sixteenth century. The oldest
title, that of Cortés as Marqués del Valle, exists now only
in Italy, but the Calimaya of Mexico, whose dean is the
Marqués de Rivas Cacho, holds a title awarded to his ances-
tor in 1616. Other seventeenth-century titles have disappeared or exist only in Spain, but many aristocratic Mexicans can claim descent from the grandees of New Spain.
Naturally intermarriage was common among the small
group of white *criollos*, who hoped to keep their families
free of Indian taint.

Most Mexican titles date from the eighteenth century,
when Mexican mines were pouring out floods of wealth
and Spain's impoverished Bourbons freely ennobled miners
who are remembered now as donors of magnificent
churches rather than as lucky prospectors. Altogether, 113

titles were granted in New Spain. What was perhaps the last was granted in 1811, clearly in an effort to hold a colony already in revolt. Many aristocratic Mexicans honor ancestors who fought against Spain in the Wars of Independence, but they are also loyal to Alfonso XIII. They mourned his death in crape-draped churches, and they celebrate his birthday with elaborate Masses. When General Francisco Franco invaded republican Spain, a few young Mexicans, believing that he would restore the monarchy, enlisted in his army. My informant added: "Mexico's nobility is equally loyal to the present King, Don Juan, and to his son, Prince Carlos, who is being educated under the supervision of General Franco."

Maximilian's empire gave Mexico no new titles, but many of his followers stayed on to grow rich and leave Mexican families with French or German names. Their children were educated in Europe, preferably in Paris, and many families followed the all-American custom of marrying their pretty daughters to titled foreigners. Such Mexicans knew Mexico only as the source of income, its people only as peons on the hacienda. But among them were true liberals who had followed the Indian Juárez, supported his Reform, and abolished titles. Aristocrats recall that even liberals—including Juárez—were quick to marry their daughters into noble families. This custom continued during the Díaz era, when many newly rich commoners—including Díaz himself—married aristocratic girls. Money is useful to support social elegance, but Mexican society includes families distinguished for intellectual or artistic rather than financial success.

Conservatives shudder away from the revolution of 1910, which ended their world. Its leaders were of two kinds. Those who, like the Maderos, were previously acceptable, maintain their social position. Others—the cartoon-type generals and politicians—are shrugged off with "Nobody knows them, I suppose they have their own society." But if few revolutionary heroes adorn high society—or would care to, as many of them would say—the social citadel is yielding to outside pressures and to explosive elements within.

The revolution and land-expropriation left many *hacendado* families relatively poor. Young men, trained to scorn work, took jobs; they are now active in business, the professions, government, and the arts, where they associate with Mexicans quite unknown to their mothers. Foreigners meet these men, who entertain so cordially that it is seldom noticed that the invitations are for clubs and not homes. The clubs are fine. The Bankers Club is said to be more impressive than any in New York or Philadelphia. A young man's club, El Caballito, frankly excludes foreigners, but the sports clubs invite foreigners, though the directors are usually Mexicans. The gayest of these is the Jockey Club, where society gathers after the Sunday races for cards, cocktails, and late buffet supper.

Mexican girls of the old families seem to have accepted poverty as a challenge. They began timidly as teachers, took paying guests, or acted as social secretaries to confused diplomatic ladies. The more daring then took downtown jobs, where their knowledge of languages was invaluable, or entered the University. Soon they were in the professions and successful as leaders. Lic. María Lavalle Urbina was the first woman to serve as Magistrate of the Federal Court. Dr. Ester Chiapa's studies of women's prisons led to much needed reforms. Several women have served as ministers to foreign lands and in international positions. Numberless teachers have contributed greatly to their country's advance. These women, from aristocratic families or aristocrats by their own competence, joined with working women to press for the vote, which was won in 1953.

A delightful example of adaptation to changing mores is

the Amor sisters. Carolina, when I first knew her, was a slim dark-eyed girl just out of the convent, who was holding two jobs. She reviewed books and music for *Excelsior* and edited *Síntesis*, a magazine of reprints, many of which she translated from French or English. Her reviews attracted Carlos Chávez, then developing the Symphony Orchestra of Mexico, and he offered her a place on his staff, which made her, in effect, the interpreter of Mexico's renaissance and a friend of its artists and intellectuals. She recalls her mother's apprehensions when she first invited a few painters to her home. But no delicate porcelain or crystal was broken, and no convention either. Out of such evenings an idea was born.

These artists were the muralists who were winning world-wide fame. But they were frescoing government buildings for laborer's wages, and they had no place to show their easel paintings. They urged Carolina to open an art gallery. So, in the English basement of her home and quite without financial backing, she began to show the "big four" painters of the revolution—Diego Rivera, José Clemente Orozco, David Alfaro Siqueiros, and Rufino Tamayo —and Julio Castellanos, whom she considers one of the greatest. Her younger sister Inés was assistant, as she had been at *Síntesis*. Before the end of the year Inés had taken over because Carolina had married Dr. Raoul Fournier and made another career. She edits two medical magazines and directs a medical publishing-house that is known throughout the Spanish-speaking world.

Carolina Amor de Fournier also finds time for a social life that is far from the exclusiveness of her mother's home. She invites to her garden home in San Gerónimo people who interest her—intellectuals, artists, foreigners, thinkers. There I met the third distinguished Amor sister, Guadalupe, known as Pita Amor from her baby nickname of Guadalupita. A tiny woman with tousled hair, brooding eyes, and sensuous mouth, she is the very picture of a poet; many critics consider her Mexico's best woman poet, if not among the best of either sex or any era. She is also considered a shocking young woman, who says what she thinks, behaves according to her whims, and dresses according to her fancy. Her poems reflect a deep sincerity and a genuine seeking for truth.

Inés, carrying on La Galeriá de Arte Mexicano, has made a reputation as critic and promoter of modern Mexican art. She is slimmer than her sister Carolina, moves more quickly, seems more intense, but she is always warmly interested and courteous. Inés will not talk about herself, but she willingly discusses the artists she has known over twenty years.

"I never doubted their genius," she said. "They could not have been such effective propagandists otherwise. I learned from them as I heard them criticizing each other's work. If they said of a new painter: 'That's a boy to watch,' I did. Often I could help financially; always I could offer encouragement." What she did comes out reluctantly. One young man who brought his drawings was wearing a suit his mother had made out of a serape. Another, whom she found dying of tuberculosis in a slum, she took to the city's best specialist. Others could put paint on canvas only because Inés—she says "the gallery"—bought both paint and canvas. It was not always easy. Mexicans still preferred to buy pictures in Europe, disdaining those earthbound Indian figures. When Rufino Tamayo first showed, *El Universal*'s art critic wrote: "Blessed are the blind." The first buyers of Mexico's modern art were from the United States, and many Mexican artists made their first success there.

Tamayo was the first to break away from the propagandist group and to live abroad. He has won many prizes, including one in Venice's Biennale 1952 and a first in Brazil in 1953. Rufino Tamayo may thus be considered Mexico's outstanding painter, and he is doubly interesting because he is a pure Zapotec Indian whose work is highly individual and very Mexican. His gay fruity colors, his unfailing elegance of design, and his sly humor are Mexican Indian and could be nothing else. Many younger painters are painting as individuals and not propagandists. Even when they fresco government buildings with the stereotyped figures, their work lacks the fire of conviction. The younger Mexican painters are best as easel painters; some of them are very fine.

Mexico's close-knit social fabric has inevitably fringed out as young aristocrats have made friends and even marriages in wider circles, and caste has become less important than brains, talent, and stimulating conversation. Many Spanish-speaking diplomats make a point of entertaining Mexican intellectuals, who are well known throughout the hemisphere, and Spanish Loyalist intellectuals who have sought homes and work in Mexico. A few intellectuals, following Diego Rivera, an outspoken Communist, talk Communism, seemingly as an anti-gringo line, but their hope for their own country seems to lie in *indianismo* as opposed to *hispanidad*.

A most articulate Indianist is the architect Juan O'Gorman, who, without a trace of Indian heritage himself, waves away all Spanish culture as an intrusion. He finds nothing good in colonial architecture except Indian influence in massive construction or fanciful decoration. "Modern Mexican architecture," he says, "must be completely adapted to regional conditions and conceived with fantasy, never functionalism." He scorns the use of glass in office buildings whose "eastern rooms are hothouses in the mornings while the western ones are ovens in the afternoons." He deplores architectural training based on study of European models and not Mexico's own magnificent ruins. His own fine stone mosaics at the Ciudad Universitaria and on the new transportation building are based on Indian styles and techniques.

This conflict between *indianismo* and *hispanidad* appears in many guises. It flared into the newspapers in 1947 when a burial was identified as that of the conqueror Cortés, whose bones were treated with respect except by Diego Rivera. That iconoclast, painting in the National Palace, depicted there a misshapen, idiotic Cortés, which he claimed was based on the actual bones. In 1949 another burial was discovered in the remote village of Ixcateopan, Guerrero, which the Indianists accepted as those of Cuauhtémoc, who is becoming their culture hero. Anthropologists who doubted that those bones were the remains of Moctezuma's gallant successor were attacked as evil, prejudiced men.

Indianismo, the desire to dignify the Indian cultural background and perhaps to replace European myths with native Mexicans, was effectively dramatized in 1953 in *El Quinto Sol (Fifth Sun)*, a pageant given under government auspices and planned as an annual event. Archæologists, artists, poets, musicians, and choreographers collaborated to present a series of ballets based on Indian legends of the emergence of sub-humans and their development into moral beings. The beautiful elliptical bowl of the University Stadium was a splendid setting for twenty-five hundred dancers, correctly or imaginatively costumed as shadowy sub-humans, sprouting green corn, jaguar and tiger warriors, and Aztec courtiers. The masses were expertly handled, though the solo and duet ballets were dwarfed by distance, and the cardboard Fifth Sun, when the hero brought it up, was ineffective under the true glowing sun. But it was altogether a magnificent show. Afterward the entire cast was taken on a motor pilgrimage to Ixcateopan to render homage to Cuauhtémoc's bones.

The foreigner finds all this puzzling; Mexican culture

and Mexican individuals are so clearly the product of both Indian and Spanish culture. But the schism lies too deep in Mexican life to be ignored. The conservative pro-Spanish and Catholic group considers the government "atheistic" because it is non-sectarian, and "Communistic" because of its social services. These believers could probably poll a majority in a free election, but the government party's domination keeps them out; they can only work indirectly through individuals in public office. Liberal pro-government Mexicans—even many who attend Mass and send their children to Catholic schools—fear a rebirth of clerical power. One said: "That would mean the loss of every good the revolution won. We can't risk it. We've got to control elections."

This ideological split creates distrust that poisons Mexican life at every level. But it is most crippling to the individual. Many young people are distraught by inner conflict—not only the universal struggle against outworn custom and parental control, but the more agonizing effort to maintain their Catholic faith while so many clerics decry the government they believe in. Daily one meets walking novels: people will often talk to a stranger. Oddly, these conflicts have not produced the social novel one might expect. Novelists shy away from their own problems and continue to depict the exploitation of the village Indian or misery in the city. Mexican poets, who often excel as lyricists, have not touched social problems. Only a few dramatists have dared to present such themes as prejudice and poverty.

Mexican writers are most notable as scholars. La Sociedad de Estudios y Letras, headed by the great stylist and beloved dean, Dr. Alfonso Reyes, produces significant books and reviews in the social sciences. Mexican anthropologists are leaders of Latin America in all problems common to Indian lands; their sociologists and economists are widely known. Mexican physicians are known throughout the world for their work in cardiology, in tropical diseases, and in some eye afflictions. Mexico has no lack of trained thinkers with the courage to lead, and with the rarer gift of understanding.

Such Mexicans will sigh: *"Ay, México es muy complejo."* Mexico is indeed complex in both its physical aspect and its population, whose problems are further complicated by the crisscross lines of its thinking. One profound student summed it up: "Our country is in formation without plan. We have no true nationality. Nothing can be discussed in the singular, and consequently there is no over-all solution for Mexico."

Clearly there is no over-all solution. But there is one conviction, shared by all Mexicans and expressed in the slogan: "Mexico for the Mexicans." This, of course, means the conservation and development of natural resources, the building of industry, the training and education of Mexicans. But it means something deeper: it means the preservation of some quality that has remained Mexican through ages of alien influences. The Mexican Indian remained himself through centuries of Spanish rule; the *mestizo*, subjected to European religion, government, and education, has somehow managed to infuse everything with Mexicanness. The modern, determined to adapt his country to the modern world and take an honored place among the industrialized democracies, hopes to retain this quality as he faces new problems.

Some problems have been solved, notably that of race. Mexicans are *mestizo*, and proud of it. The power of landowners and of foreign capital has been broken. *Caudillismo*, with its recurrent revolutions, seems to have been dissolved in common sense. Taximen on election day were saying: "We know they are stealing this election, but next time! . . ." The only talk of revolt came from certain intellectuals, who happily expended their force in talk.

Most Mexicans face their problems realistically and attack them with spirit and plenty of humor. Naturally, people of such vigor disagree on many details, but they are at one in their determination to work out their destiny in their own way, preserving their *mexicanismo*. They find this Mexican quality in the fiesta, which is at once nonsensical, gay, and sad; in the general love of color and fun, of drama and play; of everything that makes every Mexican an artist. Every Mexican also names spirituality as an essential Mexican attribute. Catholics assume that all spirituality abides in their Church, and will accept no other. Indianists refer to some mystical persistence of the glories of ancient Indian culture. Whatever it truly is, *mexicanismo* is not recognized only by Mexicans. Whoever has felt that country's strong appeal will agree that its lovable and beloved personality will prevail. Mexico will always be Mexico.

BIBLIOGRAPHY

GLOSSARY

INDEX

BOOKS RECOMMENDED FOR FURTHER READING IN ENGLISH

Beals, Carleton: *Mexican Maze*
——: *Porfirio Díaz*
Bennett, Wendell C. and Robert M. Sweigg: *The Tarahumara: an Indian Tribe of Northern Mexico*
Blasco Ibáñez, Vicente: *Mexico in Revolution*
Blom, Frans: *The Conquest of Yucatan*
——: *Tribes and Temples*
Born, Esther: *The New Architecture in Mexico*
Brenner, Anita: *Idols Behind Altars*
Brenner, Anita and G. R. Leighton: *The Wind That Swept Mexico*
Calderón de la Barca, Frances Erskine: *Life in Mexico*
Cerwin, Herbert: *These Are the Mexicans*
Chase, Stuart: *Mexico: a Study of Two Americas*
Chávez, Carlos: *Toward a New Music*
Cline, Howard: *The United States and Mexico*
Cortés, Hernán: *Five Letters*
Covarrubias, Miguel: *Mexico South: the Isthmus of Tehuantepec*
Diamant, Gertrude: *The Days of Ofelia*
Díaz del Castillo, Bernal: *The True History of the Conquest of New Spain*
Dromundo, Baltasar: *Emiliano Zapata*
Fergusson, Erna: *Fiesta in Mexico*
Flandrau, C. M.: *Viva Mexico*
Foster, George M.: *Empire's Children: the People of Tzintzuntzan*
Gallop, Rodney: *Mexican Mosaic*
Gill, Mario: *Sinarquismo*
Gill, Tom: *Land Hunger in Mexico*
Gillmor, Frances: *Flute of the Smoking Mirror*

Gruening, Ernest: *Mexico and Its Heritage*
Hays, H. R.: *Takers of the City*
Helm, McKinley: *Man of Fire: J. C. Orozco*
———: *Modern Mexican Painters*
Herring, Hubert and Herbert Weinstock (eds.): *Renascent Mexico*
Hewett, E. L.: *Ancient Life in Mexico and Central America*
Hilton, John: *Sonora Sketch Book*
Hobart, Alice Tisdale: *The Peacock Sheds His Tail*
King, Rosa: *Tempest over Mexico*
Kirk, Betty: *Covering the Mexican Front*
Kneller, George F.: *The Education of the Mexican Nation*
Larralde, Elsa: *My House Is Yours*
Lewis, Oscar: *Life in a Mexican Village*
———: *Tepoztlán Revisited*
Madariaga, Salvador de: *Cortés*
———: *Heart of Jade*
Madero, Francisco: *The Presidential Succession of 1910*
Magdaleno, Mauricio: *Sunburst*
Millan, Verna Carleton: *Mexico Reborn*
Morley, Sylvanus G.: *The Ancient Maya*
Morris, Earl: *Temple of the Warriors*
Mosk, Sanford A.: *Industrial Revolution in Mexico*
Niggli, Josephina: *Mexican Village*
Niles, Blair: *Passengers to Mexico*
O'Shaughnessy, Edith: *A Diplomat's Wife in Mexico*
Parker, George: *Guarache Trail*
Parkes, Henry Bramford: *A History of Mexico*
Plenn, J. H.: *Mexico Marches*
Porter, Katherine Anne: *Hacienda*
Prescott, W. H.: *History of the Conquest of Mexico* (with illustrations by Miguel Covarrubias)
Priestley, H. I.: *The Mexican Nation*
Proskouriakoff, Tatiana: *An Album of Maya Architecture*
Redfield, Robert: *The Folk Culture of Yucatan*
———: *Tepoztlan: a Mexican Village*
Redfield, Robert and Alfonso Villa: *Chan Kom: a Maya Village*

Reed, Alma: *José Clemente Orozco*
Reed, John: *Insurgent Mexico*
Rivera, Diego and Bertram Wolfe: *Portrait of Mexico*
Romanell, Patrick: *Making of the Mexican Mind*
Ross, Patricia Fent: *Made in Mexico*
Ross, Stanley: *Francisco Madero: Mexican Apostle*
Royer, F.: *The Franciscans Came First*
Roys, Ralph: *Indian Background of Colonial Yucatán*
Sánchez, George I.: *Mexico: a Revolution by Education*
Sanford, Trent E.: *The Story of Architecture in Mexico*
Sansores, Manuel C.: *Chichén-Itzá*
Scott, Natalie: *Your Mexican Kitchen*
Simpson, Eyler N.: *The Ejido: Mexico's Way Out*
Simpson, Leslie Byrd: *Many Mexicos*
Spratling, William: *Little Mexico*
Stephens, John L.: *Incidents of Travel In Yucatan*
Stewart, Virginia: *Forty-five Contemporary Mexican Artists*
Strode, Hudson: *Timeless Mexico*
Tannenbaum, Frank: *Mexico: The Struggle for Peace and Bread*
Teja Zabre, Alfonso: *Guide to the History of Mexico*
Thompson, Edward H.: *People of the Serpent*
Vaillant, George C.: *The Aztecs of Mexico*
Vasconcelos, José and Manuel Gamio: *Aspects of Mexican Civilization*
Velásquez Chávez, Augustín: *Contemporary Mexican Artists*
Weyl, N. and S.: *Reconquest of Mexico: The Years of Lázaro Cárdenas*
Whetten, Nathaniel L.: *Rural Mexico*

❦ ⬥ ❦

BOOKS CONSULTED IN SPANISH

Aguirre Beltrán, Gonzalo: *Formas de Gobierno Indigena*
Alvarado, Salvador: *Mi Actuación Revolucionario en Yucatán*
Azuela, Mariano: *Los de Abajo*
Barragán, María Teresa: *Wakarí*
Benítez, Fernando: *La Ruta de Cortés*
Blasio, José Luis: *Maximiliano Intimo*
Camara Zavala, Gonzalo: *Historia de la Industria Henequenera Hasta 1919*
Casasola, "Archivo": *Historia Gráfica de la Revolución, 1910–1940*
Castillo Torre, José: *El Pays Que No Se Parece al Otro*
Cornejo Franco, José: *La Calle de San Francisco*
Corral, Luz: *Pancho Villa en la Intimidad*
Duret, Lanz: *Don Francisco Montero*
Erro, Luis Enrique: *Los Pies Descalzos*
Fernández, Justín: *El Arte Moderno y Contemporáneo de México*
Gamio, Manuel: *Forjando Patria*
García Iglesias, Sara: *El Jaguey de las Ruinas*
Goyartua, Jesús: *Pensativa*
Guzmán, Martín Luis: *El Aguila y la Serpiente*
——: *La Sombra del Caudillo*
Iturriaga, José E.: *La Estructura Social y Cultural de México*
Landa, Diego de: *Relación de las Cosas de Yucatán*
López y Fuentes, Gregorio: *Milpa, Potrero y Monte*
——: *El Indio*
Marquina, Ignacio: *Arquitectura Prehispánica*
Maza, Francisco de la: *El Guadalupanismo Mexicano*
——: *La Ciudad de Durango*
Mediz Bolio, Antonio: *La Tierra del Venado y del Faisán*
Mondragón, Magdalena: *Yo, Como Pobre*
Monroy, Salazar: *La Típica Cocina Poblana*

340

Pozas Arciniega, Ricardo: *Juan Pérez Jolote: Biografía de un Tzotzil*
Rivas, Barriga: *Rio Humano*
Romero, Rubén: *Yo Fuí Rico*
Sahagún, Bernardo de: *Historia de las Cosas de Nueva España*
Sandoval, Piño: *Angela Celeste*
Sierra, Justo: *Juárez: Su Obra y Su Tiempo*
Silva Herzog, Jesús: *Ensayo Sobre la Revolución Mexicana*
Teja Zabre, Alfonso: *La Supervivencia de Cuauhtémoc*
Torre, Tomas de la: *Diario de Viaje 1544-1545* (ed. Franz Blom)
Vasconcelos, José: *La Tormenta*
——: *Ulises Criollo*
Yáñez, Augustín: *Al Filo del Agua*

GLOSSARY

abrazo	embrace
administrador	manager
aguamiel	honey water
aguardiente	Mexican alcoholic drink; like cognac
ahuehuete	Mexico's cedar tree
alacrán	scorpion
alameda	park
alférez	church official
altos	highlands
añejo	aged
aprehensión	arrest, seizure
arriero	muleteer
atole	a sweetened cornmeal gruel
ayankado	yankeeized
ayudante	aide
bacherillato	certificate given after two years beyond high school
bajío	lowlands
barrero	underground man in mining
batea	tray
bodega	cellar, storeroom
bolsa	purse
bracero	arm worker; hand
brasero	brazier
bravo	ferocious; wild
buñuelos	fritters
Caballito	Little Horse
calvario	calvary
camarín	robing-room
caminante	wanderer
campesino	peasant (country man)
caporal	ranch foreman

caracol	snail (shell)
cargador	bearer
castillo	castle
caudillo	boss
cazuela	casserole
cenote	well
cervercería	brewery
chamaco	urchin; little boy
chicle	chewing-gum
chinampas	anchored island gardens, such as Xochimilco
chirimía	the prehistoric flute
científicos	scientists
cine	movies
comal	flat clay disk on which *tortillas* are baked
conejo	rabbit
costumbre	custom
cuidado	care; take care
cumbre	peak
curandero	healer
danzante	dancer
diligencia	stagecoach
don	title meaning "noble of birth"
doña	feminine of "don"
duro	hard
ejidatario	owner of redistributed land
ejido	village land
encomendero	Spaniard to whom grant of Indians was made
encomienda	grant of Indians to a Spaniard
enfermero(a)	nurse
enramada	arbor
enredo	wrap-around skirt
estufado	inlay on wood
feria	fair
franquismo	Francoism
galopín(a)	under-boy or maid in a house

Glossary

ganadería	cattle ranch
glorieta	leafy spot
grito	cry
guayabera	a Norfolk-like cotton jacket
güero(a)	blonde
guerrillero	guerrilla fighter
hacendado	hacienda-owner
henequen	hemp
huarache	sandal
huauchinango	red snapper
huipil	woman's blouse
iglesita	little church
ilegítima	illegitimate
ingeniero	engineer
jamaica	non-alcoholic drink
jardín	garden
jícara	gourd bowl
ladino or latino	bearer of the Spanish culture
legítimo	legitimate
lengua	tongue
licenciado	lawyer
llorona	wailer
loma	hill
machismo	virility
(from macho, male)	
madera	wood
manda	promise of penance
manso	tame
médico	doctor
mil	one thousand
milagro	miracle
milagroso	miraculous
milpa	corn field
mole de guajalote	turkey with a special dark sauce
monja	nun
monote	big ape
mordida	bite; bribe
morena	brunette

nana	nurse
norte	norther (storm from the north)
novena	prayers for a consecutive period of nine days
obras	works
olas altas	high waves
orchata	drink made of ground melon seeds
paleta	ice on a stick
parque	park
partido	sharing system (of mine production)
patria	fatherland
patrón	master
patrona	mistress
pedregal	rocky place
peregrino(a)	pilgrim
petate	straw mat
piloncillo	brown sugar
piñata	pottery jar covered with paper and filled with Christmas presents
piñón	pine nut
pochismo	hybrid of Spanish and English
pocho	a Mexican-American
policía	police
portal	arcade along the front of a building
posada	inn
pozole	pigs' feet and hominy
puesto	booth
rebozo	a Mexican wrap similar to a stole
regiomontano	native of Monterrey
regular	so-so
robo	robbery
rurales	federal police
sala	parlor
serenata	band concert
servidora	servant
sidral	apple cider
simpático	appealing
soldadera	a woman camp-follower

Glossary

soledad	alone
són	tune
taco	*tortilla* sandwich
tamarindo	non-alcoholic drink
tapatío	native of Guadalajara
templo	temple
tierra chica	home land
tilma	rough cotton mantle worn by Indians
totopo	round flat bread
tránsito	traffic
vigilia	Friday's or Lenten fasting
voladores	flyers
zaguán	passage
zócalo	central plaza
zopilote	buzzard

Index

i

ii Index

Index   iii

Index

A Note on the Type

This book was set on the Linotype in Janson, a recutting made direct from type cast in matrices made by Anton Janson some time between 1660 and 1687. This type is an excellent example of the influential and singularly sturdy Dutch types that prevailed in England prior to Caslon. It was from the Dutch types that Caslon developed his own incomparable designs.

The book was composed, printed, and bound by The Plimpton Press, Norwood, Massachusetts. Typography and binding designs are by W. A. Dwiggins.

WAD